HERBCR

NATURALLY

Christina Stapley

Author of Herbwise Naturally

HEARTSEASE BOOKS

DEDICATION

To David, with love and thanks for all his encouragement, support and help, especially planning the colour pages.

Photography

Di Lewis and Christina Stapley
Snowman with wreaths and pot-pourri, Ian Clarke.

ISBN: 0 9522336 1 4

Printed in England by St. Richard's Press Ltd.
Chichester, West Sussex PO19 2TU.

With thanks to Jackie Wilson for her tireless work in editing the manuscript. Also to Gary Pilcher for preparing the graphics.

Herbs can be powerful substances whether applied as oils or in other forms. The author cannot take responsibility for reader's use of recipes or possible allergic reactions. Please note cautionary guidelines with recipes, particularly with dyes and herb candles.

CONTENTS

ILLUSTRATIONS

DIAGRAMS

Planning a herb garden

IN my first book, **Herbwise Naturally,** the subject of planning a herb garden was fully explored. In this companion volume there are details of a further 58 herbs to grow, and sufficient information to enable the reader to plant new small gardens dedicated to supplying herbs for the topics of this book. You will find herbs for flowercrafts, those which offer inspiration for needlework design, herbs with stems supplying fibres to spin and weave into cloth, herb dyes, herbs for papermaking, those with long stems suited to true basketry or shorter herbs which can be worked in bundles to form the sides of fragrant stem baskets, and lastly, herbal trees which offer timber for woodcrafts. In addition there are herbs for making wines and liqueurs, rich preserves as syrups, cordials or jellies, sweets and candies, gourmet recipes and decorations for Christmas.

As in **Herbwise Naturally,** the emphasis is placed on creating gardens of beauty and natural charm, filled with organically grown herbs to provide a healthy habitat for wildlife. Unlike the wine and liqueur and craft gardens which offer so many ingredients and materials, the treasure garden is primarily for those searching for increased pleasure in simply enjoying herbs for their beauty. Naturally, it also provides inspiration for designs in art and crafts, for all those who view it.

In this first section I have concentrated on gardening in the autumn, whether it involves planting fresh beds or harvesting from established ones. This is partly because there are numerous trees, shrubs and perennials amongst the relevant herbs which are easier to establish in autumn rather than spring. The rich harvests of fruits, seeds, berries, roots and stems are also ripe for gathering at this time. With these, the pleasures of the garden itself can live on in crafts, liqueurs and preserves, and brighten wintry days when the weather keeps all indoors.

Harvesting of roots and seeds is looked at in detail for the benefit of anyone who is new to gathering them for use. Division of plants and roots, taking cuttings and setting frost shy herbs in cold frames or giving them further protection are simply reminders of annual tasks. The lists of evergreens, herbal trees and shrubs, poisonous plants, and herbs with berries, seeds and fruits to attract birds are set out as a guide for the reader when planning beds or new areas. No doubt the choice of which herbs to plant will rest on a happy coincidence of those which will supply the needs of your own particular craft and culinary interests and those which are simply too lovely to resist. Read on noting the possibilities, and then perhaps pause for thought before making a list of possible herbs. Referring back to the height, nature and requirements of each one before beginning your plan. Who knows what further delights the garden will open for you.

The herb garden in autumn

AUTUMN can be as good a time to plant out a new garden, or to add to an established one, as spring. This is particularly so with many of the shrubs, trees and perennials suggested in this book for the craft and wine and liqueur gardens. A variety of cuttings can be taken and rooted in pots of rich composted soil in a sheltered location. (Some will require full cover against frost.) Early autumn can be perfect for taking cuttings of germander, cotton lavender and other herbs. The cuttings can be given a little extra wind protection by setting them well down into very large, deep tubs and then standing these against a hedge on its westerly side. While taking cuttings think also of the herbs which will need to be taken indoors or planted in cold frames for the winter months.

Scented geraniums, less hardy lavenders, such as *Lavandula canariensis* and *L. dentata,* French tarragon, lemon verbena and pineapple sage may require this assistance to survive if your garden is not truly sheltered. As a precaution, I also set cuttings or small plants of tender variegated or silver varieties of herbs such as tricolor sage, *Tanacetum hardjanii,* cotton lavender, bay and some delicate pinks in the cold frames. Although with Parma violets protection from frost is advised, I have found their needs better served by placing the plants between sturdy overhanging bushes in very sheltered corners or taking them into a conservatory rather than setting in cold frames. Others may be more successful with the last method, certainly when you open the lid of a cold frame filled with Parma violets the perfume is wonderful.

New hedges can be set in October and November, and paths, their edges, pergolas, arbours and other structures within the garden all made ready while the perennials are bedded down under a mulch of compost for the winter.

In an established garden, autumn – with those last harvests of fruits, leaves and seeds before the first frost, digging roots for plant division and candying or drying, is a precious time. There is always the chance an early frost may catch you unprepared. As I gather the last of the angelica leaves and youngest stems to make syrup, dig sweet cicely roots to candy, hang dry golden rod seedheads to be sprayed silver for Christmas decorations and store the late ripening seeds of *Coreopsis tinctoria* and sunflower away, I give thanks for every safe harvest.

Often in our modern lives there is the thought that it doesn't matter if you don't manage to gather all in, as you can always buy some at the shop. With many of the delights of autumn in the herb garden this is not the case. Freshly dug roots of sweet cicely, elecampane and angelica, spiced elderberry syrup, guelder rose or elderberry ink, and stocks of dried fragrant herbs on their stems must still be home produced.

Over the years as I have grown herbs I have steadily experimented more with the autumn harvest of roots, seeds and fruits - with candies, syrups and liqueurs. Many old recipes from previous centuries looked fascinating, but there was, too often, a lack of reasonable measurements from huge amounts being made for a large household - or they assumed knowledge of one step or another in the process that must have been obvious to all at the time, but is no longer common knowledge. Nevertheless, the idea of the syrups and comfits intrigued me and as my early meagre stocks of roots grew to healthier proportions and could be spared for possibly doomed experiments, so I became braver in my "instant" recipes which are generally based on old ones, rather than attempting to repeat them.

Some results were beautiful and adopted into my list of necessaries for the winter store cupboard to be repeated at least annually. Others gave startling surprises – such as finding out that elecampane root, so rapturously recommended for candying in Elizabethan times as a "kissing comfit", turns out to resemble a "Force nine Fishermen's Friend". Cough candy is an obvious use - but neat? Throats as well as tastes must have changed with the generations. Wiser, - I began candying a small amount and then liquidizing the result to use in drop form as a flavouring. Once begun, these lines of experiment can lead into new and rewarding avenues; gums of elderberry syrup to suck for sore throats being just one idea still for future exploration.

Syrups can also flavour sweets and add distinction to even a plain serving of stewed fruit. Sweet cicely, angelica and spiced elderberry are the most useful of those from autumn gathering, although once you are experienced with these, others may suggest themselves. Only a little syrup is needed, perhaps a teaspoonful per serving and this can be poured over after the fruit is cooked. For more ideas see the cookery section. Of the seeds useful in cookery - lovage, sunflower, coriander, caraway, dill, fennel and aniseed, the dill, fennel and sunflower are generally the last to be gathered. Cut the seedheads just before the seeds are ripe, hanging them in a warm, dry atmosphere over a clean length of material or paper. Enclosing the heads in paper bags can lead to mould if the atmosphere is not completely dry. If the seeds are to be saved for sowing the following year, simply dry them completely and store in labelled and sealed envelopes, jars or the used containers from photographic films which are most useful for small amounts.

Seeds of perennials and some biennials are often better sown in late summer or early autumn, than in spring. Caraway sown in this way will give seeds again within one year instead of two. Angelica should always be left to seed itself for the best results.

Harvesting roots

HARVESTING roots is a little more complicated and one of those important parts of the recipe which earlier writers often assume the reader will find too familiar to warrant instruction. Since to a modern gardener or cook this is likely to be "new ground" I will give some detail.

Those roots to be harvested are:

alkanet – as a dye

angelica – for liqueurs as fresh root, or dried as a fixative for pot-pourri

elecampane – fresh for candying in small amounts, as a dye, or dried as a fixative for pot-pourri

lady's bedstraw – as a dye

liquorice – fresh in liqueurs, fresh or dried for sweet-making

madder – second or third year roots as a dye

marshmallow – fresh for candying

meadowsweet – fresh as a dye

orris – dried and stored for 1 year before use as a fixative for pot-pourri

sweet cicely – fresh in liqueurs, or for candying, dried as a fixative for pot-pourri

For the roots to be at their best you should wait until the goodness of the plant is concentrated back below the ground. This is when the herb has been cut down for winter, and hopefully before the first severe frost. Usually I gather roots between the end of September and the beginning of November.

Often you can combine the need to divide a spreading growth of herb with harvesting the root. You may wish to leave one third in the ground, plant one third elsewhere and keep the remaining third for preparation as below. Elecampane, marshmallow and sweet cicely can all be a struggle to divide when they are well established and you are best with second or third year plants. Dig around the root first to identify which is the healthiest part and cut this away from the main root, with a spade if necessary. Elecampane has a nasty habit of snapping off, leaving you holding the top slice, which is where your preliminary digging can be helpful.

Once you have detached the root you need, carefully heel in the remainder and cover with soil, a watering with 2 drops of Bach's Rescue Remedy added to a jug of water is a good idea to help the plant over the shock if the weather is still at all warm and dry. (Bach's Rescue Remedy can be bought in wholefood and healthfood shops where Flower Remedies are available.) Take your gathered root and trim away any fibrous lengths which are too small to use, removing trapped soil with them. Cut away the top growth and wash the remaining root well in warm water. For use as a dye, simply chop the cleaned root into the dyepan and continue as instructed in the dye section. For cookery you will almost certainly wish to peel the root as if preparing a vegetable, although young root can sometimes simply be scrubbed. Discard any discoloured matter and chop into bite-sized chunks for candying or liqueurs, or slice for drying. For further candying and liqueur instructions see the relevant sections.

To dry the root the slices should be no more than 1½cm (½in) thick. Lay these on a rack and place in a warm oven on the lowest setting (no higher than 50°C) with the door ajar. It is a slow process which can take anything from 4 hours to overnight during which time the perfume of the root permeates the house. Sweet cicely smells of aniseed, while angelica is stronger and closer to the perfume of an incense. In former centuries it was carried through the house on a pan of burning coals to cleanse the air. Elecampane is also powerful compared to orris which only develops its violet perfume over the following year as the dried root matures in storage. If you feel the root is still not thoroughly dried when you go to bed, simply shut the oven door and turn the heat off, leaving it in a warm, dry atmosphere and continue the next morning for a time if needed. It can be quite difficult to be sure root slices are dried right through, so I always check mine each day for the first week, even though they are stored in airtight jars. If there is the slightest sign of softening, dry again until you are satisfied. The storage jars need not be of dark glass but must be airtight and kept in a cupboard rather than out on a shelf.

For anyone who feels hesitant about harvesting roots, simply compare the exercise to digging parsnips or carrots.They were once sliced and candied as sweets too. The recipes for syrups, sweets and liqueurs are perhaps the most precious to me for they make up the stock in my store cupboard which cannot be bought and which gives so much pleasure in the dark months of winter.

However, first things first. One old cookery book I read years ago instructed the mistress of the house first to call the gardener to the kitchen and make sure he took off his boots to be given his instructions on what to harvest. Let us turn back to the herb garden with our plans of which herbs to grow and how to care for them at harvest time, and then examine the delicious and creative possibilities for their next stage....

Herb cultivation

Divide in autumn

comfrey
cowslips
day lily
elecampane
golden rod
gypsywort
lady's mantle
lemon balm
lily of the valley
lovage
madder
marshmallow
meadowsweet

mints
mugwort
oregano
orris root
periwinkle
primrose
soapwort
sweet cicely
tansy
thrift
valerian
violets
yarrow

Frost-shy herbs (If your garden is liable to frost)

Take indoors	In cold frame	Store in sandy soil
French tarragon	young bay	dahlia
Lavandula canariensis	pineapple	liquorice
lemon verbena	sage	
scented geraniums	tricolor sage	

Herbs needing protection from cold winds

bay
cotton lavender
curry plant
pinks
rosemary
thymes
winter savory

Evergreens

bay
box
chamomile
cotton lavender
curry plant
dyer's chamomile
germander
holly

hyssop
ivy
lavender
periwinkle
rue
sage
winter savory
yew

Herbal shrubs and trees

balsam poplar	laburnum
bayberry	lilac
box	lime
bramble	medlar
broom	mulberry
dogwood	oak
elder	rowan
fig	silver birch
guelder rose	sloe
hawthorn	snowberry
hazel	sweet almond
holly	walnut
hornbeam	willow
juniper	witch hazel

POISONS in the craft garden

box	laburnum
broom (overdose)	lily of the valley
guelder rose (raw berries)	lupin (except alba)
holly	sorrel (overdose)
ivy	yew

Herb heights
Tall

bayberry	ivy
box	jasmine
bramble	juniper
broom	mugwort
burdock	mullein
dogwood	sloe
guelder	snowberry
hawthorn	teazle
holly	willow
hollyhock	yew
hop	

Medium

agrimony	gypsywort
alecost	liquorice
alkanets	lupin
buddleia mint	madder
cardoon	meadowsweet
catmint	nettle
curry plant	orris
day lily	periwinkle

12

dyer's broom
dyer's chamomile
flax
giant thrift
golden rod
gypsywort

sea holly
soapwort
sorrel
sweet gale
weld
woad

Low
bearberry
box (dwarf)
Coreopsis
curled mint
dandelion
dyer's woodruff
forget-me-not

lady' bedstraw
lady's mantle
lily of the valley
saffron
sweet woodruff
Tagetes
thrift

Herbs for sun or shade
In shade
bayberry
bearberry
buddleia mint
curled mint
forget-me-not
ivy
lady's bedstraw
lady's mantle
lily of the valley
meadowsweet
nettle
periwinkle
sweet gale
sweet woodruff
willow
yew

Sunny position
agrimony
alecost
alkanet
box
bramble
broom
burdock
catmint
Coreopis
curry plant
dandelion
day lily
dogwood
dyer's broom
dyer's chamomile
flax
forget-me-not
golden rod
guelder rose
hawthorn
hollyhock

hop
jasmine
juniper
liquorice
lupin
madder
mugwort
mullein
orris
saffron
sea holly
sloe
soapwort
snowberry
sorrel
Tagetes
teazle
thrift
weld
woad

Herb flowers
Spring
bearberry
cowslip
dandelion
forget-me-not

Early-mid summer
agrimony
alecost
alkanet
borage

honeysuckle
hop
hyssop
Iris germanica

13

hawthorn
holly
honesty
honeysuckle
Iris sibirica
jasmine (yellow)
lilac
lily of the valley
periwinkle
primrose
rosemary
sloe
sweet cicely
sweet gale
sweet woodruff
violets

bramble
broom
cardoon
catmint
clary sage
curry plant
day lily
dogwood
dyer's broom
dyer's chamomile
dyer's woodruff
elder
fennel
guelder rose
gypsywort

jasmine (white)
lady's bedstraw
lady's mantle
lavender
meadowsweet
mullein
pinks
roses
Santolina
soapwort
Tagetes
thrift
thymes
violas
woad

Late into autumn
Coreopsis
dahlia
elecampane
golden rod
hollyhock
lavenders
lupin
marshmallow
pot marigold
tansy

Herbs for berries, seedheads & fruits to attract birds

angelica
bramble
burdock
cardoon
dill
dogwood
elder
fennel

guelder rose
hawthorn
holly
ivy
juniper
sloe
snowberry
sunflower

teazle
yarrow
yew

The Wine and Liqueur garden

SUCH a selection of herbs can offer a rich and rewarding garden with plenty of interest in foliage and flowers during each season. The most striking evergreens - juniper and rosemary are almost essentials for liqueurs, and the spring beds beneath the flowering rosemary can be bright with primroses, violets and cowslips for spring wine-making. These are soon joined by the dancing crowns of delicate white sweet cicely flowers held on thin stems above the lacy, fern-like green of the leaves, as if held above a rising water-line for safety. A herb of many uses, sweet cicely will serve to sweeten sour fruits in wines, add flavour to fruit punches and give a liquorice taste to liqueurs made from the root.

Its partner from woodland glades, also requiring a shady corner, is the sweet woodruff which, together with the pretty hawthorn blossom heralds the May sunshine and festivities. Sweet woodruff flowers are perfect miniature white stars modestly displayed only a few inches above the ground, while white or the later red hawthorn blossom, known also as "may", will be high on the hedge or an overhanging branch. Every bit as glorious as sloe blossom whether seen "en masse" or as individual flowers. Before these have faded, the golden variegated foliage of the lemon balm is growing tall to be cut for its harvest together with flowering lemon thyme to make a perfect dinner wine. As yet, the young stems remain neat as the nearby pinks open clove-scented flowers to perfume the air, waiting for their own harvest for syrup and liqueur with the first red roses.

Golden and variegated meadowsweets brighten the dark corner behind the house wall, where the *Iris germanica* opens its extraordinary flowers with such zest that they "pop" like a gun going off. Beneath the overhanging thatch the peppermint grows strongly in a narrow bed. The essential oil content, and therefore the flavour, is increased by an occasional nettle peeping amongst the dark stems as a companion plant. Both are held in a firm line by the drainage trench between the eaves and the lawn. Peppermint for liqueur and nettle for beer or wine, form strange but productive "bedfellows".

Borage and pot marigolds, latecomers in this northerly facing, shaded part of the garden, add splashes of colour in the raised beds between the growing angelica, dill, alecost and mugwort. Bees are buzzing around the thyme, hyssop and biennial clary sage by high summer and last year the honeysuckle was filled with the excited flutter of young thrushes, safe within its abundant growth.

The roses have already faded when the elecampane raises its dish-like flowers to the sun at over five feet high and the Vanessa butterflies swoop to enjoy its savour, as the birds come to take their fill of ripened angelica and dill seeds.

A Craft garden

THE craft garden can be looked upon as a self-sufficiency exercise, simply to provide materials for dyes, basketry, paper-making and wood-turning. It may be that the idea of conveying your talent for design in craft within the framework of the garden itself appeals to you. Or the garden and the plants within it may hold your main interest while their uses and inspiration are an added bonus. Whichever path you follow into making a craft garden, and whether you are wishing to supply materials for a single craft, or all eight suggested in this book, planning your garden will be an opportunity for creativity in itself. Planting herbs which you discover for the first time in these pages could also extend your interests and inspire you to experiment with new craft projects which, in turn, lead to fresh plantings. Although I already enjoyed basketry and needlepoint even before I began gardening, my use of natural materials and home dyes in these crafts sprang from my appreciation of the herbs.

The wondrous diversity of herbal trees, shrubs, perennials and annuals offers a garden which can be enclosed by tall hedges of useful trees and shrubs, decorated by those which are truly ornamental providers and, in summer, cover every inch of space you wish to provide, so that there is little room for weeds. My own country garden seems perfectly in keeping with its surroundings being bounded by a mix of common, variegated and purple elders, red dogwood, hawthorn, holly, broom, willow, snowberry and bayberry. A smaller town garden might be equally served by planting variegated holly, ornamental elders, purple, silver, gold or cut-leafed - broom and red dogwood. At the centre of a lawn, a weeping willow or weeping mulberry makes a lovely focus point. Guelder rose, hazel and thornless bramble are all within my garden along inner boundaries, together with mock orange and a range of tall herbs such as hollyhocks, sunflowers, fennel, mullein and biennial clary sage. Interest is added to a trellis screen, which divides this area from the vegetable garden, by covering it in decorative ivy, golden hop, white and yellow jasmines and honeysuckles.

A covered arbour might be constructed for your "working seat" in the craft garden, to be shaded by any or all of these, or by a beautifully scented climbing rose to sweeten the air as you work. Remember that in this garden area you will wish to do more than simply sit to watch the birds, butterflies and bees attracted by the herbs. Therefore leave extra space on a flat area of path or grass to set up a table to work, a spinning wheel, a tapestry or embroidery frame. A place reserved in some shade is helpful in hot summer weather when you will not want to have hot, sticky hands as you handle home-dyed wools or silks, or pressed flowers.

If you enjoy home dyeing you will have noticed already that the smell (it really is stretching the truth to mention perfume, except for a few herbs) of the dyepan is strong for an enclosed kitchen. A barbeque-type hearth offers the opportunity to simmer the wool or fabric and dyes outdoors (unless very close neighbours are likely to object), so adding to the pleasure of the exercise. Dyeing should always be done on a sunny, dry day to be sure of drip-drying the dyed material outdoors and testing it for light fastness in sunlight.

With these pointers in mind, other aspects of the garden can be considered. Since all of the herbs you will be growing are for harvest they will need to be easy to reach with no bed more than 1.2m (4ft) wide and since some of the dye plants in particular benefit from raised beds, the edgings to these need to be considered.

Depending upon your "craft" interests, you might favour a fancy tile edging reminiscent of Victorian flower gardens, alongside brick paths. Good imitations with neat designs are now available at a fraction of the price of the real thing. Clipped box, cotton lavender, germander or lavender hedges could be set to outline the beds with geometric precision forming a patchwork pattern contrasted by corresponding shapes of coloured paving stones, brick, grass or bark. Or an interest in basketry might inspire you to weave low hurdles of hazel or ash to edge the beds, linking the craft garden with one of medieval times when these wattle hurdles were set around gardens, or to encircle individual bushes, herb plantings or trees.

At this time there remained much of the spirit of the wild meadow in gardens, with low-growing flowers often left amongst the grasses to be enjoyed, or, when greatly valued, set on little hummocks of earth called "tuffets" to be seen better and not trodden down. It was one of these "tuffets" which provided a seat for Miss Muffet in the ancient nursery rhyme. Clearly this was in the carefree times when gardening required a minimum of effort and no-one had invented the repetitive task of mowing the lawn.

The mead of flowers, wild strawberries, violets, lily of the valley, heartsease, daisies, forget-me-nots and cornflowers inspired tapestry designs and in some paintings we see the ladies portrayed working at their frames in the serenity of the garden. An idyll we too can enjoy in our quiet moments. If it seems the weather was always better in those days whereas today a little shelter might be required more often than not, then a summerhouse overlooking the garden would give the opportunity to sit in warmth with no sudden breezes to blow your design away just as you have set out your carefully pressed flowers on the graph paper. The sun appearing again from behind the cloud which seems ever-ready to creep across the sky just as I am settled in the open, may tempt you back out to study the contrasts of one herb against another in the craft garden. There, companion plants might inspire a new approach to the theme.

On many occasions I have gone to the garden on one simple errand only to be side-tracked by the sight of another herb, perfect for harvesting, which will take up my time for the rest of the day.

So it is, having set the dyepot on the heat again to simmer, and hung a finished batch on the line to dry, we might venture forth into the garden around, searching out those flowers which could be portrayed with the colour already achieved. Yellow is the easiest colour to obtain and there are numerous yellow flowers amongst the herbs for your designs, from winter yellow jasmine and spring light, creamy primroses through the summer flowers of broom and curry plant to the early autumn, sunflower and golden rod.

The craft garden can have many flowers, in fact more than any other herb garden for it includes such unlikely plants as dahlia and *Tagetes* as dye herbs; sunflowers and hollyhocks for long fibres for spinning alongside the delicate blue-flowered flax; lupins and mullein for paper-making, with nettles and fennel adding their fibres; thymes and hyssop for making stem baskets, lavenders for country favours and fans woven in the style of corn dollies; elegant flowers for pressing and needlework design - lily of the valley, pinks, heartsease, roses, honeysuckle and many more; and lastly those for drying, both for arrangements and making miniature, framed knot gardens – tansy, cotton lavender, peppermint, eau-de-cologne mint, oregano and red yarrow.

There is nothing like a craft garden to make you fall in time with the seasons. An appreciation of each harvest as one follows on from another can lead to a better understanding of nature and of your inner self. Each craft has its true season, when there is a time to enjoy it to the full. Dyeing is mainly done in full summer, although there are a few dyes ready to harvest in winter, spring and autumn, and dried flowers, bark, roots etc can always be used. Having harvested the flowering thymes and hyssop, you may wish to make up stem baskets as soon as the materials are dried, when you are full of enthusiasm for the project, or they may be kept for a week or month or two. Lavender favours must be made in the heat of summer when the lavender is perfect for harvest and newly picked. The perfect excuse to sit in the sunshine, or beneath the shade of your arbour and listen to the bees buzzing as you work.

Pressing flowers is a lovely pastime since you may give it a few minutes here and there or much longer, according to your daily round. The most pleasure may be gained if you make a regular hour at intervals through the year, however, as this will give you the greatest variety of flowers and leaves and form a pleasing record to look back on in the winter months as you make up cards, pictures or decorative items from your pressed materials. Harvesting and drying bunches of flowering herbs takes little time on a daily or weekly basis through the summer and will give you a fascinating stock of materials for arrangements and miniature knot gardens when the days are dark, wet and boring in winter.

On bright winter days you may wish to cut and prepare your ivy, elder, dogwood and other basketry materials and make baskets from the honeysuckle or golden hop you have stored beneath the hedge from autumn. Wood stored to season for woodturning is a longer process. All of your stored materials, pressed flowers, sketches, paintings or photographs from each year form a treasurehouse of design inspiration which may emerge in finished projects as embroidery, needlepoint, miniature knot gardens, flower arrangements, carved or turned wood, baskets, pictures, decorations on ceramics, decorative papers, ink, home produced cloth and so much more.

It is not so much a matter of "How does your garden grow?" as "How does your garden help you to grow?"

A Treasure garden

ALL gardens are to treasure: whether bursting with the promise of new buds and bright spring flowers in the face of uncertain weather, in their full glory as bees and butterflies alike plunder the generous stores of nectar and pollen, or as they offer ripened harvests of roots, seeds and fruits in autumn. In each garden there are certain plants the gardener treats with especial care and feels proud to have grown. Often these "treasures" have either very ornamental flowers or finely variegated leaves.

In the treasure garden that I have set out for my own enjoyment, the variegated gold and silver leafed herbs have become the focus of my scheme, with occasional beautiful flowers such as the polyanthus "Gold Lace". The idea for this "treasure garden" came initially from the silver moonlight gardens which are so effective both in the gathering dusk or moonlit splendour of warm summer nights and on cold, dark days during winter when their silver brightens the dark earth.

After a season of growing only silver herbs, I decided to complement this beauty in creating my own private hoard of gold, silver and bronze leafed plants in a small area where they may give the finest contrasts to really stunning effect. A central tree, or a planting of several to border the "treasure garden", can set the scene. The balsam poplar has rich, golden leaves which first open from slightly sticky and fragrant buds in spring, when other trees are cautiously holding back. Unchecked, it will grow to a considerable height, but it can be well pruned each year to maintain manageable growth while supplying stout stakes for basketry at the same time.

Pretty alternatives could be the variegated elders - the gold or silver leafed, either of which can be kept trimmed back to a shrub rather than a tree. For a dense, bushy growth to give shelter to the garden and be appreciated quickly, silver or gold leafed holly bushes can be bought 1-1.2m (3 or 4ft) tall and interplanted for contrast. They can also offer a little shade for lower plantings and add touches of beauty in every season.

Cultivating gold or silver leafed varieties of favourite herbs and flowers has been a popular idea for centuries. In particular, the Elizabethans, who delighted in contrasts of texture and colour in their gardens and welcomed any opportunity to surprise and impress their guests, prized such beauties as gilded rosemary. For years I searched for this rarity around the country and have finally found a source. The silver leafed still eludes me. Elizabethans must have found it equally difficult for some contemporary writers suggest painting evergreen box or rosemary with gold leaf to obtain similar effects. We are assured it washes off quite slowly over a period of weeks. No doubt the real gold and silver plants were much treasured.

Then there is the joy of being given a real "treasure" of a plant in the form of a cutting or seeds by a friend - my white flowered honesty with creamy golden splashed leaves was one of these. Another friend with a love for old-fashioned flowers and herbs, who had brought her own treasures from a Chelsea flower show years before, gave me variegated meadowsweet. This is one of my carefully nurtured favourites. The red stem with gold and green deeply serrated leaves, set in artistically pleasing pairs, brightens dark shady corners in the garden and bears creamy flowers later in the summer, at a rather lower height than those of the common meadowsweet.

Chance finds when out to buy other herbs can be wonderful surprises; variegated tansy was one of these for me, with variegated rue from the same shopping trip. Variegated rue is less permanent than the tansy as it tends disappointingly, to revert to green in some summers, but the tansy has delicate, feathered leaves, closer to the plain tansy than the curled, with striking splashes of creamy yellow in the foliage. Variegated lemon balm will also hold its golden bounty provided it is not placed in shade. A little cover from very hot sun is, however, required for lemon balm as the golden edges of the leaves can scorch brown and be spoiled.

More commonly for sale, but none the less of a treasure, is the hardy golden sage which may look sad after a hard winter, but with judicious pruning (which at the same time provides cuttings) it can readily be revived into healthy, bushy growth. By contrast, the tricolor sage with its creamy, pink and silver grey foliage needs complete protection from frosts and cold March winds to survive.

The wholly golden herbs - golden marjoram, lemon thyme, feverfew and meadowsweet - can be set against the pure silver herbs to good effect. Of these, curry plant seems to stand cold winds better than silver cotton lavender; both give a wealth of easy-to-raise cuttings. For extra impact amongst low-growing herbs, the dwarf

19

forms of each can be recommended. Dwarf curry plant may be difficult to find but the *Santolina nana* is more readily available and has neat, compact silver growth. The crisp brilliance of "silver posy" thyme at its best is my next prize, needing well-drained soil and protection from easterly winds. The silver leafed tansy, *Tanacetum hardjanii,* a far cry from its tall, green and rampant relative, remains low-growing, but is particularly subject to frost, or extreme weather conditions, whether wet and cold or dry and hot. Taller and most effective of the silver herbs is the *Artemisia* "Silver Queen". Other artemisias, wormwood, *A. absinthum* and sea wormwood, *A. maritima,* are also suitable.

Lavenders provide some varieties with distinctly silver rather than grey leaves, but *Lavandula canariensis* has all the qualifications of a real treasure since it is difficult to obtain, needs to be overwintered with care indoors as it comes from the warmer climes of the Canary Islands, and is delightful in fragrance and appearance with finely toothed, almost feathered, silvery leaves. Papillon lavender is a hardier herb with extremely ornamental flowerheads, much closer to stoechas lavender than other varieties.

Although not consistently silver leafed through the year, a mint which could be considered for this garden is the buddleia mint, which has flowers and leaves resembling buddleia. It was previously known by the rather less impressive title of horsemint. The silver grey in the leaves is more in evidence later in the season than in spring. Other mints are the gingermint which has regimented stripes of gold on its green leaves, is comparatively low growing as a mint and bears tiny crowns of purple flowers around the stem at each of the upper leaf nodes, softening its summer image in a charming manner. The taller pineapplemint also has variegated leaves with pretty cream edges or sometimes whole cream leaves amongst a soft green.

If you have a pergola or fence, or build a "covered way" between the beds of silver and gold, then golden hop may use this backdrop as a support on which to drape its splendour through the hot summer. A towering Scotch thistle rising before it makes an impressive partnership. Cardoons can also be grown here, although their leaves are only mildly silvered. The *Eryngiums,* Miss Willmott's ghost and sea holly show their silver character only in their second year. Sea holly is temperamental in germination away from its native habitat of sandy, salty soil, but will rise from an "ugly duckling" of a green plant in the first year to a tall, mature herb with branching stems like grand candelabra's bearing spiny silver ruffs about the flowerheads, in the second or third season. An area of silver leafed sorrel, with small spear-shaped leaves can be kept low to the ground and edged to good effect with a row of dwarf golden box, perhaps with a young golden bay rising from the centre.

Whether you complete your hoard of "herb treasures" by adding an imaginative touch of spice with silver leafed old fashioned pinks, such as "sops-in-wine" with their rich, clove perfume, or a scattering of rare and lovely flowers - perhaps gold and silver laced polyanthus or auriculas - may you keep on finding new joys to add over the years.

A little nut tree bearing only a silver nutmeg and a golden pear may be too much to hope for, but we may all have the opportunity to nurture a rare treasure one day. . .

Wine and liqueur garden

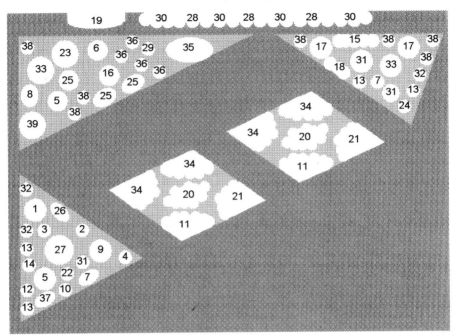

1 agrimony	21 lemon balm
2 alecost	22 liquorice
3 angelica	23 lovage
4 anise	24 marjoram
5 biennial clary sage	25 meadowsweet
6 bog myrtle	26 mint-curled
7 borage	27 mugwort
8 broom	28 nettle
9 caraway	29 pineapplemint
10 chamomile	30 peppermint
11 clove pink	31 pot marigold
12 coriander	32 primrose
13 cowslip	33 rose
14 dill	34 rosemary
15 elecampane	35 sweet cicely
16 gingermint	36 sweet woodruff
17 honeysuckle	37 thyme
18 hyssop	38 violet
19 *Iris germanica*	39 wormwood
20 juniper	

Treasure garden

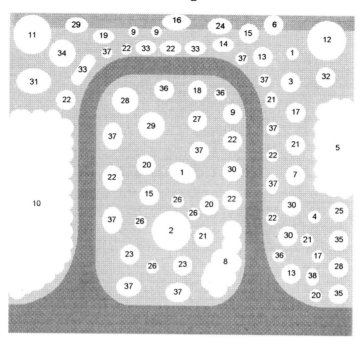

1 **Artemisia** – Silver Queen
2 balsam poplar
3 biennial clary sage
4 box-golden
5 buddleia mint
6 cardoon
7 catmint
8 cotton lavender
9 dwarf cotton lavender
10 curry plant
11 dogwood-variegated
12 elder-variegated
13 fennel-bronze
14 feverfew-golden
15 gingermint
16 holly-golden
17 honesty-variegated
18 horehound-white
19 **Iris pallida**-variegated
20 lavender-Papillon or Stoechas

21 lemon balm-variegated
22 marjoram-golden
23 meadowsweet-variegated
   (or golden)
24 milk thistle
25 mullein
26 polyanthus-gold lace
27 rue-variegated
28 sage-golden
29 sage-purple
31 sea holly
32 Scotch thistle
33 silverweed
34 sorrel-silver leaf
35 tansy-variegated
36 tansy-silver
37 thyme-golden
38 thyme-silver posy
39 yarrow-silver
   leafed

Craft garden

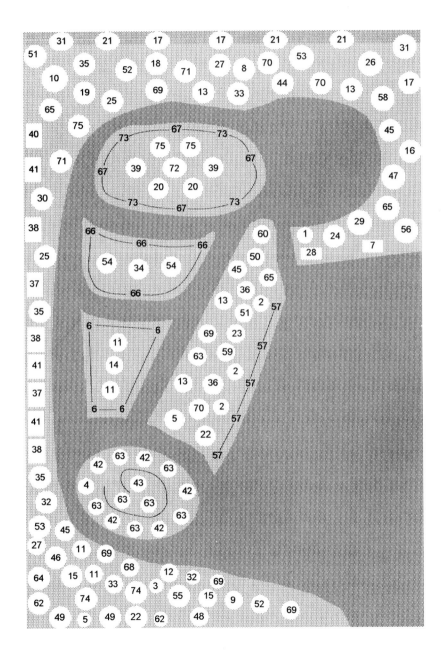

Craft garden

1 agrimony
2 alkanet
3 bayberry
4 bearberry
5 biennial clary sage
6 box
7 bramble
8 broom
9 cardoon
10 comfrey
11 *Coreopisis tinctoria*
12 cotton lavender
13 cowslip
14 curry plant
15 dahlia
16 day lily
17 dogwood
18 dyer's broom
19 dyer's chamomile
20 dyer's woodruff
21 elder
22 elecampane
23 fennel
24 flax
25 forget-me-not
26 golden rod
27 greater burdock
28 Guelder rose
29 gypsywort
30 hazel
31 hawthorn
32 heartsease
33 helichrysum
34 holly
35 hollyhock
36 honeysuckle
37 hop-garden
38 hop-golden
39 hyssop
40 ivy
41 jasmine
42 lady's bedstraw
43 lavender
44 lily of the valley
45 lungwort
46 lupin
47 madder
48 mallow
49 meadowsweet
50 mullein
51 nettle
52 oregano
53 periwinkle
54 pinks
55 sea holly
56 sloe
57 snowberry
58 soapwort
59 sorrel
60 statice
61 St. John's wort
62 sunflower
63 *Tagetes*
64 tansy
65 teazle
66 thrift
67 thyme
68 Tudor immortelles
69 violet
70 weld
71 wild strawberry
72 willow
73 winter savory
74 woad
75 water avens

Common name	Latin name
agrimony	Agrimonia eupatoria
alecost	Tanacetum balsamita
alkanet	Alkanna tinctoria
bayberry	Myrica cerifera
bearberry	Arctostaphylosa uva-ursi
bog myrtle	Myrica gale
box	Buxus sempervirens
bramble	Rubus fruticosus
broom	Cytisus scoparius
buddleia mint	Mentha
cardoon	Scolymus cardunculus
catmint	Nepeta cataria
coreopsis	Coreopsis tinctoria
curled mint	Mentha
curry plant	Helichrysum angustifolium
dandelion	Taraxacum officinale
day lily	Hemerocallis flava & fulva
dyer's broom	Genista tinctoria
dyer's chamomile	Anthemis tinctoria
flax	Linum usitatissimum
forget-me-not	Myosotis symphytifolia
fullers teazle	Dipsacus fullorum
golden rod	Solidago virgaurea
greater burdock	Arctium lappa
guelder rose	Viburnum opulus
gypsywort	Lycopus europaeus
hawthorn	Crataegus monogyma
holly	Ilex aquifolium
hollyhock	Althaea rosea
hop	Humulus lupulus
ivy	Hedera helix
jasmine	Jasminum grandiflorum
juniper	Juniperus communis
lady's bedstraw	Galium verum
lady's mantle	Alchemilla vulgaris
lily of the valley	Convallaria majalis
liquorice	Glycyrrhiza glabra
lupin	Lupinus albus
madder	Rubia tinctorium
meadowsweet	Filipendula ulmaria
mugwort	Artemisia vulgaris
mullein	Verbascum thapsus
orris	Iris germanica
periwinkle	Vinca major
red dogwood	Cornus sanguinea

saffron	Crocus sativus
sea holly	Eryngium maritimum
sloe	Prunus spinosa
snowberry	Symphoricarpus albus
soapwort	Saponaria officinalis
sorrel	Rumex acetosa
stinging nettle	Urtica dioica
sweet woodruff	Asperula odorata
tagetes	Tagetes patula
thrift	Armeria maritima
weld	Reseda luteola
willow	Salix
woad	Isatis tinctoria

Key to abbreviations

A annual   S shrub
B biennial   T tree
P perennial

Agrimonia eupatoria   **P**   **AGRIMONY**

A familiar plant of the hedgerows, agrimony is often to be seen together with St. John's wort, betony and yarrow in the long grasses at the roadside. On dry chalky hillsides and high meadows it may appear only a few inches high, in perfect miniature. In damp ground the 60-75cm (2 to 2½ft) reddish stems bear "spires" of tiny yellow flowers in midsummer resulting in the common name of church steeples. The flowers are followed by small cone-like sticky burrs which attach the seeds to any unheeding passer-by in autumn, in order to spread the plant. This clinging property has given another name for the herb, sticklewort.

The herb's medicinal uses were known as early as 2,600 B.C. Eupatoria in the Latin name is thought to be in honour of Mithridates VI Eupator, King of Pontus (100 B.C.). Agremone or argemoney may have referred to white specks in the eye which agrimony treated. It has also been a wound herb, removing thorns and clotting the blood; a "liverwort"; and, in Anglo-Saxon times when it was known as "garclive", it was applied to wounds, warts and snake bites. The seeds should be sown in autumn for best results. My own plants self-seed most effectively in the gravel path, suggesting moisture can be important in the early stages. Once they have four leaves I transplant the seedlings into soil in a sunny position. In damp, good ground the herb will grow taller with very attractive, deeply indented, hairy leaves. Set amongst its wild companions, yarrow and St. John's wort, in the craft garden, it will be supported in high winds and less likely to curl over, catching at unsuspecting visitors who walk close to the flowerbed. Agrimony leaves and flowers, together with citrus fruits and ginger, used to be made into a "lemonade", taken for colds, adding another name to its list, that of lemonade flower.

The herb is found in Asia, Europe, Canada and the U.S.A. Sow the seeds some 25cm (9in) apart, close to the surface where they are to remain, or closer together in a moist seedtray outdoors, transplanting later. The leaves can be gathered in summer together with the flowering tops for wine. The tops and stalks may be used as a dye. In autumn the seeding spire is cut down and mature plants may be divided.

The especially fragrant, *Agrimonia odorata* is a larger garden plant with a scent reminiscent of apricots which can be dried for pot-pourri or scented pillows.

Alchemilla vulgaris   **P**   **LADY'S MANTLE**

THE leaves of lady's mantle, with their elegant, deep folds and frilled edges, are of course responsible for its name. It must have been easy to see the resemblance in the days when ladies still wore mantles, or cloaks. The real beauty of these almost circular leaves, which can be several inches across, is, to my mind, the drops of dew or rainwater which collect in the cupped centres.

There are numerous varieties of lady's mantle, both wild and cultivated, many of them being native to the American Andes. In Britain and Northern Europe 14 varieties can be found, some in very limited habitats, Yorkshire and Teesdale favouring several. *Alchemilla alpina,* wild in northern England and Scotland is popular in gardens for rockeries, hanging baskets or pots. With silvery edges and undersides to the leaves together with a low growth, it can be included in the silver garden to some effect. *Alchemilla mollis* is the cultivated plant, while I have seen

Alchemilla vulgaris, the true herb, growing wild in north Yorkshire some 22-30cm (9 to 12in) from a short, black root. It is this plant which is harvested for medicinal use.

The flowers are minute and of a delicate greenish yellow which later fades to buff parchment. There is no attraction in their colour, but their petite perfection is magical to those who take the time to stop and examine them closely. They are lovely as dried flowers, although very fragile.

Lady's mantle prefers some shade with clay or chalky soil and the *Alchemilla mollis* is complemented well by purple sage as a companion plant. With the two growing together in abandoned profusion at a path edge, the sage shades the roots of the lady's mantle, which appears holding "bouquets" of flowers on 30-45cm (12 to 18in) long stems above the purple foliage.

The leaves of the two make an interesting combination when intermixed and the spreading habits of both tend to be discouraged as they challenge each other for dominance. Lady's mantle seed can be gathered, although it takes careful and regular observation to determine exactly when it is ready, as the seedheads are so small. Sow the seeds in either spring or autumn, or leave the parent plant to self-seed. A mature plant can also be divided in the autumn, but spring will often reveal several tiny seedlings alongside the parent plant which can be transplanted to a more suitable spot when large enough.

Alkanna tinctoria   B or P   ALKANET

THERE are a confusing number of alkanets, some of which appear very like forget-me-nots, while others are closer to a borage, as they are of the *Boraginaceae* family. The native British form is *Anchusa officinalis,* a soft, hairy plant of varying height with narrow leaves on angular stems bearing violet flowers in July. This form is a biennial. There is also an evergreen alkanet, *Pentaglottis sempervirens,* with deeper green leaves and of a sturdier, bristly nature. This perennial flowers from early summer onwards and, in the days of Culpeper was naturalised in the West Country and Kent.

Alkanna tinctoria, which is the main dye plant, has largely been cultivated in Central and Southern Europe, where it is a native. It is also known as Spanish Bugloss or Dyer's Bugloss and grows to about 30cm (1ft) tall. The leaves are long and narrow as with other forms, and the flowers, either blue-purple or pale yellow, appear in full summer. The root is the part of the plant harvested to produce the red dye in contact with oils, waxes and spirits of wine. The roots of Dyer's Bugloss may be particularly large and are dug in autumn from mature plants and have been used to stain wood, leather, marble or wax. Alkanet dyes wool and has been the dye for paper used for acid/alkaline tests. It has also produced colouring in lipstick or rouge. (See dye section.)

Althaea rosea   B or P   HOLLYHOCK

THE hollyhock is an essential part of any cottage garden or herbaceous border. It is equally at home in the back of a herb garden bed, since hollyhock flowers were formerly given medicinally, reminding us of the common mallow family relationship of the hollyhock and marshmallow.

The dark, purplish flowers are those best for dyeing wool. The tall hairy stem which may be 3-4m (10 to 13ft) high has been used both for paper making and to provide fibres for spinning.

The hollyhock, or "holyoke" as it is recorded in early times, originated in China: and reached Europe possibly as late as the 16th century. Gerard, writing in the 16th century, mentions growing the double purple-flowered form and wrote then that these were common everywhere. The hollyhock is now cultivated throughout Europe and in America.

In all but the most sheltered situation, hollyhocks will need to be staked against high winds during their second year, as even these sturdy stems are not sufficient to hold up the many brightly coloured flowers which form at either side of their upper length. The flowers open from mid-summer into autumn above the large, heart-shaped leaves which are grey underneath.

As with all mallows there is a tendency to develop rust on the leaves caused by the fungus, *Puccinia malvacearum.* This may be prevented or treated at an early stage with a horsetail infusion made by putting 4 tablespoons of dried horsetail into 2.3 litres (4 pints) of water. This is brought to the boil and simmered for 20 minutes before setting aside for 24 hours and then straining. The recipe is further diluted to 9 litres (2 gallons) of water before spraying it over the mallow leaves. Treat again each week for several weeks.

The flowers can be gathered as they first open, or the plant left to go to seed. As the seeds ripen, gather these, either cutting down the stems for compost, or leaving them in damp shade to ret for the fibre extraction. (See herbs for fibres.) Seeds sown in autumn or the following spring germinate freely in most soil types. Feed well during the second year if growing for fibres.

Anthemis tinctoria   P   DYER'S CHAMOMILE

AN attractive plant for borders, or even to make hedge-like divisions between other low-growing herbs, dyer's chamomile flowers on and on through the summer. The yellow or cream daisy-like flowers, which declare it to be a member of the *Compositae* family create attractive splashes of colour amongst the deep green of weld, in the craft garden. The spreading and seeding habits of dyer's chamomile also make it a plant to be kept in check after the first year and it is as well if many of the flowerheads are harvested at their peak for dyeing wool. In this way the number of seedheads is drastically reduced. Excess flowers can be set to hang dry and stored in a dry, dark environment to be used months later.

Dyer's chamomile seeds germinate readily whether saved and sown in the following spring, or left to fall naturally in autumn. The young seedlings should be set some 30cm (lft) apart, to make an almost continuous line, or dotted at larger distances amidst yarrow, weld, alkanet, lupins or other herbs. Growing to a height of 60-90cm (2 to 3ft), they could be placed behind the lower growing forget-me-nots, *Coreopsis* and *Tagetes.* The foliage consists of finely divided leaves which might be seen as needle-like versions of the heavier tansy; yet still less delicate than those of Roman chamomile. Their pungent scent is typical of the family. The golden flowers attract hoverflies and useful predators to the garden in a similar manner to those of the deeper orange marigolds and they are a friendly, if slightly invasive gardeners friend for the edges of the vegetable patch. In a mild winter the clipped mounds of their lower leaves survive, making welcome patches of green where they outline bare patches of soil which await the presence of annuals.

Arctium lappa   B   BURDOCK

RARELY thought of as a garden plant, burdock thrives on waste ground, often at the edges of ditches, or near water where the ground is relatvely rich. It seems almost a defiant gesture to take it into the garden, for neighbours will surely think it a weed, unless you have a wild area where it might seem at home. Despite the difficulties which my springer spaniel has with occasional burrs in her coat (the name "lappa" meaning "to seize" needs no explanation at seed-time,) I like to grow burdock in the craft garden, for it is actually a most useful herb. Since the plant can be gathered when in flower for use as a dye, it is only necessary to leave a burr or two to seed for new plants in the following year.

The tonic qualities of burdock will be well remembered by those who have enjoyed dandelion and burdock as a drink in spring. A specific for kidney diseases, burdock is cleansing and the young shoots can be steamed in a similar manner to asparagus and eaten, or candied, as with angelica. Also in spring, the roots of second year plants may be dug and roasted to make a "coffee" drink. The name "love leaves" comes from an old practice of eating the young stalks raw as an aphrodisiac. The large leaves, rough later in the year, can be smoked as a form of tobacco and gave the plant another common name, "Gypsy's rhubarb", from their shape.

Greater burdock is plentiful in southern Britain, while the lesser form, *Arctium minus,* is found in the northern regions.

In good conditions, with nitrogen rich soil, the deep, vertical roots of greater burdock will support plants of up to 2m (7ft). It is more usual to see them around 1-1.5m (3 to 5ft). Both plants can yield a dye. Several varieties are natives of Europe, North America and Asia. The pretty, maroon flowers may easily be missed when so many brighter blooms clamour for your attention from July through to September. They are, however worth seeking out in their wild situation if you have not noticed them before, decorating the stately branched stems like so many young thistles. These are followed by the burrs which, if left, will remain through the autumn.

Arctostaphylos uva-ursi   P   BEARBERRY

THE common name of "mountain box" tells us a great deal of the nature of the plant, which thrives on barren, mountainous heaths, with an additional, alpine form as far north as Arctic regions and in coniferous woods where the temperature is cool. It is tempting to place such an attractive, sprawling herb in full sun to cover the top of a wall or bank, but the wall should, at least, be north facing. *Uva-ursi* prefers an acid medium, unlike most other herbs and so will benefit from a buried tub of its own composted soil in the garden if it is set amongst herbs with an alkaline preference.

The glossy, leathery leaves are evergreen and borne on trailing, creeping stems with an initial height of only 15cm (6in). It is a native of the British Highlands, parts of Europe, Asia and North America. The white and pink, bell-shaped flowers appear in early summer to be followed by red berries, which on moorland provide food for grouse. Unlike many dye herbs, *Uva-ursi* gives colouring from the leaves rather than the bright berries. In her book, **The Colour Cauldron,** Su Grierson notes records of its use for grey and black dyes in Norway and Sweden, as well as the bluish-black obtained in Scotland from harvesting the leaves at flowering time. The herb has also had other uses in tanning leather, dried in tobacco mixtures and prepared as a medicinal plant. The Physicians of Myddfai in Wales mention it in the 13th century.

Armeria maritima   P   THRIFT

AS the Latin name suggests, thrift grows in its dwarf form as a native plant on cliffs overlooking the sea, although inland it can also be found in gravelly, mountainous areas. It grows wild in Europe, Asia and North America. There is also a taller form cultivated in gardens which gives an excellent harvest of long-stalked flower heads to be dried for flower arrangements. The clumps of the tall, grass-like leaves should be divided at least every other year for the better growth of the exceptionally pretty globe-like flower heads, which appear as if packed all over with tiny pinkish purple flowers waving on a single bare stem. These are almost as attractive later on in the summer as seedheads when the colour goes from the petals and they appear as a whitish "paper" shadow of their former glory.

Gerard mentions thrift, then called, "Our Ladies' cushion", as a native of salt marshes which was used to edge herb beds. He writes they are esteemed for "their beautie and pleasure", rather than a use being sought in physic. In Tudor times, the lesser form was popularly grown in Britain with the plants set close together for the best effect from the massed evergreen leaves. These became thickened by the regular clipping and could readily be shaped. After knot gardens went out of fashion thrift remained as an edging plant but was allowed to flower and the pink, purple, red and white flowers became well known.

In the modern herb garden, where thrift likes to be in full sun, the flowers make an additional contribution in summer by attracting many insects, including bees and butterflies. The medicinal use which was eventually found for its antiseptic qualities has now been discontinued in home treatments as applications can result in allergic dermatitis. It has also been given as a treatment for obesity.

Artemisia vulgaris   P   MUGWORT

THIS must surely be the most elegant of the wayside herbs. Tall and stately in maturity, with such deeply cut leaves that they seem almost fringed. The beauty of mugwort is too often spoiled by the neglected nature of its surroundings. The herb has a talent for growing in the most dry, dusty, inhospitable places. You will see it alongside busy roads where it takes on a cloak of grey dust, or close to the seashore amongst shingle and debris.

In full sun in the garden, it can be seen to advantage, brought from a "Cinderella" existence into the limelight to be appreciated. It is hardly surprising the herb has been credited with magical powers in Europe and Asia. Eating "muggins" in May has been said to keep away poison, fire, bills, consumption, beasts and "disorderly besetments".

The small, pale, yellow-white flowers which cluster about the upper stems in July and August are subtle and can be gathered to be sprinkled over food as a condiment (to be avoided by pregnant mothers) before they fade into tiny white balls of seeds. To propagate mugwort, the seeds should be left to scatter naturally, or gathered as they ripen and sown straight away. Seeds which are kept have a poor germination rate.

Alternatively, the mature plants can be divided in spring or autumn as they gradually spread over a larger area. Mugwort is not invasive in the enthusiastic manner of mints and tansy, but it will make steady progress if left to itself.

The herb is distributed through Europe and Asia and naturalised in North America where it can be found in eastern states as far south as Georgia. It is happy to grow in poor, sandy or chalky soil and will reach a height of about 90cm (3ft), almost doubling this size when in rich ground. As the plant grows taller the white undersides of the leaves will become more apparent, hinting at the close relationship this herb has with wormwood and other members of the *Artemisia* family. Mugwort is one of the gentler members of the family group, being included in beers as a bitter herb and its soft leaves having been used over centuries to bind sore feet or pad shoes to stay weariness. It is still sufficiently pungent to act as a useful pest deterrent, the essence of mugwort being used in insecticides. It has a reputation for keeping midges away as well as moths. The root is dug in autumn, the "coals" which form about them being the old root which is very salty. The Japanese used these to make moxa cakes to be smouldered on the patient's flesh. This treatment is also followed in traditional Chinese medicine with powdered mugwort cones set on a slice of garlic to smoulder above acupuncture points.

Asperula odorata   P   SWEET WOODRUFF

A pretty, delicate woodland plant, woodruff is a favourite of mine beneath the lilacs and in the shade, covering the bare lower stems of the bog myrtle. The edges of the leaves which form divided "ruffs" about the thin stems at intervals look as lovely when the herb is "iced" with frost as they do beneath the tiny white flowers. These top the stems in late April or May at around 10-15cm (4 to 6in) and might be imagined to have been added in cross stitch.

As a ground cover, sweet woodruff needs little attention, merely the protective shade of the taller plants around it and an autumn mulch of compost from the herbs, with a little leaf mould. Take care strong manure laid beneath roses does not come into contact with the herb. Over many years I have never known it to suffer from pests or disease, only to shrivel in unfaltering drought. It may take time to establish, but once set in a suitable habitat the herb will steadily increase.

Cut woodruff back during flowering to dry with the full scent of new-mown hay. This perfume is brought out by the drying process and once made it such a popular strewing herb. Gather it at its best for flavouring wine or use in insect repelling pot-pourri mixtures. Sweet woodruff should not be taken in large quantities, when it will produce symptoms of toxicity.

It is a native of Europe, Asia and North Africa and will germinate readily if the seeds are sown in autumn. Alternatively, established plants may be divided in late summer. A close relative, Dyer's Woodruff, *Asperula tinctoria* can be grown in the dye garden. The leaves are thinner and more pointed so that the general effect is rather less attractive than that of sweet woodruff. Dyer's woodruff will stand a sunnier position and has tiny white flowers on slightly taller stems later in the summer. The roots yield a red dye.

Buxus sempervirens   S   BOX

TO most people, the name box conveys the idea of a neat, dark green, compact, low-growing hedge around a bed of herbs. Some will be familiar with taller box hedges but we rarely see box growing more than 2m (7ft) in Britain. It is however, native to all of Europe, North Africa and Western Asia where the tree bark, wood and leaves has the most powerful medicinal properties. In favourable conditions box can grow up to 7m (24ft) when it becomes an evergreen tree rather than the familiar shrub. Box woods were once common in Europe, with trees living to 600 or 700 years. A former famous site in Britain was on Box Hill near Dorking, in Surrey. The wood, being very hard, was much in demand for making musical instruments, boxes, chess pieces and so on. The root was also popular with cabinet makers and turners.

Felling of such slow-growing trees soon reduced the supply drastically. Branches of box are no longer used to give the blessing on Palm Sunday, nor are they put up in houses when the Christmas holly and mistletoe are taken down. Buxine contained in the bark and leaves was once used to treat fevers, but is not a safe home remedy. Box has also been used in homoeopathy to treat rheumatism.

My own box hedge took almost four years to come together to a height of some 15cm (6in) from cuttings of hedge clippings. Having set 120 of these first into hormone rooting powder and then into a prepared shallow trench at the edge of the herb bed, with a little sand and compost added to the chalky soil already there; I kept them watered during dry periods for almost 2 years. My care was rewarded, for almost every sprig took, giving a length of hedge some 8.4m (27ft). Each year in the late spring or early summer the tiny hedge gives minute clusters of yellow green flowers. I cut these away as I trim the hedge, but they would otherwise turn to small egg-shaped capsules which contain the fruits. For medicinal purposes the leaves and bark should be gathered before flowering. The low, garden varieties have little of the medicinal promise of the Asian trees.

There are a number of varieties available to keen gardeners, with golden and variegated forms now relatively common. There is also a silver. In the writings of Sir Hugh Platt in the 16th century, we find he recommends gardeners should paint the plain box with gold leaf to gild it. Clearly one needed to be resourceful in those times.

Convallaria majalis   P   LILY OF THE VALLEY

THIS was one of the first gifts I received from a new neighbour as I began making my present herb gardens, and remains a special favourite. The common names of "May lily", "Our Lady's tears" and "ladder to heaven" all capture the sweet quality of the pure white bell flowers as they first open, usually early in May, to grace the lush greens of the surrounding young herbs. Joining with the white sweet woodruff and often the white crowns of sweet cicely flowers, which also enjoy the shady north side of the house, they form a trio of apparent purity and innocence.

The effect is not to be trusted with this herb, for all that. It contains a powerful cardioactive glycoside similar to digitalin in foxglove and has been used to treat the same medical conditions. The herb is harvested for medicinal use as the flowers open. Poisonous when misused by humans it can also be a danger to young puppies if they are adventurous enough to dig up the root and eat it. In its favour, lily of the valley helps to restore cut flowers and set in water with them will make a longer lasting arrangement.

Growing lily of the valley in the shade of trees, where it reaches about 15-20cm (6 to 8in) high, ensures a supply of the natural mulch of leaf mould which would keep the rhizomes fed in a wild state in woodlands. Beneath shrubs, it should be given a mulch in autumn and once established will spread by runners. Generally the herb likes to be in well drained soil, but it can survive even solid clay if sufficient humus and peat is added. The wide green leaves, so attractive in early summer, will fade to bronze tatters by the time the orange-red berries are ripening with their precious seeds inside. If you are not gathering the leaves for dyeing wool, nor taking up the roots after flowering to divide them, then a little careful planning can surround the unsightly autumn herb with variegated mints or other leafy, shade loving herbs.

The medicinal herb is a variety native to Europe, East Asia and North America. Other species are native to Eurasia. Gardeners in Britain began an enthusiasm for special varieties early, it seems. Pink and red varieties of lily of the valley were already grown in 1597. By 1770 the Rev. William Hanbury writes of red, striped, double and double white varieties. Today "rosea" and a variegated form are available.

Coreopsis tinctoria   A   COREOPSIS

THESE pretty, bright flowers will make brilliant splashes of colour in the herb garden towards the end of the summer, joining the *Tagetes* and dahlias. Either the red or yellow flowered *tinctoria* yield a red dye as this comes from the anthers. Bolder and taller than French marigolds, they have a smiliar pattern and quality to them, although the flowers are rather more open. The plant is a native of North America. The seeds need to be sown early in the year under glass. They appear to germinate sooner if sown within 3 days of a new moon. Keep the young seedlings under protection until the last danger of frost is passed, gradually hardening them off. They are tender morsels for slugs at this stage too, and so need to be surrounded by bark chippings which have been treated with essential oil of pine. Do this by putting two drops of essential oil onto cotton wool and placing this in a plastic bag with the bark chippings or rough sawdust. Seal the bag and leave for 24-48 hours for the material to absorb the fragrance. Alternatively drip the same essential oil into a jar of

Vaseline and stir it in well. Keep the jar sealed for 24 hours before smearing the treated Vaseline around the edges of pots containing the plant, or onto bark to be used as before. Snails will also find this repellent. Alternatively a barrier of spiny herbs such as rosemary or horsetail can be used. I have tried rings of teazle heads but the slugs manage to avoid these. Once planted out, some 20cm (8in) apart, keep the young plants watered if the weather turns very dry, until they are well established. Continue to protect from slugs.

In good soil the plants will grow to 45cm (18in) tall, with the many flowers opening one after another from mid-late summer, having tiny, tightly packed buds on tall, slender stems. The narrow leaves have a wispy, insubstantial quality, although they are not divided. In some years, when a late frost has held up planting out and has been followed by dry weather, it seems a race with the first frost as to whether the seeds will develop and ripen sufficiently to be gathered and sown in the following spring. It is best in such conditions to leave the first flowers to go to seed and gather from later blooms for dyeing.

Cornus sanguinea   S   RED DOGWOOD

ALTHOUGH an attractive shrub all the year round, red dogwood really comes into its own during the winter months. Especially if the bushes are set in front of a screen which is covered in winter jasmine to add bright yellow flowers amongst their branches, underplanted with silver curry plant, or a mass of snowdrops, which are equally effective. Cuttings taken in the autumn will root readily and in two-three years will give bushes of 1.5-2m (5 to 6½ft), large enough to offer the first young stems for basketry.

The white flowers decorate the bushes in July, following the nearby roses and often while some of these are still out, the berries will be forming. These turn from, small, dark and rather uninteresting blobs into large white berries, occasionally still alongside the flowers. The seeds within need to be sown in autumn or stratified in the fridge before sowing. Although a cold February may be all that is needed. The oval deeply veined leaves have an autumn gift of beauty turning from bright green to a lovely red.

The name "dogwood" may have originated in a rude comment by Parkinson that the fruit was not fit to be given to a dog. Another use was found for the berries however, which yield an oil for soapmaking.

Crataegus monogyma   T   HAWTHORN

PARTICULARLY in a country garden, it is a pleasure to enjoy the blossom and fruits of our native hawthorn within a hedge. In my own garden, part of the hedge is kept clipped down and gives only a few blossoms, while at the bottom of the garden taller growth is pruned back only every other year on alternate trees. In this way there is sufficient blossom to gather some for a tasty liqueur, once popular with cooks for flavouring cakes – and to gather fruits in autumn for wine, liqueur and preserves. Left to itself, hawthorn will grow to some 10m (32ft). It is a hard wood which polishes well and the root wood is used to make boxes and small articles (See craft section).

May blossom as it is also called, is one of the great joys of late spring and early summer. Each flower bears numbers of red-topped stamens as tall central decorations, cupped by the five white petals in a delicate arrangement. Hawthorn, as its name suggests, is sufficiently prickly as a hedge to deter animals from pushing through, and if kept well clipped when first planted, will make a strong barrier. To imitate an old field hedge it should be interplanted with hazel, brambles, elder, blackthorn and perhaps wild roses - a veritable larder for the autumn.

Beyond clipping and layering by an expert for a superb hedge, hawthorn will need little attention to give the fruits for your use. Another name for it has been bread and cheese tree as the leaves and fruits were commonly eaten. Medicinally, a tincture is administered as a cardiac tonic and to reduce high bloodpressure. This use is found also in Russia and the hawthorn grows wild across Europe, North Africa and Western Asia. Should you wish to grow hawthorn as an ornamental tree then you may prefer the red-flowered form *C. laevigata,* "Paul's Scarlet", with beautiful red blossom which opens a little later.

Crocus sativus   Bulb   SAFFRON CROCUS

SAFFRON is an ancient dye and medicinal herb. The Romans might well have introduced it to Britain in the first instance, since they used it not only as a dye, but gathered the grass-like, grey-green leaves to strew the floors during public meetings as a fragrant herb. It has certainly been valued as a dye, cosmetic medicine and perfume. It comes originally from Asia Minor and has been cultivated from Persia and India to China since very early times. Later cultivation spread to France, Italy, Germany, and finally England.

A romantic tradition tells us that a crusader smuggled saffron bulbs back to Britain within his staff during the reign of Edward III. Whether or not this is so, saffron came to be an important crop, grown at Saffron Walden, and became naturalised near Derby and in parts of Yorkshire.

In my chalky soil with underlying clay, saffron is a reluctant herb which has never been long-lived for all the varying sites in the garden I have set it. The bulbs need to be well drained, planted 10-15cm (4-6in) apart and have plenty of sun. Summer is the best time to plant them out and their best harvest of orange-red stigmas from the blue-purple flowers comes in the September of their third year, after which it may be variable. Gather these in the morning as with other herbs, drying them ready for use. The corms can live for 15 years in good conditions, but unless you can provide the right sandy soil, it is safer to lift them after flowering, breaking away the small cormlets which form on each corm to replant as extra stock. If you are seriously wishing to harvest your saffron for use, it will need a great many to produce even a small quantity with only 3 stigmas per flower. Shelter from frost and cold north-east winds is also important along with keeping a watch for disease in older corms.

Medicinally, saffron tea was given to treat measles, palpitations and female obstructions, and the herb has been used as a dental analgesic. It is reputed to give mirth, occasionally to the point where the patient is recorded as dying of laughter. (Chinese herbal medicine uses it against depression.) Saffron remains an expensive herb to buy, unless you are fortunate enough to travel to Spain or Egypt for your supply.

Cytisus scoparius   S   BROOM
(Also Sarothamnus scoparius)

I always feel there is a joyful air of complete abandon about a broom bush in full flower. As a European native, it grows on sandy commons, in woodland clearings and even on rocky hillsides. At the coast broom can flourish wet with sea spray. Perhaps it is the aura of these wild places that can be detected by those sensitive to such things as it stands tall in wide garden beds or in a shrubbery. With the sun bringing out the brilliant yellow of the petals in early or full summer, and the great sweeps of slender branches with their small, inconspicuous short leaves, arching, or reaching up into the blue sky, it seems to enjoy just, being. A thriving bush will certainly give a plentiful harvest both of the uncomplicated two-lipped flowers for wine or dyeing and immediately afterwards of the green shoots for basketry.

Indeed, the bush needs to be cut back at this time or it may produce too many seed-pods in eager enthusiasm and exhaust its strength. In the days when the seeds were roasted as a coffee substitute, this may have been encouraged. A broom bush set too close to a path can also become a nuisance if not controlled, as it taps passers-by on the shoulder, even when they are a good 2m (6ft) away. Broom grows taller than the gardener too, if left to do so, possibly 2.5m (8ft). The herb has made an intensely practical contribution to all manner of crafts. The harvest of twigs has been used for thatching, basket-making or bound together to form brooms, giving the plant its name as this was such a common use. The leaves yield a green dye and the bark gave fibres for papermaking, while the wood has been valued by cabinet makers for veneering. Broom has also been used in tanning leather.

Gathering the flowers for wine, or as a dye, has been mentioned, and the buds were once pickled and eaten. The medicinal drug was gathered from the young branches before the flowers came, or the flowers might be picked to treat kidney disorders. The drug is powerful and should not be administered without trained advice and certainly avoided by pregnant women. The seeds may be harvested and sown as soon as they ripen rather than keeping them for the following spring. Sandy, acid soil is best. The bush can also be layered.

In addition to its practical craft applications, broom has also been used against witches and elfin lovers, to say nothing of being slipped into a husband's drink to ensure his sound sleep while the wife goes to her very human lover!

Dipsacus fullorum   B   FULLERS TEAZLE

STATELY and majestic in full growth, teazles will make an excellent addition to a tall border planted amongst shrubs. The thick spiny leaves form intriguing cups next to the sturdy, ridged stems, holding water for some time after rain. One can imagine small toads and frogs using them as tiny swimming pools, but their true function seems elusive. The name *Dipsacus* is from the latin **dipsao**, "to be thirsty", and refers to this special property. The common teazle grows wild throughout Europe and in the Mediterranean countries, where its water store may be more necessary. If the flowerheads which form at the top of the tall stems, sometimes 2m (6½ft) or more above ground, are left to go to seed, you will have a plentiful supply of self-sown plants in the following spring.

The flowers are a pretty, pale lilac and draw the bees in great numbers. In fact I have found it necessary to beware of setting these giants too close to the path as the year they stood as fine sentinels at either side of the entrance to the serenity garden, several people were stung by the bees which they accidentally disturbed. Once the bees have taken their fill from the flowers and the seeds have ripened, the small birds will be the next visitors to these plants. Goldfinches, in fact all manner of finches and other birds, tackle the spiky heads to remove the seeds. The flavour must be exceptional, for they are not removed without a struggle, as can be seen from the feathers which hang from the spines when the birds are gone.

The Fullers teazle heads have been used to tease wool in readiness for spinning and to give the brushed effect to baize for billiard tables. They therefore make an interesting addition to the craft garden, one which is useful for flower arrangers who can gather the seedheads even after the birds have taken their fill - or before the seeds ripen if young plants will be unwelcome. I have also found them a useful barrier to keep rats from nesting in the thatch and cats from sitting in delicate herbs.

Eryngium maritimum   B or P   SEA HOLLY

A herb to be enjoyed - in more ways than one. A native of Europe, I have seen sea holly growing wild in the soft sands on Norfolk beaches, in South Wales above the shore and in pockets of sand on southern beaches. Kent and Essex shores once boasted considerably more of the herb. I have yet to find a wild plant taller than 30cm (1ft). In the garden, in well-drained sandy soil, they can grow to 90cm (3ft) high, with many branches bearing the thistle-like flowerheads above their spiny ruffs of leaves, like so many candelabras. The change from soft, green leaved, low plants in the first year to tall stems producing smaller leaves with impressive points very like holly in the second or third year, is quite striking. Particularly as after the tiny pale blue flowers open in July or August to draw the bees, reminding passers-by of small teazles, these upper leaves turn silvery with a metallic sheen in certain lights.

Once established the herb is easy to grow, simply needing good drainage and a sunny position. Persuading the many seeds to germinate can be more of a difficulty and I have resorted to adding salt and sand to the soil in order to provide more suitable conditions. Observing the rule of sowing seeds at the time of the new moon may also be helpful, and autumn sowing is more successful than spring. Established plants can also be propagated by root divison in spring.

While dividing the aromatic roots, some can be gathered, either to boil and eat roasted, rather in the way of parsnips – the flavour my surprise you, or to add sliced to preserves, or candy. Candied eryngo root was once a great delicacy, to say nothing of aphrodisiac and the town of Colchester was famous for these "kissing comfits" in the 17th century. They are mentioned by Falstaff in Shakespeare's play, **The Merry Wives of Windsor.** In Anglo-Saxon times, the root was also prescribed for the King's evil, mending broken bones and melancholy. Its medicinal use has since been discontinued.

There are numerous cultivars. In the 17th century the herbalist, Gerard, already grew three and there are now many *Eryngiums.* Miss Willmott's ghost being one which has come to the fore recently. Several of these might be included in the craft garden for flower arrangements.

Filipendula ulmaria   P   MEADOWSWEET

ALTHOUGH my first contacts with this hardy herb in the wild where it grows
along marshy stream edges and in dank woods, did little to endear it to me, I have
come to appreciate it with time. The scent of the pretty, cream coloured, frothing
flowers in summer is not one I enjoy, yet dried it was an important strewing herb in
Elizabethan times and reportedly also one of the Queen's favourites. A Cumberland
name for the herb, "courtship and matrimony" may refer to the sweet scent before you
touch the flowers and the rather different perfume as they are crushed between your
fingers. Meadowsweet was, however, also a popular strewing herb in churches,
particularly for weddings. It is a native of Europe and Asia and has been introduced
into North America where it thrives in wet woodlands in the eastern states and
Canada. In my garden it grows well in areas of solid clay which retain the water for
a long time after spring and are inhospitable to many herbs. Meadowsweet needs
watering during persistently dry spells, and is best with light shade unless you can
keep the roots permanently wet.

In a garden situation, the fine red stems with large, deeply-divided leaves, green
above and whitish beneath, can be seen to good advantage. The flowers which were
also the first source of salicylic acid in 1839, from which aspirin was synthesized,
have an anti-ulcer activity and once flavoured mead - a use remembered in the
common name of "meadwort". If they are not harvested between June and August as
a dye source or to be dried, watch for insect infestation which may follow in hot, dry
conditions on the flowerheads as the seeds develop, turning them grey. In many wet
meadows this plant is truly "Queen of the Meadow", taking over large areas. As
established plants start to spread, their area can easily be confined by digging some
roots each autumn to yield a grey-black dye for wool. If, on the other hand, you are
wishing to extend the patch, the roots may be divided at this time. Seed can be saved
but should ideally be sown in a sheltered spot and in autumn rather than spring. The
young herbs need to be spaced some 20-30cm (8 to 12in) apart. They will flower in
their second year.

In a dark corner beside water, the variegated or golden meadowsweets are
perfect for a stunning effect amongst mints and sweet woodruff. Digging these roots
for dye may be practical but I have never experimented, for spare plants are always
requested by friends for their gardens. The smaller upper leaves deserve to be pressed
and given pride of place in flower pictures. The variegated plants will give fewer
flowers and are rather shorter in growth, rarely reaching above 60cm (2ft) while the
wild herb grows to 1.2m (4ft) in damp ditches.

Galium verum   P   LADY'S BEDSTRAW

A delicate herb which in the wild seems hardly to draw attention except when
flowering in high summer. You are most likely to have noticed it when
sunbathing on a dry, grassy hillside, as it often appears in miniature in this situation,
with fine stems bearing tiny golden yellow flowers in thick clusters. These honey-
scented blooms have been crushed to colour cheese and butter and the juice of the
leaves acts as a rennet substitute for cheesemakers, giving it the common name of
"curdwort". Dye also comes from the stems and particularly the creeping rhizome of

this herb which belongs to the same family as the commercialized dye, madder. Lady's bedstraw was much used for dyeing in the Scottish Highlands.

In deeper, richer soils, lady's bedstraw may reach 90cm (3ft) in height and often passes unnoticed amongst wild grasses at the roadsides. Then, the woody stems appear square and the leaves noticeably hairy as they grow in whorls below the panicles of flowers. A European native, lady's bedstraw has proved its adaptability in spreading as a weed in the eastern states of America. To increase plants in the craft garden, divide the runners or sow the rough seeds in autumn in well-fed ground with a little shade. Or grow lady's bedstraw simply for interest in a rock garden where it will remain a smaller plant. The scent of hay from the dried leaves and stems made it a popular herb to be mixed with bracken and insect-repellent herbs for stuffing mattresses. This early use is probably responsible for the tradition attached to its name that the herb formed part of the bed for the Virgin Mary at the birth of Jesus - hence "Our Lady's bedstraw".

Genista tinctoria   S   DYER'S BROOM

A pretty, comparatively low-growing broom, generally no taller than 1m (3ft), dyer's broom makes an attractive bush for the centre of a herb bed. The branches come low to the ground and are quite densely covered with the small, green, spear-shaped leaves. The shrub, also known as dyer's greenweed, may remain evergreen in a mild climate and produces yellow flowers which proclaim its membership of the pea family from midsummer into the early autumn. These are followed by long dark pods of the seeds which can be sown in autumn where the plant is to grow, or saved and set in pots or a seed-tray the following spring, with some protection from frost. This gives a head start to the tiny plants which grow slowly even in the sandy soil they prefer. They will flower and produce a harvest in their second year.

Native to Europe and Western Asia, dyer's broom grows mainly on heaths or in open woodland where it can enjoy light shade or full sun. It is especially associated with the Lake District in Britain in "Kendal green", the name of the green dye produced by overdyeing the yellow from the herb with woad. This process also gives the herb an additional name of woadwaxen. In North America it has been naturalised in New England and other parts. Dyeing has not been its only application. In some places, the stem fibres were spun for cordage and coarse cloths. In the kitchen, dyer's broom has provided flower buds to be pickled in imitation of capers. Medicinally, the herb has been used to treat rheumatism, gout and sciatica. The seeds are quite strongly purgative, and kitchen or medicinal use should be avoided while pregnant or suffering from high blood pressure.

Glycyrrhiza glabra   P   LIQUORICE

THERE is something rather intriguing in the idea of growing sweets in your garden, particularly to children. I have known little ones announce they would like to come back to my garden after dark to dig them up. Whether they expect liquorice root to emerge from the soil as round Pontefract cakes or liquorice shoelaces I'm not sure. Unusual in gardens, liquorice has an ancient history of cultivation for its medicinal use. It was known to the ancient Egyptians, Greeks and Romans, and was cultivated in early times in China, Persia and Turkey, having its origin in the

East. Records of its appearance in Central and Western Europe seem to be much later, perhaps in the 15th century, while the Dominican Black Friars brought it to Pontefract in Yorkshire where the medicinal root came to be appreciated as the familiar sweet.

It is now found wild in parts of Europe, North America (where it was introduced in the 17th century,) Russia and Central Asia. Liquorice actually likes to grow close to the sea, although it will thrive inland in deep, rich, sandy soil. Pieces of root with complete buds can be set about 10-15cm (4 to 6in) deep and 90cm (3ft) apart in spring. The linear arrangement of the slightly sticky green leaves along the stems proclaims the herb's membership of the pea family, and the delicate lilac-blue flowers, which follow in July or August on stems up to 1.5m (5ft) tall, are also typical in form.

My grandfather, who grew up in Lincolnshire, remembered picking the reddish-brown seedpods which follow the flowers as he and his friends walked through fields of liquorice on their way to school in early autumn. Where frost is a problem, the plants can be lifted in late autumn, some root harvested and the remainder kept protected against frost for the winter. In late March or April these can then be replanted. Left in situ the roots can grow branching rootlets of 1.2-2.4m (4 to 8ft).

Hedera helix   P   IVY

MANY gardeners plant variegated ivy to enliven a dark wall or fence. Few, I suspect, welcome the leathery green-leaved climber from the woodlands, our native ivy. It can, however, be attractive against a light flint wall or even covering an old tree stump or long-abandoned fence post. The honey coloured flowers are small but in autumn will attract bees to the rich nectar which at times may actually drip from the flowers. The berries which follow ripen through December and January, being ready for harvesting between then and early March. It is easy to put off gathering them on bitter days, since the dyepot will wait for another time, but remember the birds will soon eat the ripe berries while you delay.

The creeping ivy which carpets some woodland ground is the most useful to gather for basketry, since it is often sufficiently pliable to use immediately, simply stripping the leaves. It bears roots at intervals from the stems which anchor it to the soil. Ivy found clinging to the bark of trees puts out fibrous shoots with sucker-like ends which attach it to the tree bark and can reach into cracks to draw sap and nourishment. This ivy hangs in festoons from upper branches and is older, 10 years or more; its maturity witnessed by flowers and berries which do not occur on the younger creeping plants. Ivy is a very long-lived herb, surviving for more than 500 years in good conditions. It enjoys a mild climate, but has no particular soil requirements, being naturalised in the temperate regions of the world. Indeed, the content of ivy pollen in prehistoric remains has been used as an indicator of past temperatures.

The mature woody stems can grow to almost 30cm (1ft) in diameter, large enough to provide turned items, such as goblets and ivy cups. The wood is very porous and absorbs colour from wine which may have led to the belief that it was also absorbing the alcoholic effect. Formerly, an infusion from the leaves was drunk to remedy an excess of alcohol. The leaves are gathered in autumn just before flowering for medicinal application and have been used in poultices to treat rheumatism and neuralgia. A tincture is extracted for medicine. The berries are no longer taken and may cause blistering and so for safety wear gloves when harvesting them. Ivy is poisonous in large doses, especially the berries. A further use is to simmer them to produce a decoction as a fabric or hair dye.

Variegated and ornamental forms of ivy have been grown since ancient times. Pliny, writing in the 1st century A.D., mentions a silver variegated ivy, and centuries later John Evelyn recommended clipping ivy into ornamental shapes. In the 19th century this was taken to extreme lengths when the herb found its way not only onto balconies, but into drawing rooms where portable bowers of decorative ivies might be set over couches.

Helichrysum angustifolium   P   CURRY PLANT

AN easy perennial to grow, curry plant makes very effective hedging where it is trimmed and controlled. A height of around 20cm (8in) will keep it bushy and the spiny-leaved stems neat. Left untrimmed the bushes will grow to 45cm (18in) or more and can be trained back against a wall to intermingle with winter jasmine for a lovely effect in the winter months. It is a particular asset to any "silver garden", designed to be viewed at its best by moonlight. Hedges in a winter garden also add a freshness and form which is even more delightful beneath a light frost. Although older plants will recover well from quite heavy frosts, keep young cuttings protected during their first winter.

Cuttings may be taken in late summer after flowering, or in early spring. These may be set alongside pea rows to some advantage as they discourage birds from eating them. Alternatively, cut stems can be laid amongst the plants. They can also be used in a similar manner to protect the yellow buds of Primulas and primroses which birds seem to find so attractive.

Clipping in early summer will, of course, remove the possibility of flowers. The yellow blooms should be harvested for dried flower arrangements when the yellow buds are first opening in July and August. Later they take on a white papery effect at the edges and will not dry well at this stage. The scent of curry can be quite intense close to a bed of these plants on a hot day as the sun draws out the fragrance, or when the plants are touched.

Not a familiar herb in the historical sense, curry plant is looked upon as a newcomer from Southern Europe. The dwarf form, *Helichrysum angustifolium nana,* is rarely seen but worth searching for to place in a miniature garden. It is likely to become more widely available as the curry plant itself is appreciated and planted in modern herb~gardens.

Hemerocallis fulva   P   DAY-LILY

THE day-lily, so-called because each flower lasts only a single day, used to be much more common along the roadsides than it is now. It is still found in many cottage gardens and is as familiar in Europe as it is in China. The herb appeared there in 12th century paintings and was known as the plant of forgetfulness. A close relative, *Hemerocallis esculenta* was grown as a vegetable in the East and

H. aurantica flowers are also eaten boiled, in batter, or pickled. In England, both *H. fulva* and *H. flava* were cultivated in the 16th century and the flowers freshly picked. They might also be dried as they opened and later simmered to produce a yellow, or blue-green dye.

The plant takes its place in the craft garden not only as a dye, but additionally for the abundant supply of lily leaves which are quite as good as those of the iris for soft basketry. Growing to some 60-75cm (2-2½ft) high, they have taller flower stems rising singly above the leaves. These are cut low to the ground in early autumn after flowering, when the herb can also be divided to increase your stock and the bulbs replanted. Dry the leaves on a rack in a warm, dry place and store to be soaked and used in coiled mats and baskets.

Humulus lupus   P   HOP

CENTURIEs ago the hop was a kitchen herb, rather than the farm crop I remember as a child growing up in Kent - or the ornamental, rough-stemmed climber we see all over the country in gardens. Hops only came into use in brewing in the reign of Henry VIII, and were much resisted as a replacement for the bitter gruit ale herbs of alehoof, mugwort, alecost and so on at the beginning. Including hops in brewing was thought by many to spoil the taste, lead to tormenting desires and endanger life. Those who were for the change actually replied that hops were a cure for quarrelsome natures and might control sexual desires. The understanding that resins in the hops are antibacterial came much later. A native of Europe, parts of Asia and North America, hops grow naturally in damp, rich soil amongst thickets of willow and alder, or in hedgerows beside ditches. In either situation, the tendrils climb over nearby bushes and trees to a distance of 7.5m (25ft), and although requiring plenty of water, also appreciate a sunny aspect with shelter from north-east winds. Today they are also grown in Australia and New Zealand.

In autumn when the greenish-yellow flowers are ripening in the "cones", these can be gathered and dried, giving the familiar heavy odour which is soporific in sleep pillows. At the same time the plant can be cut right back to benefit growth the following spring and provide plentiful basketry material. Golden hop is as good a supplier of basketry stems as the common hop and can be grown over an archway or tall pergola. Odd short lengths of stem clipped away at this time will also provide a pinkish dye when simmered for an hour. A third craft use is to ret the stems in a similar way to flax to provide fibres for spinning and weaving into a coarse cloth.

To increase your hop plants, divide the roots in spring or take stem cuttings in early summer and plant out at 30cm (1ft) intervals. The hop will twine in a clockwise direction as it grows. If you are planning to attract butterflies to your garden then the hop will help to bring the lovely comma.

Ilex aquifolium   T   HOLLY

THE familiar English holly was, in earlier times, known as "hulver", "holy tree" or "holme", only taking the name of holly in the 17th century. An evergreen tree, it can grow to over 10m (30ft) tall and is native to Europe where it is often seen in oak and beech woods. It also grows from Western Asia to China and can thrive in most soils, provided they are reasonably well drained and have the goodness which in the wild is supplied by the mulch of leaves on the forest floor.

Holly trees are frequently found in old country gardens where they may once have been planted, because, according to superstition, they protected the house from lightning. Equally well, conservationists might include a holly tree in their garden plan to attract bees to the deliciously fragrant flowers in early summer. These are tiny, a dull white, and quite inconspicuous, appearing on the previous year's growth. There are times when only the sudden burst of perfume draws attention to them. They may be unisexual or bisexual. Holly is also recommended in butterfly gardens as it attracts the perfect tiny holly blue to dance in your garden in late spring. The shiny, tough leaves may have very fierce spines at the edges or be smoother. Folklore in some parts of the country taught that the smooth leaves were from "she" holly and the spiky leaves from "he" holly. I have found both types on the same tree and have read that the smoother leaves have actually been produced in times of drought, or as the tree has become old and is failing in its upper growth.

The leaves are gathered for medicinal use in early summer and infusions were formerly made of them to treat fevers. The berries which ripen in time for Christmas have been used medicinally but are violent in their purging effects and small children should be warned not to eat them. The fermented bark from young shoots, used to be mixed with oil to make birdlime and exported as insecticide.

Full grown trees supply a hard, white wood which needs to be well seasoned before producing attractive turned articles, or pieces for inlay work which may be stained. Young trees take a number of years to reach this size, however, for holly is very slow growing. My own holly hedge, planted four years ago, is just beginning to make real progress; young hollies planted out may take at least two seasons to recover from their change of habitat. I have mixed golden, silver and blue holly with the common variety, and will, in years to come, have a thick, protective hedge all year round. If holly needs trimming back this is best done in spring, remembering you may be removing the possibility of berries that year.

Iris germanica   P   ORRIS

THIS plant, also called "German iris", has deep blue flowers veined with purple, and a yellow "beard". The scent is as sweet as the beauty of the flowers might tempt one to believe I am always disappointed that they do not last longer, for often it seems there is a spell of wet, windy weather just as the irises flower, which also takes the white lilac and turns it into shrivelled brown remnants. The *florentina* variety of *Iris germanica* may have white flowers tinged with violet and a yellow "beard", but the colours of the flower can vary. My own plants have striking lilac coloured flowers.

Two years ago I was fortunate enough to watch one of these large buds spring open, and hear the amazing "popping" sound which is produced by the sudden unfolding; louder than a broombud bursting. Both irises will give the aromatic root which is matured for one year after it is dried before being ground as a fixative in pot-pourri. *Iris pallida,* with blue flowers, is grown in Provence for its sweet perfume and also provides orris root.

Native to Southern Europe and naturalised over Central Europe, Persia and

Northern India, orris grows in most soil types, but likes a sunny site with good drainage. The rhizomes can be divided in early summer or after flowering, setting each piece with its new bud of growth horizontally along the ground, close to the surface with the roots down into the soil. These will give large, sword-shaped leaves in the following year. The flower bearing stalks can be 1m (3ft) tall.

Orris root may be harvested after flowering and is dried as small cubes to be stored. These are matured for a year and then ground. The resulting scented powder has been popular for centuries in toilet powders, as a dry shampoo, or in dental preparations. Medicinally it has been taken as an infusion for diarrhoea. A definite contribution to "civilized living", we find orris used in Elizabethan times in making "Swete cloth" adding its characteristic violet perfume. Later in history those who might give offence to ladies with their garlic or tobacco-laden breath could always chew on slivers of orris root to sweeten their approach.

Isatis tinctoria   B or P   WOAD

THE picture which springs to most people's minds when woad is mentioned is one of the ancient Britons brandishing weapons, their bodies painted with woad for battle. No doubt the body paints which might be obtained from mixing woad with lye, or ashes from the fire, were quite impressive, if sometimes grey instead of blue. There was another possible reason for using woad at this time however, the herb is a styptic and was frequently used medicinally in ancient times. Painting the body with a herb which can help to stop the bleeding from anticipated wounds and frighten the enemy into the bargain, must have made woad the perfect "battledress".

In the garden, set some 25-30cm (10-12in) apart, woad is an attractive plant with large, pointed leaves, sometimes reaching 30cm (1ft) in length in their second year. The leaves are more of a blue than green with a thick, lighter coloured rib down the mid-lines. The rosette of the first year leaves produces a tall, pale stalk with pairs of leaves at either side, up to 1.2m (4ft) tall in good ground by the second summer. The mass of flowerheads of tiny, golden yellow flowers (lovely in a pressed flower display,) appears in June or July. These are followed by large black seeds which resemble shortened broom buds and can be carried some distance if they fall on a windy day. (Gerard described them brilliantly in his herbal as "little blackish tongues".) The seeds can be soaked before sowing, in rich compost, from February onwards. They will do best planted out in chalky soil and will not grow as tall, or seed as readily in clay. Two or three harvests of leaves are possible from mature plants in a season. These must be hand gathered, leaving the stem undamaged with a leaf or two for its continued growth. The leaves remain in good condition through the winter period.

Should you wish the herb to become a perennial, the seedheads must be cut from the plant before they ripen, in fact immediately after flowering is best. Doing this also helps to avoid attacks by an insect which delights in infesting woad, *Aphis brassicae*. Membership of the *Brassica* family makes woad quite a hardy herb, with some 50 species across a large area of Europe, Northern Africa and Asia.

Woad appears to be native to Europe and of course has been cultivated as a dye there and elsewhere for the past 2,000 years. We find it cultivated in Egypt early in the Christian era and then in Japan, China, North Africa and Tibet. In Britain it was widely cultivated in medieval times and enjoyed much popularity in the Elizabethan era, when it was also imported. There were considerable drawbacks to the industry which polluted the air as the woad leaves, which had been hand pulled, crushed at the woad mill and the pulp dried in balls; were then fermented. In addition, woad exhausted the soil where it was grown in quantity and polluted the streams, so that the woadmen moved on from time to time. Elizabeth I hated the smell of fermenting woad and decreed it should not be processed within 5 miles of her estates, or of city markets. When dyers received the dried, fermented woad, they fermented it a second time, so polluting the atmosphere yet again. This second process gave an interesting by-product - the "flowers" of woad, from the blue scum floating in the vats which was used as a blue paint by many early artists.

Despite its problems, woad was not superseded by indigo until this century and remains a stronger dye which is also used as a starter for indigo dyeing. In fact they contain the same glucoside, indican, which in both cases converts to a blue dye as the fabric is exposed to oxygen. Large areas of East Anglia were once woad farms. Glastonbury, Norwich and Lincolnshire have also been associated with woad dye production. The last woad mill was in Lincolnshire and closed in the 1930s. As a medicinal herb, woad had long vanished from the scene, although it still appears in the **London Dispensatory** for 1654. Amongst earlier uses we find woad leaves, woolly fibres, or root given for haemorrhage, St. Anthony's fire, tumours, ulcers, jaundice, snake bite; problems with the liver or spleen, and scurvy.

Jasminum grandiflorum P JASMINE

FEW flowers are sweeter than the fragrant white flowers of jasmine as it grows against a south-facing wall in the summer sunshine. It is little wonder that the herb has been cultivated in large quantities for perfumery. The best time to appreciate its fragrance is at daybreak or dusk, which makes it the perfect climbing plant to encourage around a bedroom window. Jasmine will also grow against pergolas or lattice fencing and is steadily spreading green branches over the covered way in my garden. Persuading it to flower profusely in a less sheltered situation is, however, not always successful. One plant can survive for 15 years and cuttings are easily taken in late summer or spring to plant in other sites if this problem is encountered. Jasmine, which in rich soil may produce excess green growth rather than flowers, can be cut back and the cut lengths of stem used in basketry. The smaller leaves press beautifully.

Jasmine probably originated in Southern Asia and may have been brought to Europe from the East Indies by the Spaniards in the 16th century. Since then it has been grown for perfumery in France and Italy, as well as in Palestine, Syria, India and Egypt. It has been suggested that the great stone which was rolled in front of the tomb of Jesus in the Garden of Gethsemane (which may translate as jessamine or jasmine) was one used within a trough to extract the oil from jasmine grown in the Garden. In recent times, jasmine oil has been extracted by maceration in oil or by enfleurage. The French oil is the most expensive.

Jasminum nudiflorum is the Chinese winter jasmine, a familiar perennial in British and American gardens. The brilliant yellow flowers make a most welcome display in the winter months, providing dried flowers to decorate spring pot-pourri, and in the autumn, cut green stems for basketry.

Juniperus communis   T   JUNIPER

I have always associated juniper bushes with cold, scrubby moorland and high hillsides in the north where their growth can be stunted by the fierce winds and they appear to cling stubbornly to life. Bringing a male and a female juniper into my garden, where they grow in adjoining beds in the chalky soil they prefer, has opened my eyes to taller possibilities. Juniper trees can reach 12m (40ft) in Norway and Sweden, although in Britain they are unlikely to grow to more than 2m (6ft). The female juniper which I planted at 60cm (2ft) high four years ago is already over 1.5m (5ft), but has suffered in high winds and needs firm staking in order to cope with this spurt of growth. The male, close by, has been more cautious, being some 45cm (18in) shorter and is a far sturdier tree. For a time I thought they might not be compatible, since no berries appeared. Finally they reached maturity, delighting me with the first cone-like flowers on the female tree, and equally pleasing catkins on the male branches. Later that year, several tiny green berries appeared on the female, to mature and ripen only slowly to contain three tiny seeds.

The branches spread from the upper growth of the male, giving the impression of broad shoulders; this growth habit is less marked in the female tree but can still appear as raised arms in a protective or threatening gesture - depending on the observer's mood. The many branches have reddish woody stems graced by needle-like growth which stroked downwards is soft and appealing, and brushed the other way reveals vicious spines.

Juniper has a wide distribution from the Mediterranean climate across Europe into Norway and colder areas of the Soviet Union. In North America it is found on dry hillsides from Canada to New Jersey and in the mountains of New Mexico. Much used, the berries are germicidal and juniper has been thought of for many centuries as a protective tree. In medieval times it was burned at funerals to keep evil spirits away and in times of plague purified the air. In fact it is a helpful tree to grow close to the house door or windows as it exhales odours which are antiseptic and balsamic.

The other widely known use for the berries has been in making gin. They were exported in large quantities from Scotland to Holland for this purpose. The wood has been used in curing meat; and gum sandarach or "pounce" as it was once commonly called, used in scented preparations, was made from juniper.

Linum usitatissimum   A   FLAX

A very ancient plant, flax has been grown for 7,000 years, the oldest region of cultivation being the Middle East. Modern forms are thought to have come from the pale flax, *L. bienne,* which had lilac tinged flowers and was grown by the Romans in the Mediterranean and Britain. Blue or white flowered flax is a pretty addition to any herb garden or herbaceous border, where from June into high summer the shy flowers can tease the proud gardener by closing just as an interested visitor comes along, even though it is still afternoon. Tradition explains their coy flowering habits by saying they only open at the time of day when they were first sown. With testing this unlikely theory in mind, sow the round seeds (larger, but similar to coriander) at a recorded time in March or April in deep, good soil which is well-drained. Adding potash from burnt sunflower stalks is a help to the flax which should not be sown repeatedly in the same area year after year.

It is a great joy to me to see the increasing number of fields of flax, which seem to billow in the summer breeze with waves of blue flowers followed by greyish foliage as they turn in the wind. Flax for linseed production is sown thinly and left for the oval, oily seeds to mature. Grown for fibre, the plants are sown closely together, forms with fewer branches to the stem are encouraged. The erect stems, 1.2m (4ft) tall, are reaped in August when the blossom has fallen and the stems are yellowing, but before the seeds ripen. The bundles of fibres are then retted and treated to extract the fibres for spinning. For those who buy a strick of flax to spin, it is intriguing to think that the thick bundle of long fibres consists of flax stems which were grown side by side through the summer and have been kept together throughout the preparation.

Lupinus albus   B or P   LUPIN

THE white-flowered lupin, *Lupinus albus,* is referred to here. some lupins have poisonous seeds whereas the white-flowered *L. albus* bears seeds which are given to animals as fodder and are not dangerous in the uses given below. Do **not** experiment with other cultivated varieties in these ways. The white lupin may have originated in Egypt and most certainly was grown by the ancient Egyptians. The Greek, Theophrastus and Roman writer Pliny, each refer to the seeds as food. The Romans grew the lupin both for food and as a medicine, and the seeds were soaked to apply as a "plaster" to ulcers. In later times, powdered seeds were included in cosmetic face packs.

Native to parts of Asia and Southern Europe, and cultivated in North America, the white lupin grows to only about 60cm (2ft) tall and has a long taproot and smooth typical lupin leaves with a whitish underside. The white flowers are followed by tough pods containing 3-6 white seeds. When these "pop" they can do so with a force that sends seeds to the far corners of a small garden. The white lupin likes sandy soil and needs little attention in the first year, being harvested in the second summer. All of the lupin family are useful for fixing nitrogen in the soil, but *Lupinus angustifolius* is the variety favoured for enriching the soil, being dug in as the flowers are forming, or shortly afterwards.

The seeds of the white lupin *L. albus* can be eaten with the bitter parts removed and were once ground into flour and made into bread. They have also been roasted as a coffee substitute. White lupin seeds can yield an oil which has, in wartime been incorporated into margarine. Mrs. Grieve, in her wonderfully detailed book, **A Modern Herbal,** mentions a "lupin banquet" in Hamburg in 1917 when all the above forms of lupin products were served, along with lupin soup, cheese of lupin albumen and lupin liqueur. The guests washed their hands with lupin soap, returning to a table covered by a lupin fibre tablecloth and had lupin-fibre paper and envelopes available. It almost seems a garden of lupins might be the key to self-sufficiency.

Herb cultivation

Silver and gold in the Treasure garden

(Below) Craft garden

Herb cultivation

(Top left) *Dyer's chamomile*

(Left) *Alkanet*

(Below left) *Burdock*

Agrimony

Dyer's woodruff

(Top right)
Lily of the valley

(Right) *Box*

(Below right) *Thrift*

Bearberry

Herb cultivation

Dogwood

(Top left) *Teazle*

(Left) *Hawthorn*

(Below left) *Coreopsis*

Broom/Mullein

iv

Dyer's broom

(Top right)
*Variegated
meadowsweet*

(Right) *Sea holly*

(Below right) *Ivy*

Liquorice

Herb cultivation

Curry plant

(Top left) *Hop*

(Left) *Day lily*

(Below left) *Iris germanica*

Holly

Flax

(Top right)
Gypsywort

(Right) *Buddleia mint*

(Below right) *Woad*

Juniper

Herb cultivation

Sloe

(Top left) *Bog myrtle*

(Left) *Iris sibirica*

(Below left) *Bayberry*

Curled mint

Lycopus europaeus   P   GYPSYWORT

AN unusual plant in gardens, the herb grows to some 30-45cm (12-18in) tall and has rather elegant, deeply-toothed, opposite leaves. The tiny flowers which cluster around the stem at the leaf axils appear to be pink at first glance, but are actually white with touches of purple. They are pretty without drawing undue attention. With the sun behind it, the herb can be very attractive and is not unduly invasive in a flower bed, despite being closely related to the mints. Gypsywort spreads gradually with a creeping rhizome.

The wild herb is native to Europe and Western Asia. It was taken to North America most probably as a dye for cloth, for the flowering tops have been used to give browns (with ammonia and iron,) while the addition of iron results in a greyish black. The fresh juice from larger quantities of the herb will give a black dye for wool or linen. The common name is thought to have come from the gypsies' use of the herb to imitate a deeper tan on their skin. Quite why this might be necessary for them I do not know.

Gypsywort will be more at home in damp soil, although it likes the sun. Alongside meadowsweet, bog myrtle and bergamot, it has the needs of a plant that naturally grows along lake margins or in marshy ground. If you have only a small patch of gypsywort, the flowering tops can be collected for the dye when they are at their best, which is generally in July or early August. The plant is then divided in autumn or spring, since if you are using it as a dye, you will be denying it the chance to set seed.

Medicinally it has been used fresh or dried to combat haemorrhaging, treat an overactive thyroid condition and act as a sedative. It is no longer in general use in herbal medicine.

Mentha crispa   P   CURLED MINT

MOST people's first reaction to this mint is one of dismay. The elaborately curled nature of the rounded leaves makes them look as if they have been gathered at the edges. The immediate association to most gardeners is that the plant must have been attacked by insects to produce these symptoms. The mint is, in fact, in perfect health and has a steadily spreading growth to prove it. The fragrance of curled mint is very strong, matched by the powerful taste when the mint is used in wines. My own favourite partnership for curled mint is with blackcurrants when both flavours remain equally enjoyable in the fermented wine. It is this pungency which recommended it, along with peppermint, for liqueurs, and places the plant firmly in the garden area dedicated to wines and liqueurs, rather than a cookery bed.

As with all mints, the leaves should be harvested for drying just before the plant flowers. If left to do so, it will produce the typical tiny pink-purple flowers of the mint family around the stems at the leaf axils and the leaves will quickly deteriorate. The cultivation is also the same: needing moist, rich ground and containment of some kind before long. The herb grows to about 30-45cm (12-18in) tall in these conditions. It can be divided in spring or autumn at the roots.

Unlike other mints, *Mentha sylvestris,* known latterly as "horsemint" and now given the rather more elegant name of "buddleia mint", has silvery qualities to the leaves. Its habits are similar, needing only the luxury of damp ground to spread quickly across the flowerbeds. The soft, almost furry, whitish leaves can be most attractive as a background to low-growing bright annuals. My buddleia mint has found a home in the treasure garden where it provides the perfect contrast to golden thymes. If allowed, this mint produces pointed spikes of lilac coloured flowers which resemble buddleia and will also attract butterflies to the herb garden. It grows to about 30-45cm (12-18in) and can be propagated by dividing the root in autumn or spring.

Myosotis symphytifolia   A - P   FORGET-ME-NOT

THESE charming, low-growing plants are perfect to soften the effect of formal planting. With a little shade they will quickly seed themselves at random, offering pastel colours of blue and pink, with creamy white in their flowers. The *M. symphytifolia* has been given medicinally as a syrup for pulmonary infections and is especially associated with treating problems of the left lower lung.

The soft rosettes of leaves of the garden forget-me-nots are especially at home with a little shade. The plant likes moisture, although there is a slightly different wild form which is the true, water forget-me-not, *M. scorpioides.* This is an evergreen perennial which flowers from early summer to the autumn and grows to about 26cm (9in) high. It can be propagated by root division. There are a number of varieties, some annual, some perennial, which between them can give flowers from spring to mid-autumn with mild conditions; they also supply a wonderful source of tiny flowers for pressing.

The field forget-me-not, *M. arvensis,* is an annual or biennial, suited to dry conditions in the garden and could be included in a wild area with grasses. The creeping forget-me-not, *M. secunda,* is short and hairy compared to the others, sending out runners which root. It is a good ground cover on peaty, acid soils, flowering in the height of summer. There is also an early forget-me-not, *M. ramosissima,* a changing forget-me-not, *M. discolor,* with yellow flowers which deepen to pink, blue or even violet, and many more. Since there are 50 species growing in temperate climates, there are many fascinating differences to be found in the wild forget-me-nots, if we look carefully. Propagation of forget-me-nots is best left to nature unless you are particularly concerned for the survival of a rare variety. They readily seed themselves, but seed can be gathered and sown in a seed tray in late summer.

Myrica cerifera   S   BAYBERRY

A hardy shrub in poor, well-drained ground, bayberry is widely distributed in Europe and America. Its other common names of wax myrtle, candleberry and waxberry tell us all we need to know of its once widespread use to give an aromatic wax for candlemaking. The secondary applications, in manufacturing soap and Bay Rum hair dressing, have not been acknowledged in the same way. The clusters of grey berries which ripen on the bush in autumn are harvested and boiled, and the resulting liquid cooled and strained to extract the solidifying wax. This is made into greyish-green, spicy fragranced candles and was once also used for sealing wax. The water which is strained off is a useful dye.

The bayberry generally grows to a height of about 3m (9ft) in British gardens; on the East Coast of America, where it is a native and grows as far south as Florida, it can reach a full tree growth of 10m (30ft). In these conditions it is evergreen, although in colder climates it may lose some leaves during winter and become deciduous. The long, rather pointed leaves are a light, attractive green and the flowers appear in spring or early summer as catkins.

Bayberry is a lovely addition to a shrubbery or as part of a hedge in the craft garden, where it may yet benefit from the sunshine. It appears to thrive in either moderately dry or wet soil conditions. The fibrous bark of the herb has been used medicinally for gargles, in snuff for nasal catarrh and in poultices. Small pieces can also be chewed for toothache.

Myrica gale   S   SWEET GALE

A fragrant miniature willow in form, "sweet gale" or "bog myrtle", as it is also known, makes an unusual and attractive shrub for an area in the garden which can offer rich, moist, acid soil. A herb of marshland and the edges of bogs, as the name suggests, this delicate-leaved herb will need shade in most gardens. I have tried unsuccessfully to nurse well-watered plants in the sunny craft garden and find they thrive only in one of the raised wine and liqueur beds with peat added, where they enjoy almost constant shade. Here, a planting of sweet woodruff beneath the bare, reddish-brown lower branches as a ground cover makes a lovely combination. Sweet gale is native to North west Europe, Asia and North America, as far south as Virginia and is deciduous, losing its slender, pointed leaves in autumn, leaving the small berries which were once gathered and added as a seasoning to stews. In good conditions it can grow to 2m (7ft) high, but in most gardens is more likely to remain at around 1m (3ft).

Divide the root or take stem cuttings in spring, before the catkins of yellowish flowers decorate the bush. It may also spread by means of suckers, but the seeds have a poor germination rate. Plants may change sex from one year to another.

Once protected by law in Britain, when its leaves were gathered to flavour beer, it was widespread in the New Forest, other wet heathland and the Fens. Gale beer was brewed in Yorkshire using the leaves which are gathered in late summer. The leaves and twigs might also be mashed and boiled in salted water to extract the wax which is produced in tiny glands along their edges. It is unlikely you will be able to grow sufficient quantities in your garden to make an incense scented candle at home. The fresh or dried leaves can also be used for their yellow dye, once popular in all parts of the British Isles; twigs are often included for a golden hue. The last, now redundant use of bog myrtle gave it a lost common name of "flea wood"; as it was included in bedding to repel fleas.

Nepeta cataria   P   CATMINT

A favourite with cats, catmint is a pretty and fragrant addition to a collection of silver-grey herbs. The heart-shaped leaves are closer to grey than silver, although whiter on their underside and covered in soft down. It needs little attention apart from harvesting which can be done from early summer when the pink flowers decorate the tops of the square, 45-90cm (18in to 3ft) stems. Catmint is native to Europe, East and West Asia, being a hardy plant in most situations. There are numerous cultivars with miniature varieties and some have blue flowers. These generally retain the pungent fragrance, slightly reminiscent of mint, which intoxicates some cats to ecstasy. To propagate catmint, the plants can be divided in spring or autumn, stem cuttings can be rooted, or the seeds collected and sown during the following spring. There is a tradition that plants grown from seed are left alone by cats which seem only too eager to roll in the herb when it has come from a rooted cutting. Cat attraction or no, it can be included in an area of plants to bring butterflies and at the same time assist in keeping rats at a distance.

Although related to the mints, catmint does not spread in their rampant, distinctive way and consequently can tolerate considerably drier soil. The flowering tops, as well as providing an exciting toy filling for kittens and cats, have been harvested as a medicinal herb. In the form of a tea catmint has been given for fevers, nervous complaints and colic. It should be noted, however, that a large dose of the warm tea can prove an effective emetic. The leaves have also been eaten in small quantity for toothache or smoked for bronchial complaints, when it occasionally produced hallucinogenic effects.

Prunus spinosa   T   SLOE

SLOES may be gathered wild as a dye, to be frozen before cooking very slowly with honey to make preserves or puddings, for medicinal uses or to make sloe gin - which some regard as medicinal. It is also a pleasure to grow the trees in the hedge of a large country garden, making a particularly apt outer border to a craft garden. The trees, which grow to some 4m (13ft) are exceptionally pretty when covered in the delicate white flowers, before the first leaves open. Of course when the flowers are in a mass and at their best, this is also the time of the "blackthorn spring" which appears to coincide exactly as tradition says, with piercingly cold weather. If you are very fortunate and live in Southern England your sloes may attract the rare brown hairstreak butterfly; from Oxfordshire to Northamptonshire there is again a small chance of drawing the equally rare, black hairstreak butterfly. Tortoiseshells are more likely visitors.

The blackish branches bear vicious spines as well as alternate, oval leaves, and so the young trees need to be set at the back of a bed where they will not catch passers-by. Often by late summer the large, spherical berries are well developed and turning from green to bluish-black. They need the frost to ripen them fully for use, or they will be desperately bitter. Immediately after the first frost they should be picked, or the birds will start to eat them. Within the green centre is a stony seed. The trees are more usually spread by suckers than seedlings, and sometimes one tree will give rise to a whole thicket. The sloe is native to Europe and commonly found in wild hedgerows. An old saying tells us "An Elder stake and a blackthorn ether will make a hedge to last for ever."

Blackthorn has been the source of many decorative walking sticks in the past and excess bark was used in manufacturing ink. The berries release a pinkish dye, which is likely to fade with strong light, but the undiluted juice can be squeezed from the berries before they ripen to produce an ink which is fast.

In the garden, a double form of *P. spinosa* may be preferred, or a *P. spinosa purpurea,* which has purple leaves.

Reseda luteola — B — WELD

WE may often see weld growing wild on roadside verges and in old quarries. It is a native of Europe, and at home both around the Mediterranean and in Britain, growing mostly in sandy soils. This is *R. lutea,* the wild form, which does not grow quite as tall as the cultivated *R. luteola.* Weld is a very ancient dye herb, and has been found in the remains of Neolithic settlements in Switzerland.

The cultivation of weld in Britain many centuries later was widespread in Kent, Essex, Herefordshire and Yorkshire. There is nothing quite as fresh as the young green of cultivated weld leaves and stems, unless, perhaps it is spinach. Young, first-year weld plants are attractive with rosettes of lanceolate leaves splayed tidily around the base of the herb at soil level. In the second year these small plants can grow quickly to 60cm-1.5m (2 to 5ft). They produce fleshy stems with long, narrow, thickened leaves topped by masses of tiny greenish-yellow flowers about the upper stem. Perhaps this sudden spurt of growth is one reason for the common name, dyer's rocket.

An essential part of my dye patch in the craft garden, weld leaves and tops give me both a useful yellow dye and a good green. Both are of a high quality and meet the herb's past reputation as a commercially viable dyeplant. In addition to yielding simple colours, weld has been used in combination with madder to give orange; with dyer's broom to obtain Lincoln green; and with woad or indigo, again for greens. The plant bears many seeds if the flowering tops are not harvested in summer and will seed itself quite readily.

Since it is a biennial, it is necessary from a harvest point of view to keep seedlings and mature plants side by side. In fact, keeping them intermixed is helpful in that the tiny young plants may dry up in well drained soil in a hot early summer and benefit from the shade of their older "relatives". Otherwise sow the plants in slight shade and moist soil. The form of the flowers reveals the herb's membership of the mignonette family, but sadly there is no enjoyable fragrance from weld. It has no real credit as a medicinal herb, although in the past it may have been used against the plague and venemous bites.

Rubia tinctorium — P — MADDER

A famous dye plant, madder can hardly be left out when planning a craft garden. At the same time, madder needs a good deal of space and some patience before it can be harvested for use. As a herb I find its growth strangely fascinating with the angular, gawky prickly stems to 1m (3ft) tall and whorls of hairy leaves. These may "ambush" nearby taller plants which are then used to support the continued growth of the madder. The rough character above ground is contrasted by the smooth almost polished effect of the reddish roots. These are long and cylindrical, growing out profusely in all directions, as if from a Medusa's head, until they seem to colour the soil. Madder prefers to have a sunny, well-drained situation with well-fed and deeply dug alkaline soil. The greenish-yellow flowers are small and inconspicuous in summer and may pass unnoticed. Their earlier presence, however, is confirmed by the round, purple berries that follow. Some dye evidently pervades the plant for it is a slightly gruesome fact that animals grazing on madder will develop red bones and birds eating it can have their claws and beaks similarly coloured.

The roots, which will easily break away as you try to lift a plant, can be divided in autumn or spring, either time being correct for harvesting. The root takes two to three years to mature sufficiently to give a strong dye and so it is as well to take plant divisions each year, marking the plants with dates, to assist when harvesting for dyeing wool or cotton. The herb can also be increased by layering the trailing stems to encourage them in growing fresh roots.

Indigenous to Asia Minor and South east Europe, madder is particularly associated with its home in Turkey from the term "Turkey red" given to the fast and bright dye from the root. Madder has been used in India since prehistoric times and was exported from Baghdad to Western Europe. It was later cultivated on a large scale for the dyeing industry in France, the Netherlands and Central Europe as well as in Britain.

Rubus fruticosus   S   BRAMBLE

THIS familiar hedgerow native of Europe has a magical quality in that it binds modern man to the far past. It is the only remaining hedgerow harvest still popular even with city dwellers on day trips to the autumn countryside. The berries, luscious, after a wet end of summer and shining in autumn sunshine, have been picked since neolithic times, giving us an amazing link with prehistory. A number of magical rites to cure disease are associated with brambles, whether crawling through circles made by the curving stems to cure boils or rheumatism, or gathering blackberries at appropriate times of the moon to give protection against evil.

Brambles can beome rampant in a garden patch as each shoot which curves down to the ground is liable to take root - a fact which is all in its favour if you happen to be growing it to supply lengthy stems for basketry. I grow the thornless variety **Rubus biflorus** to eliminate the hated task of dethorning them first. Either bush will, of course, attract butterflies with its pretty pinkish-white flowers in summer. These include the grizzled skipper in Southern England and Wales and, in my garden, the white admiral, gatekeeper and ringlet.

From late summer through the autumn, the fruits ripen from green, through red, to rich black, often in several successive batches, giving tasty bramble and apple puddings, bramble jelly and a pink dye. The young shoots, roots and leaves can also be harvested in spring and early summer to give green, orange and grey-black dyes for wool or linen. Harvesting the long, trailing stems for basketry should be done in early autumn when the bush has fruited and you are tidying your garden patch ready for winter. Simply strip the leaves, leaving the stems in a dark, damp corner under a hedge in order to "fade" them in preparation for soaking and weaving. The reddish-brown stems will fade a little, but remain an attractive shade for stakes. A single bush gave me a harvest of several 3m (9ft) lengths a year ago. The central fibres of the stems have also supplied twine in the past.

The alternate leaves have been used medicinally to treat burns and scalds or in decoction form as a mouthwash or gargle for infections. Or the leaves and flowers can be picked together for tea. Juice from the young shoots has been applied to wounds as a healing agent, and even powdered root bark and leaves given for diarrhoea.

Rumex acetosa   P   SORREL

THIS is a herb which seems, like rue, to attract either a great love or hatred. There are those who would not be without fresh sorrel for their salads and those who cannot bear the acidic taste, or find it upsets them. Certainly anyone who suffers from rheumatism or bladder stones should not indulge in a diet rich in either common or French sorrel - *Rumex scutatus*. Sorrel has a high oxalate content which makes it a dangerous herb to take in large quantities, and there have been a few cases of poisoning. Native to Europe, it is a herb of the meadows, especially thriving where the soil is rich in iron, with the French variety enjoying a drier environment than common sorrel. Either will benefit from being cut back at intervals, in order to stimulate fresh growth of the arrow-shaped green or red tinted leaves for salads.

Left to grow to a full height of 60cm-1.2m (2 to 4ft), sorrel produces spires of reddish-brown flowers in summer, followed by three-sided nut-like seeds. The herb attracts the small copper butterfly, an unusual and lovely visitor to gardens. It isequally well placed in the kitchen garden (I grow it in a raised vegetable bed), in a physic or a dye garden. Medicinally, it has been given as a diuretic, astringent and bitter tonic. The very old and very young are best avoiding it. The leaves have also been applied as poultices for some skin complaints. In the dye garden, sorrel offers green, brown, pink and yellow dyes from the tops with a variety of mordants. A silver leafed sorrel is now available which makes a pretty addition to a small garden along with other variegated herbs. This is a miniature version which does however spread in a similar fashion to common sorrel. Either can be further increased by dividing the roots in autumn.

Salix   T   WILLOW

IF you are fortunate enough to have a cool and fairly wet corner in your garden, then you may enjoy growing one or two willows to give young stems for basketry. They do not have to become sizeable trees (willow can grow to over 18m (60ft) since you will be cropping them regularly and therefore keeping their height under control. The white willow with its wonderfully graceful long, greyish leaves is the source both of basketry material and the medicinal drug, salicin. The bark is gathered in September for medicinal use and the leaves when harvested have proved mildly calming and sleep-inducing in an infusion. In the bath, they also help against rheumatism. Soft charcoal is made from the wood and the basketry use has led to willow being cultivated on a commercial scale in certain areas, in addition to its profusion in the wild along streams and rivers throughout Europe. The female flowers are on separate trees to the male and are in smaller catkins with a nectar-producing gland. If there is one tree that has ever made me wish I might have a talent for sketching, it is the willow. Although I feel the most sensitive portrait might be to capture the ballet of its moving form in a painting on silk.

Historically, it is interesting to read that Culpeper mentions the writings of a Mr. Stone, who notes the efficacy of the bark in treating fevers. Culpeper predicts that the price of the Peruvian bark then in use being likely to rise, this knowledge might prove of use in the future. Little could he have imagined that two centuries later willow was indeed to be at the centre of pharmacological progress when the salicylic acid isolated from the bark earlier in that century was produced synthetically in 1852.

To return to the basketry use - Somerset is the area where most basketry willow osiers are grown. If growing them yourself, cut them back in the third year after planting and each year from then on. If the ground is sufficiently wet you should be able to cut lengths of between 1 and 2m (3 to 6ft). You may do this in early autumn while the sap is still rising, storing them in water for a time to maintain their supple nature, or harvest during the winter. (See the basketry section for further preparation.) Weeping willow wands can also be cut for baskets.

Saponaria officinalis   P   SOAPWORT

THE joyous aura of the herb is perhaps expressed in one of the common names of "Bouncing Bet". For the 60-75cm (2 to 2 1/2ft) tall stems, bearing seemingly heavy white or pink flowers from mid-summer onwards, do appear to bounce merrily in the breeze, tending to lean over a little as the summer advances. The plant gives no scent either from the leaves or flowers and has been taken into cultivation for its usefulness - in producing a soapy washing solution for delicate fabrics from the saponin content of the leaves or root - rather than for its attractiveness.

Native to Southern Europe and Western Asia, and naturalised in northern climes, it was introduced to North America by settlers, to supply soap for washing and shampoos. I have seen it growing wild in hedgerows close to farmhouses, where it has presumably escaped from earlier gardens. I grow it in my own garden for use, where I have found that the herb enjoys moisture but will not thrive well in sodden ground. It does not necessarily require any great richness in the soil. Soapwort can be propagated from seed sown in spring, or by dividing the roots in autumn, when part may be harvested for drying and use. The best results are from the combination of soapwort and hard water. The pale, green veined leaves can be gathered to make up in a decoction for spot cleaning or shampoo throughout the summer. In solution this is sufficiently gentle for old fabrics, but do try a test piece first.

As a medicinal herb, it has a use in local compresses for skin diseases, together with some possibly dangerous roles in internal use as an expectorant and cholagogue. The saponin content makes it a remedy to be used internally only under medical supervision.

Scolymus cardunculus   P   CARDOON

GROWING cardoons has been a fascinating education for me, and in a way an introduction to the Victorian kitchen garden, in reading about the method of elaborately winding a band of hay around the stalks to prepare them for harvest. The cardoon is a close relative of the artichoke, indeed some people argue it is an artichoke rather than a herb. However, two thousand years ago Pliny wrote of its medicinal properties, while its further uses as a dye and as a substitute for rennet in cheese-making since then support it in the herbal category.

I first included the cardoon not in the vegetable patch, but in the treasure garden, for its distinctive, spiny grey leaves and wonderful globe-like seedheads. Even without special feeding the plants grew to some 1m (3ft) tall and could have been much larger had I grown them as for a vegetable. Before the seeds come the flowers, and with them another fascination – that of watching even bumble bees tumbling about within the amazing depth of the purple petals. A section of the flower might well resemble a punk Mohican hair style, for each slender petal seems to stand straight upwards, leaving the bee unable to climb out from amongst them.

Save the seeds from your cardoon for the following spring and sow several in a pot of soil in the warm in late March or early April. Pot on singly when they reach 4 leaves and plant out when the danger of frost is passed. If growing cardoons for the table, then it is a good idea to dig a trench as if for artichokes or sweet peas, feeding the young plants well. For ornamental purposes in the craft garden, however, this is really not necessary. The stalks are "earthed up" with the hay band in September, about a month before gathering to eat. More seeds can be sown up to midsummer for successive crops, the last being in the following spring. These would need to be protected from winter rain and cold to do well. Do not forget to gather any seedheads after a spell of dry weather when they can be dried for decoration and a few seeds saved for the following spring.

Solidago virgaurea P GOLDEN ROD

A welcome display of bright colour in late summer, golden rod has found its place in many flower borders as a herbaceous plant; growing some 60-90cm (2 to 3ft) in height. In fact it is better known in this role than as a herb, despite the common name of "woundwort". In past centuries *Solidago* enjoyed a high reputation as a healing plant. As such it was imported from the Middle East to be applied to gangrenous wounds and for other medicinal uses, until, as Gerard writes, it was discovered growing wild at Hampstead wood. The monetary value dropped immediately from the 2s 6d (12 /2p) formerly asked for a single ounce to a point where, as he confirms "no man will give halfe a crowne for an hundred weight of it". Later, familiarity with its eager spreading habits - which lead it to dominate even a large flower bed in a couple of seasons - brought some contempt on the part of gardeners it seems. Dry woodland and heaths can still support the herb which thrives in acid, calcareous soils. In a garden, it can easily be propagated by root division in spring or autumn. Cut back the tan stems in autumn after they have lost their pointed green leaves.

The modern golden rod was cultivated from *Solidago canadensis* introduced from North America by John Tradescant the younger in the early 17th century. The delicate and pretty bright yellow flower sprays press beautifully for design and craft purposes, or they may be harvested to make a tonic wine. In the meantime, the bees and other insects will crowd in to visit them as soon as the tiny buds open. These are followed by a mass of seedheads with the softest down imaginable, quite suited to the most delicate of arrangements. They can be successfully retained on the stems by spraying with silver or gold paint or a clear hair lacquer.

S. virgaurea is a native of Europe, North Africa and Asia, while *S. canadensis* which grows to 2m (6ft) has spread and hybridized in America to the extent that there are now over 100 different species there. A number of these were involved in trials to produce a golden rod 4.2m (14ft) tall which might form a natural alternative source of latex for manufacturing rubber for Henry Ford. His friend Thomas Edison succeeded in this task, although the process of making "golden rod rubber" was expensive and soon overtaken by synthetic rubber. A set of car tyres were, however, produced from golden rod and presented by Henry Ford to Edison. The spreading roots can be divided in spring or autumn, or the seeds sown in spring, for if your interest extends beyond crafts or winemaking you will need more than a single clump. A possible tendency to mildew can be counteracted through the summer by occasional feeds with horsetail tea. (See page 29, hollyhock.)

Symphoricarpus albus   S   SNOWBERRY

WHAT a joy the plump, white berries are in autumn and early winter until the birds eat them, or they are harvested for dyeing wool. These follow on from pretty pink, bell-shaped flowers in late summer. The slender, tan coloured stems are attractive too, when the oval, green leaves have already left them with the autumn winds and frost. Highly suitable for a garden hedge, snowberry is also useful for providing basketry stakes when the distinctive colouring of the stems can be appreciated in a durable basket. I have therefore used snowberry to divide my craft garden from the orchard. Since the shrub is good at spreading by suckers, a little careful management can encourage the hedge to thicken quickly, with unwanted suckers providing a crop for basketry needs.

The snowberry is a native of Europe, naturalised across North America and grows as far north as Iceland. In Britain it has often spread into the wild from gardens and can be found along old railway embankments. The shrub can grow to a height of 3m (10ft) in good conditions, but can also be kept trimmed down to about 1m (3ft) if liked. Plant new hedges between October and February, taking stem cuttings by pulling the tiny sideshoots away with "heels" to encourage growth in March. These may be dipped in hormone rooting compound and given some protection for a time by setting into pots of composted soil with polythene bags over the top. This will keep the soil moist and protect the shoots from possible bitter winds until leaves open on the stems and the danger of frost is passed. Alternatively the pots could be kept in a greenhouse for protection. Plant out in early May.

Tagetes patula   A   FRENCH MARIGOLD

THESE may come as a surprise in the herb garden when they are normally thought of simply as bedding plants. I first included them as companions to my precious pinks and carnations to protect them from eelworms and then became fascinated by their wealth of bright flowers and dye possibilities. Since then I have found the lemon and tangerine gem to be brilliant dyes for wool. These tiny dwarf French marigolds, growing to no more than 15cm (6in) tall, generally known only as *Tagetes*, are indeed best suited as border edgings. They make a brave show of being well defended with their strong smell, one cannot call it a perfume, and yet when the slugs are about, they go down one after another. *Tagetes* came from Mexico originally and not surprisingly are extremely susceptible to the British unpredictable cold spells after spring has tempted us to plant out young seedlings. The larger varieties of French marigolds were introduced to this country in 1573 by the Huguenots.

Needing extra care, they are best grown from seed in seedtrays in a heated greenhouse, or better still indoors until they are well established. A little hardening off on sunny days will prepare them for the shock of being out in a coldframe overnight for a while before planting out. At this point some sort of slug defence is advisable and I use Vaseline which has had 2 drops of essential oil of pine added to the jar and stirred in, smeared around the top of pots or trays. (Leave the scented Vaseline sealed in the jar for at least 24 hours before using it.) Both slugs and snails find this scent repulsive and the Vaseline will hold it, while making it more difficult for them to reach the plant into the bargain. In a bed the same mix can be smeared onto bark chips and set into the soil around the plants.

Tagetes are helpful when planted with carnations and pinks as protectors against eelworms, also to edge vegetable beds, keeping certain pests away. In the dye garden they provide cheering patches of colour against a backdrop of predominantly green weld, alkanet, gypsywort or other herbs. They can also be very attractive surrounding a single dahlia.

They produce so many flowers through the summer, one after another, that it is not difficult to pick a bowl of them for dyeing wool yellow or orange, while still leaving sufficient for a good show of blooms. In a poor season remember to leave some of the early flowers to go to seed to be sure of collecting your own mature seeds for the following year, before the frost takes the plants.

Tanacetum balsamita   P   ALECOST
(Formerly *Chrysanthemum balsamita*)

ALECOST, also known as costmary and bible-leaf, is a modest plant perhaps most suited to its last name. The grey colouring of the long, pointed leaves, the inconspicuous nature of the scent unless the leaves are bruised, and the unassuming, daisy-like flowers make it a chance discovery amongst other herbs. It is a pretty, sweet herb however, and worth including in a garden for wines, ales and liqueurs, or a fragrant garden, for the pleasure of its presence.

The name alecost came from the frequent use of the herb in the early ales, along with other gruit herbs. Costmary comes from an association with the Virgin Mary, as many white flowered herbs are dedicated to her, and bible-leaf from the dried leaves being used as bookmarks in family bibles for their sweet, mint-like scent. They were also laid amongst linen to keep moths away and can be included in pot-pourri or sweet pillows to good effect.

Alecost grows to a height of about 60-75cm (2 to 2½ft) with long, thin stems bearing fewer leaves beneath the clusters of flowers which resemble both feverfew and chamomile. Despite the latin *Tanacetum,* which may alarm those who have grown tansy, *(Tanacetum vulgare)* with its rampant spreading habits, alecost does not grow rampantly over other plants in the flower bed. The root can be divided in spring or autumn and the increase in size during the season is generally modest. The herb may be planted in full sun or partial shade with equally good results, but is best set with other sturdier herbs such as pot marigolds to give surrounding support in windy weather. Mrs. Grieve in her **Modern Herbal** says alecost is a plant of the Orient, introduced in the 16th century. However, it seems to have been very common in gardens before that and was included in 15th century cookery recipes as well as medieval ales. Thomas Tusser, in his **Five Hundred Points of Good Husbandrie** published in 1580 includes it under strewing herbs.

Taraxacum officinale   P   DANDELION

THERE is far more to the common dandelion than is evident from its modern role, which is generally as an amusement for little children in blowing away the downy seeds while chanting "one o'clock, two o'clock" and so on. This charming pastime, which has delighted little children for centuries is remembered in one of the herb's common names, "Peasant's clock". Another, "mole salad", reminds us that the leaves are edible, if generally exceptionally bitter for modern taste.

For tender young leaves which can be enjoyed in green salads, grow a cultivated variety of the herb in well-fed, rich soil, and keep them from flowering by removing all flower buds. Having been sown in spring, the clumps of dandelions can also becovered with pots to blanch them for better flavour. Leaf harvest lasts from spring until September. The roots are dug in the autumn of the second year when they can be scrubbed and dried in thick slices on a baking tray in a moderate oven until dark brown. Store in an airtight jar and grind as required. The dandelion is found almost all over Europe, growing from a few centimetres up to 40cm (16in) the name being derived from the French **"Dent de lion"** which refers to the toothed edges of the leaves. It is also a native of northern and southern temperate regions, Central and Northern Asia and North America. The flowers make a delightful wine and the leaves and roots included in beers have always been known for cleansing the blood, particularly when partnered with burdock. First mentioned by Arabian physicians in the 10th century and appreciated also by the Welsh physicians of the Myddfai, the dandelion contains health-giving minerals (it takes three times the iron from the soil absorbed by other plants); silicic acid, valuable for bones, nails and hair condition; sulphur and vitamins A and C in high amounts.

The herb is very old, pollen from its bright yellow flowers being found amongst pre-Neolithic remains, but its virtues are barely touched on by some herbalists, such as Gerard. Culpeper however, notes the herb is much eaten in spring by the French and Dutch and comments rather acidly that foreign physicians are not as selfish as ours with information on the virtues of plants - presumably putting the dandelion in the category of preventative medicine. He also recommends dandelion for jaundice, urinary problems, agues and fevers. The milky sap has been painted onto warts to clear them. Oozing as it does from the stem or root, it tends to congeal into a rubbery substance. This has been investigated during wartime shortages as a commercial source of latex for rubber production. For this reason and the possible use of the flowers as a dye, the dandelion may find a place in the craft garden as well as kitchen or medicinal beds. When siting the dandelion row, it may be helpful to remember that the plants give off ethylene gas which acts to retard the green growth of surrounding herbs, while it encourages the development of flowers and fruits. This would make them good companions for tomatoes, for instance. Their leaves provide food for the clouded buff moth.

Taxus baccata   T   YEW

THOUGHT to survive for more than a thousand years, the yew's exceptional life expectancy means that its growth is correspondingly slow. It is native to Europe, North Africa and Western Asia. Old yew hedges make wonderful protective shields around gardens, with a wide path between them and thirsty herbs. However, set as a garden hedge, which is its most likely role, or as a specimen tree which can be shaped into impressive topiary, it needs a few years to appear really established in the garden plan. Care should be taken when siting yews near areas where small children are likely to play as it is very poisonous and deaths have occurred in recent times. The needle-like leaves are the most poisonous part, containing up to four times as much of the alkaloid taxine in winter as they do in summer, and the berries are also a danger if the seed inside is eaten. The drug acts swiftly producing symptoms of vomiting, cramps and diarrhoea, followed by unconsciousness and death from cardiac arrest often within an hour. Horses are particularly susceptible to eating the needles, dying within a matter of minutes.

Over a period of centuries, the tree can grow to 20m (65ft) in height and make a considerable, shady spread of branches. The girth of the trunk is massive by this time and I recall visiting a churchyard at Nantclyn in North Wales where a pulpit had been carved out of the trunk of an ancient yew, with steps cut into the side of the tree to reach it. Yews have a common association with churchyards, one popular reason given for this is the former use of yew in manufacturing bows for archers. (Archery practice also took place in churchyards in former centuries.) It may have been a useful site for a poisonous tree away from fields where animals might be poisoned by eating the leaves. Earlier still, the yew was an object of worship along with the elder, and the sacred groves could be converted to Christian worship by siting the church amongst the sacred trees. There is much superstition attached to this tree and its folk name of "the tree of death" is a reminder of magical as much as poisonous powers.

In winter, when its dark branches are lightened by a scattering of snow, with occasional red berries still left from the onslaught of the birds, the yew can look beautiful. On the trunk, flakes of red bark may be outlined artistically by frost. The heartwood of the yew gives a good dye and the wood is most effective in its markings when turned, although of course a hard wood to work with (see the craft section).

As spring approaches, the small yellow stamens of the cones of greenish male flowers are more attractive than the scattered female flowers which may not appear on the same tree.

If there is an old yew within several hundred yards of your garden it is quite likely you will find tiny seedlings appearing courtesy of the birds, who having eaten the berries, leave the seeds together with their droppings on your flower beds. I have numerous such "gifts", which I am allowing nature to grow on for me, moving them to a permanent site as they reach about 15cm (6in) high. Trimming is all the extra care they will need.

Urtica dioica   P   STINGING NETTLE

EVERY garden of sufficient size should have a nettle patch for at least two good reasons. The first is to use the cut nettles in liquid feeds and to add heat to the compost heap, contributing to the better growth of the other plants. The second is its role as a food for the many insects and particularly butterflies, which find the leaves attractive. For their needs the nettle patch is best sited on a sunny, south facing bank of good soil. The herb is the only food-source for the peacock and small tortoiseshell butterflies; it also feeds the lovely red admiral amongst 30 different insects. In a craft garden, the nettles may be planted for use as a dye from the leaves or roots, for paper-making, or as a source of fibres to spin into cloth. If we add harvest of the nettle for wine and beermaking and kitchen use, you will soon appreciate the value of the herb. It is hardly surprising it was blessed by St. Patrick for its many services to man.

In a small garden where there is not space for a whole patch of nettles, they may be dotted here and there, next to mints, sage, marjoram or a single angelica to increase the content of essential oil and therefore the flavour of their companion herbs. In an orchard, nettles beneath apple trees may aid ripening of the fruit. Beekeepers should also note that nettles were traditionally planted close to hives to discourage frogs.

Like the yew, the nettle is dioecious - that is, it has male and female flowers on separate plants. Venturing out in the early morning may reward you with the rare sight of the male flowers giving impressive "explosions" of clouds of their pollen as the anthers spring outwards when the flower opens. The roots spread quickly without the need for young seedlings however, and for reasons of harvest and to encourage the butterflies with young growth, they should be cut down in early June, before they flower, unless being grown for spinning. In order to grow tall nettles for long fibres, around 1.5-1.8m (5 to 6ft) a good, rich, moist soil is necessary, preferably in a ditch. It is in part this requirement that has discouraged growth for nettle cloth on a commercial scale, despite many experiments. The nettle is native or naturalised through most of Europe and temperate Asia as far as Japan. It can be found in parts of North and South America, Australia and New Zealand. The famous sting of the nettle can be cured by the application of juice from docks, or certain other herbs. The nettle also carries its own antidote in the juice inside the stem: crushing the stem with a stone can release this to relieve the pain when there is not a dock in sight. The same formic acid which stings so severely has an important use too, in stopping bleeding, although admittedly you might need to be hard pressed to wish to use it.

Verbascum thapsus   B   MULLEIN

I have childhood memories of seeing mullein growing tall into the sky from the ruins of a red brick wall, looking quite magnificent. This was in Buckingham and I remember mullein being known in the family, as "The Buckingham plant" for years afterwards. Such is the impression that can be left by a really fine specimen. The association of mulleins and old brick or stone walls seems to be most successful, both from a visual point of view and from the plant's needs, as it will thrive in stony, alkaline ground (particularly limestone) which is well drained. The plants may need staking against the wind, however, should they rise from the top of the wall, rather than the lower pockets of soil at the base of the stonework. Mullein can grow to be around 2m (6ft) tall and the lower "velvety", grey-furred leaves can spread over 60cm (2ft) quite easily.

The name mullein may have come from the Latin *mollis* which describes the soft nature of the leaves, and the common British names, "feltwort", "donkey's ears" and "blanket leaf" also refer to it. So soft are the leaves that they once padded poor children's worn shoes. The other name of "candlewicks" directs us to the use for the highly inflammable white down growing from the leaves, which was stripped off and roughly twisted to make wicks for lamps. In fact, sometimes the whole tall spire of flowers and smaller leaves was dipped in suet and burned as a light, giving rise to yet another affectionate name, "Our Lady's candle".

In the centre of a raised garden bed or along a wall behind other herbs in the craft garden, mullein adds character and height. The yellow flowers, which are small and densely packed together around the spire of top growth, tend to open one by one, making harvest (for the medicinal mullein oil or pressing) tedious when the weather is changeable. It does result in a long flowering period, however, and the flowers can be dried in a warm dark place, below 40°C. An infusion of the flowers with lye gives a golden hair dye. The leaves can also be dried and were once smoked as a treatment for tuberculosis.

This native plant has one enemy which seems to find the herb whatever strong scented companions I plant close by - the mullein moth caterpillars. Each year I take care to examine the foliage for their small black eggs which hatch out into voracious caterpillars with distinctive yellow and black markings in early summer. If the eggs or very young caterpillars are not successfully removed at this time then the plant will soon be ruined, the leaves resembling moth eaten fragments of blanket.

Viburnum opulus   S   GUELDER ROSE

ONE of the happy surprises in the herb craft garden to those who know nothing of its practical uses, the guelder rose is recommended both by its low maintenance needs and highly decorative nature in more than one season. Both of these factors most certainly contribute to its frequent choice in plantings with red dogwood around public and commercial buildings. The Guelder rose was first imported to Britain in the 16th century from the area on the German/Dutch border, known as Guelders - hence its name. Native to Europe, North Africa and Northern Asia, it grows wild in woodland clearings and at wood edges, often along roadsides, enjoying a sunny position.

The white flowers are particularly distinctive from early summer, borne in a series of flat-topped clusters, which appear to be edged with a "broiderie anglaise" effect of open, five-petalled sterile flowers standing out on short stalks around the dense, fertile centre. The guelder rose can grow to 4m (13ft) tall, in calcareous soils, when it will dominate even a large craft bed. However, it is relatively slow growing when compared with those other members of the *Caprifoliaceae* family, elder and honeysuckle.

In autumn, as the maple-shaped leaves turn through gold to crimson, the berries will already have ripened to an attractive, brilliant red. At this point I gather them to make guelder ink. Although fresh berries, which contain viburnine, are poisonous, cooking destroys their dangerous character. Medicinal preparations from the berries have been used to treat cramps, asthma and tension. The bark, also known as "cramp bark", is greyish, and the young branches, trimmed back in early autumn may be used in basketry. The guelder rose may easily be propagated from cuttings taken at this time, or the ripe berries left to yield their seeds which should be sown outdoors in late autumn or early spring as they need the frost to germinate.

Vinca major   P   PERIWINKLE

THE periwinkle family contains numerous decorative plants which are grown in flower gardens to cover unsightly walls, or trail as an attractive ground cover beneath tall shrubs or trees. Their rampant stems bear oval, evergreen leaves and the flowers of different family members may vary from white to the common blue or purple and dark red. The flower forms are generally star-like with five rounded or pointed petals. The periwinkle is a familiar part of the English garden and they may be indigenous, but could equally well have been introduced from Southern Europe by the Romans.

The flowers may already be in evidence as early as February on their single stalks. The periwinkle continues to flower as the stems arch their way across the available ground, taking root at intervals. If you are in even more of a hurry to propagate new plants than the periwinkle itself, then stem cuttings can be taken in spring or autumn.

In the craft garden, the periwinkle earns its place as a source of basketry material as the trailing stems stripped of their leaves are useful weavers, easily gathered at any point in the year. It might be well placed under a hedge of other basketry materials. As a herb, periwinkle finds its main associations with magic, although its medicinal applications have come to the fore in modern times with the related Madagascar periwinkle being a source of an anti-cancer treatment. *Vinca minor* was grown in physic gardens for wound drinks and the crushed leaves were applied to wounds.

The sorcerer's violet is a common name for periwinkle, which was an ingredient in love potions and spells. In the Anglo-Saxon leechbooks, it was recommended to be picked "when the moon is nine nights old, and eleven nights, and thirteen nights and thirty nights, and when it is one night old". With its easy growth habits, and evergreen nature, it was also looked upon as a plant of fertility and used for garlands both on coffins and for the condemned on their way to execution. In the 14th century, the herb was powdered with earthworms and houseleek and given to quarrelsome husbands and wives in their food to bring peace and love between them. Quite who inflicted this treatment upon them is not clear, nor whether it was taken willingly. Personally I can't imagine coming back for a second helping and perhaps this is the way in which it worked.

Geographical distribution of the herbs has been taken from: *The Encyclopedia of Herbs and Herbalism, edited by Malcolm Stuart, published by Black Cat, 1987, A Modern Herbal. Mrs. M. Grieve. FRHS, published by Jonathan Cape, 1931 and The Illustrated Flora of Britain and Northern Europe by Marjorie Blamey and Christopher Grey-Wilson, published by Hodder and Stoughton, 1989.*

Herbs in Wine-making

MAKING wines at home is a pleasure I remember my parents enjoying and I now use the same large, earthenware crock in which my mother's spiced elderberry port looked, and smelled so inviting. With recipes, the crock and an appreciation of wines passed down, wine-making has a sense of retaining family connections for me, as well as offering the constant invitation to experiment for myself.

I do not consider myself an expert, nor am I concerned to be up to date with methods, for I have found others coming to me to learn the older ways of adding fresh yeast on toast and steeping herbs for longer. The flavour from a plastic bucket, unfortunately, is not the same as that given when the wine is made in earthenware, although at times I have to resort to using both. If you do use earthenware, the glaze must always be undamaged.

Wine-making is a pleasant hobby for anyone who has a little time now and then. Ingredients should always be gathered when they are at their best - on a sunny day in dry conditions. Whenever possible harvest herbs, fruit and vegetables from your own garden, as these can be prepared immediately. Gather herbs and flowers into a basket rather than a plastic bag which will encourage rapid wilting.

Every stage from picking the ingredients to drinking the wine should be a pleasure. Occasionally, when a time consuming task is necessary, such as destalking elderflowers or berries, spread the work by inviting friends round to help. For most people it will be a novelty, at least on the first occasion. Avoid elderberry stains on the carpet by making this a garden party, perhaps a prelude to a barbeque.

Little equipment is needed for wine-making: a large crock (preferably with a lid, although it can be covered with a clean cloth) or a plastic fermenting bucket; a couple of demi-johns as each will be in use for several months at a time, and a bored cork and bubbler fermentation lock for each; corks, bottles (recycle if possible), plastic tubing to syphon when bottling, a nylon straining bag, sterilization tablets for preparing demi-johns etc. and a bottle brush to aid cleaning.

Every piece of equipment must be exceptionally clean; demi-johns, fermenting vessel, bottles, fermentation lock, syphon etc. must all be sterilized to avoid infection from bacteria.

Over the centuries, wines have generally been made of almost any fruit or vegetable which gave an abundant harvest. A more careful selection should be made with herbs however; some have very distinctive flavours, and occasionally powerful properties, that might give unlooked for results. Herb wines were often made with their medicinal qualities in mind. Dandelion, nettle, elderflower, mint, parsley and rosemary were all credited as health-giving, whether as blood cleansers, tonics, digestives or in helping arthritis.

The herbs in the table have all been made into wines in the past and I have given some indication of the nature of the wine they produced. Certain old favourites such as cowslip and primrose are, sadly, only practical for a very few of us to make. Neither flower should be picked in the wild as they are protected by law and it is up to the keen gardener and wine-maker to grow as many of these plants as possible in their own gardens, from seeds on sale. A stock can soon be built up, dividing the plants and allowing them to seed each year, and a large garden or orchard can provide sufficient for a modest quantity of wine.

Where flower wines are made, all the green parts should be removed from the backs of the flowers.

Herbs for Wine-making

Herb	Part used	Harvest	Wine type
agrimony	flowering top	July	dry, white
angelica	whole plant	June-August	dry, white
broom	flowers	July-August	med, white
Calendula	flowers	June-Sept	sweet, white
carnation **(Dianthus caryophyllus** only)	petals	June-July	sweet
chamomile (no more than 18)	flowers	May-Sept	dry, white
coltsfoot	flowers	March	dry, white
cowslip	flowers	April-May	dry, white
dandelion	flowers	April-May	dry, white
elderflower	flowers	May-June	sweet, white
elderberry	berries	Sept-Oct	sweet, red
golden rod	flowers	Aug-Sept	dry, white
hawthorn	flower	May	dry, white.
hawthorn	berries	Sept-Oct	sweet, fawn
honeysuckle **(Lonicera periclymenun** only)	flowers	July-Aug	sweet, white
lemon balm	leaves	June	dry, white
limeflower	flowers	July	sweet, white
lovage	flowers	July	dry, white
meadowsweet	flowers	June	sweet, white
mints	young tops	June	sweet, white

Herb	Part used	Harvest	Wine type
nettle	young tops	April-May	dry, fawn
oak leaf	leaves	June 21-July 7	dry, white
pansy	flowers	May-Aug	med, white
parsley	leaves	June-July	dry, white
primrose	flowers	Feb-April	dry, white
red clover	flowers	July-Aug	sweet, red
rose	petals hips	June-July Oct-Nov after frost	sweet, red dry, fawn
rosemary	flowering tops	Mar-June	dry, white
saffron	stigmas	Sept	white
sage	leaves	May-June	dry, white
thyme	flowering tops	July-Aug	dry, white
violet	flowers	Mar-Apr	sweet, white
woodruff	flowers	May	dry, white
yarrow	flowers and leaves	July-Aug	dry, white

Having looked at the list and thought about the herb ingredients available to you, it is as well also to think about those herbs that will have strong flavours before making your choice. Some, such as sage and rosemary, are best steeped for a few days in a wine already made, or partnered with a fruit to counter some of the strength of the herb and complement it. In addition, sweet cicely may be used in its sweetening role with tart fruit wines such as damson, while the combination of angelica and rhubarb, so good in cookery, can also be repeated in wine-making.

Dandelion, carnation, pinks and roses will need to have the white tips of the petals cut away to keep the wine from becoming bitter. This is a time-consuming task, but not as bad as one might imagine, as the flowers can be laid in lines and sliced through several at once. Roses should be from the **Rosa gallica** family. **Damascena** is the best for flavour.

Elderflowers and elderberries need time to destalk, but both are so invaluable and delicious that I never begrudge their preparation.

You are most unlikely to be able to grow saffron in any quantity, never mind cope with the harvest. I couldn't resist including it however, as so often saffron is a forgotten herb and the wine could still be made in hotter climes than the British Isles.

Lime tree flowers come from the lime, *Tilia cordata.* If you are fortunate enough to have a lime tree in your garden, collect only flowers and bracts, not the sticky leaves which attract aphids. The flowers need to be sun-dried before use to bring out the rich, honeyed flavour.

Amounts of flowers in old recipes often dismay the beginner. Picking a gallon of pansies or primroses is unthinkable, even if your garden had so many. However, I have seen various recipes for the same flower wine adding from 1.2 litres (2½ pints) in volume of flowers to 4.5 litres (8 pints) of water. It is therefore always worth experimenting with a smaller amount and perhaps extra ingredients for flavour.

Measure flowers in a kitchen measuring jug unless you are lucky enough to have an old wooden grain measure in the house. Do not push them down when measuring, simply give the jug a tap now and then to stop large airpockets forming between them. In the case of chamomile, however, I have included a caution not to add more than 18 flowers to a wine as their flavour is very strong and in excess can be really unpleasant.

Other herbs not mentioned on this list may be steeped in wines, wine cups and fruit punches, or partnered with fruit or vegetables in wine-making. The leaves and stems of salad burnet, leaves of sweet cicely, fennel, scented geranium *(Pelargonium),* lemon verbena and dill, borage flowers, caraway and coriander seeds, have been the most popular. Angelica seeds, lemon balm leaves, sprigs of rosemary, flowering sweet woodruff, clary sage tops, hyssop leaves and flowers, meadowsweet leaves, and juniper berries can also be steeped in white, or, in some cases, red wines.

In the recipes below I have tried to give a wide selection of flavours and both red and white wines. From this base you will be able to create new recipes with your own favourites. I have particularly enjoyed blending herbs with fruits to give richer tones and, as in the past, use some of the surplus harvest from the garden.

The first part of the basic method is always the same-that is, to prepare the herb and fruits or vegetable, add sugar and any spices and citrus fruits, and, usually, to pour boiling water over them. Some recipes require fruit in particular to be simmered to extract the juices; this, however, also kills the natural enzymes which would normally break down the pectin, so clearing the wine. (This can result in a very active, frothy fermentation aided by the pectin, and a cloudy wine later which will need extra decanting, filtering and possibly finings added at a later stage.)

Campden tablets are helpful in destroying wild yeasts present in elderflowers in varying degrees from year to year, and in fruits. Add according to the recipe, or instructions on the packet, remembering to crush each tablet in water first.

The sugar used is almost always white, either caster or granulated, lkg (2-2½1b) per 4.5 litres (8 pints) will give a dry wine, while up to 1.8kg (41b) produces an increasingly sweet wine. The alcohol content will generally be 15% or more.

To return to our method, when the liquid, which is now referred to as a must, has returned to bloodheat, then a slice of toast is made (being careful not to burn it) and left to cool slightly before spreading with fresh baker's yeast. I have found consistently better results in using this rather than dried wine yeast. Occasionally, however, it can lead to cloudy wine later. If you cannot obtain fresh yeast, then for preference follow the directions on wine yeast, rather than use dried yeast intended for baking.

Once covered, the brew is left for 24 hours by which time the yeast should be working well in the wine. The slice of toast with its yeast is carefully removed and the wine stirred. The wine should froth, showing the yeast is already working on converting the sugar to alcohol and carbon dioxide, as it uses the oxygen. If you are in the least doubtful about the progress at this stage, add a handful of chopped raisins to boost the fermentation. These will also enrich the wine. I like to use the large, plump muscatel raisins, bought from a healthfood shop where they will have been sun-dried without harmful chemical additions.

My parents consistently left their wines to stand at this stage for days longer than most modern recipes require, stirring the wine with a wooden spoon twice daily (never use metal with wines). The spiced elderberry port in particular will illustrate this. From their results I can only conclude this is right, although for reasons of having sufficient crocks to go round in the busy summer season I tend to leave mine for 5-10 days, rather than 10-21 days. The longer time also allows more opportunity for bacteria to enter the wine, which could result in a large batch of vinegar later.

Keeping the wine covered and in a clean atmosphere at an even temperature of about 70°F (21°C) is important. Do not stand even an earthenware crock in direct sunlight, or too close to a fire of any kind, or it may become overheated.

With the wine working well, strain out the fruit, spices, peel or other additions and pour into a prepared and slightly warmed demi-john. The wine can be syphoned from one to the other until close to the bottom if there are no flower petals or small spices that might pass along the syphon pipe. After this, you will need to strain the remaining wine, leaving the dregs to be discarded. I well remember a cautionary tale from my grandmother's wine-making when she was loathe to throw away the plump raisins from a brew and fed them instead to her chickens. My grandfather was not at all pleased to find drunken poultry staggering about later in the day!

Fill the demi-john past the height at which it begins to narrow to the neck, but not completely to the top, and fit the bored bung with fermentation lock inserted. After a few minutes, you should see the first bubbles rising through the boiled water in the fermentation lock.

With red wines, it is important to cover the sides of the demi-john with brown paper, as strong light can make the wine fade during fermentation. Of course, if you plan to stand the demi-john in the bottom of your airing cupboard this will not be a problem. Always stand it on a tray until you are sure the wine will not overflow - something I have only known to happen once - and be sure to label each one. Having found a safe home for the fermenting wine at an even temperature, you will need to wait for between 3 weeks and 6 months before the fermenting ceases and it is ready for the next stage.

If there is a heavy sediment you may wish to rack or syphon the wine into another prepared demi-john and allow it to settle again in a cool place for a further 3 months before bottling. Or you may, like me, be far too impatient and syphon it straight into the bottles. Again choose dark bottles for red wines and place the syphon tube so that the wine runs gently in down the side of the bottle rather than splashing into the centre, producing bubbles. Fill the bottles to the lower part of their necks. The best time to do this is when the weather is quite settled, unless the temperature in your home is well controlled. To carry out the task during a thunderstorm is not recommended, although to avoid certain phases of the moon no longer appears to be an important instruction amongst keen winemakers!

Store the bottles on their sides in a wine rack in a cool place which will not have any sudden fluctuations in temperature. Very occasionally, I have known a single bottle discharge its cork and contents during exceptional weather and I keep the rack where such an incident would not be a disaster. If you make sparkling wines, these must always be bottled in very strong, recycled cider or champagne bottles and the corks wired.

Wine will benefit from being kept for 12 months before drinking, although a few are ready before that time. Do not pour away a wine tasted after a short time if you are not satisfied with the flavour, it may well improve. Wine that is too sharp can be sweetened by adding a few raisins to each bottle while wine that is too sweet can be aided by starting a fresh fermentation in a demi-john to remove unused sugar still in the liquid. In desperation, add a few sprigs of flowering rosemary for 4 days and then remove the herb. The flavour of the rosemary will almost certainly cover an unwanted taste.

Testing the wine, choosing those we will offer to visiting friends, hiding a bottle or two of real favourites in an inaccessible place to ensure they will be kept for a year or two, when they can be triumphantly opened as real treasures – these are some of the joys to come. Wine-making can take as much, or as little time as you wish to give it. You may make only one or two gallons in a year or over 50, according to your enthusiasm and storage space. What you cannot do, of course, is sell it without a licence.

In the following recipes I have presumed the reader has studied, or will return to, the advice in the previous pages on the basic method.

The first wine is one that I particularly enjoy as a table wine. It is not as dry as you might expect, although of course with a little less sugar, you could make it so. It partners fish well or makes a light dessert wine. The tartness of the rhubarb is overcome by the angelica, which also adds a slightly "muscatel" flavour.

Rhubarb and angelica
1.8kg (4lb) rhubarb stalks, cleaned and sliced thinly
350g (12oz) angelica stalks and leaves
1.4kg (3lb) white sugar
a handful of raisins
4.5 litres (8 pints) of water
25g (1oz) yeast
Cut up the washed angelica stems and leaves into 1.7 litres (3 pints) of water in a large pan and set over a moderate heat. Slowly dissolve in 450g (1lb) of sugar. Boil gently for about 20 minutes. Meanwhile, slice the rhubarb into the crock or

70

fermenting bucket and add 900g (2lb) of sugar. Pour the cooked, sweetened angelica and liquid over the rhubarb and sugar, and add a further 2.8-3.4 litres (5-6 pints) of boiling water to make up to 4.5 litres (8 pints). Stir in a handful of raisins or sultanas. When the liquid has come back to bloodheat, make a slice of toast, spread with fresh yeast and float this on the liquid before covering with the lid. After 24 hours remove the toast with a slotted spoon, pressing out the liquid, stir with a wooden spoon and cover.

Stir twice daily for 4 or 5 days, then strain and pour or syphon into a prepared demi-john which is slightly warm. Fit the bung and fermentation lock as directed above, label and stand in a warm place where there will be an even temperature. After a few minutes the first bubbles should pass through the water in the fermentation lock.

When the wine has finished fermenting follow the further instructions above. This wine generally takes between twelve and eighteen months to reach its best flavour. It can be drunk before then, but do keep some for the full period.

Soon after the rhubarb and angelica wine is made, the lemon thyme will be flowering and ready for harvest. This is another wine with a full flavour; good as a table wine with white meats, fish or vegetarian dishes. The soft, tonic effect of the lemon balm is enlivened by the slight tang of thyme.

Lemon balm and thyme

8 cups of torn lemon balm leaves and young tops
a handful of lemon thyme sprigs, (preferably flowering)
rind of 1 large or 2 small lemons
1.35kg (3lb sugar)
4.5 litres (8 pints) water
25g (1oz) fresh yeast
toast.

Peel the lemon or lemons finely with a potato peeler and put the lemon peel, sugar and 3.4 litres (6 pints) of water into a preserving pan (non-aluminium). Heat gently to dissolve the sugar, stirring all the time with a wooden spoon. Simmer for 20 minutes. Pour carefully over the torn lemon balm leaves and thyme sprigs in the fermenting bucket. Add 1.1 litres (2 pints) of boiling water.

Leave to cool to blood heat. Pour in the lemon juice and stir. Toast a slice of bread on both sides, allow it to cool a little and then spread with fresh yeast and float this on the liquid. Cover well. Leave for 24 hours when the toast should be removed gently with a slotted slice. Stir again with a wooden spoon and cover. The must should bubble as you stir it.

Stir twice daily for the next 4 days, then strain and pour or syphon into a prepared demi-john which is slightly warm. Fit the bung and fermentation lock as directed above, label and stand in a warm place where there will be an even temperature. After a few minutes the first bubbles should pass through the water in the fermentation lock.

When the wine has finished fermenting follow the further instructions. This wine may well be ready in 9 months rather than a year, but do not be tempted to drink all of your stock without waiting to savour the flavour of some which has truly matured.

As the lemon balm and thyme wine is syphoned into the demi-johns, already the roses will be opening and the first strawberries will be ripening. Another harvest is ready for use. The roses should be red and heavily scented. This wine is predictably rich and quite sweet. It takes a little longer than the lemon balm and thyme wine to mature. Keep for at least a year before tasting.

Strawberry and rose petal wine

20 red roses
1.15kg (2½lb) sugar
450-700g (1 to 1½lbs) strawberries
3 Campden tablets
1 orange
1 lemon
4.5 litres (8 pints) water
25g (1oz) yeast

Dissolve the sugar slowly in 2.8-3.4 litres (5 or 6 pints) of water in a large preserving pan over a low heat. Add the destalked and washed strawberries and simmer for 10-15 minutes. Having picked the 20 scented red roses, lay each on a chopping board and cut away the white heels of the petals by slicing across the base of each flower in turn. Lay these in the bottom of the fermenting bucket. Crush 3 Campden tablets and add. Pour over the strawberries and hot liquid, making the quantity up to 4.5 litres (8 pints). Then add the juice of both the orange and lemon. Leave for 24 hours before adding the fresh yeast spread on toast, as otherwise the Campden tablets will stop fermentation. As before, leave the toast and yeast floating on the surface for 24 hours, before removing the toast with a slotted spoon. The must should now be bubbling. Stir twice daily for a further 5 days and then syphon or pour the strained wine into a slightly warm demi-john. As above, fit the bung and fermentation lock, seal and label before standing in a warm place for fermentation. Keep the bottled wine for at least a year to allow the rich, sweet flavour to mature. A lovely dessert wine.

This next wine has a beautiful colour from the petals of the pot marigold (**Calendula**) flowers. The combination of these with the fresh peaches gives a rich, luxurious quality, both in the appearance of the wine and its very special taste. It has the added advantage of being ready to drink a little earlier than many other wines. A sweet, fruity wine, it may be enjoyed alone or with dessert at a dinner party.

Marigold and peach wine

5 ripe peaches
425ml (¾ pint) in volume pot marigold petals pulled from the heads
juice and rind of 1 lemon
1.15kg (2½lb) sugar
4.5 litres (8 pints) water
25g (1oz) yeast

Cut the washed peaches into thick slices, keeping the skin on, but discarding the stones. Put these, with the washed marigold petals, rind and juice of the lemon and the sugar, into the fermenting bucket. Pour over the full volume of boiling water, stirring at the same time in order to dissolve the sugar. When this has cooled to bloodheat, add the fresh yeast spread on toast as above, covering with the lid for 24 hours. Then remove the toast with a slotted spoon, squeezing the liquid back into the must as you do so. Stir twice daily for 7 days before straining and syphoning or pouring the wine into a slightly warmed demi-john. Fit the bung and fermentation lock, label and store in a warm place as before for fermentation.

Among the rosé and red wines are some of the richest and most delicious. The wine below is lighter than the others and has a lively, sparkling nature which makes it perfect for special occasions. One of my favourites, this delicate sweet wine is perfect to serve with a dessert - in the evening with home-made candies or chocolates for special occasions - or simply when you need a treat.

Redcurrant and pineapplemint

675g (1½lb) of redcurrants
6 bushy sprigs of pineapplemint, each 20cm (8in) long
1.15kg (2½1b) of sugar
4.5 litres (8 pints) water
25g (1oz) fresh yeast
toast

The sprigged redcurrants should be left to stand in a bowl for 24 hours after picking. Put them with the sugar and washed, torn herb, into the fermenting bucket. Pour over the boiling water, stirring with a wooden spoon until the sugar has dissolved and crushing the fruit against the sides. When the liquid has returned to bloodheat, toast a slice of bread on both sides and when cooled a little, spread with fresh yeast. Float on the liquid and cover. Leave for 24 hours, then remove the toast carefully with a slotted slice, stir and cover again. Stir twice daily for the next 3 days, then strain and pour or syphon into a demi-john as above, leaving in a warm place. As this is a rosé, you will want to surround the demi-john with brown paper to exclude the light, or keep it in a warm, dark cupboard, to prevent the colour of the wine from fading. Again, this is a wine which is unlikely to need a long maturing time, but will benefit from it.

As the redcurrants are harvested, you may already be picking blackcurrants and these will make an even richer wine. To counteract the powerful blackcurrant flavour and balance it a little, I decided to experiment with mint. Peppermint and curled mint are the two most strongly flavoured members of their family, long associated with liqueurs, and this narrowed my choice. Fearing the peppermint might not altogether blend with blackcurrant, I made curled mint my final selection. The result, even at the stage of syphoning into the demi-john was very promising and with maturity a year later, the wine proved a real winner. The full flavour of the blackcurrant is appreciated first with the mint almost as an after-taste, but fully as strong. A little of this wine may be spared now and again for the base of celebration fruit salads or other desserts, but you will most certainly wish to keep a good stock for cold winter evenings, to drink by the fire with friends.

Blackcurrant and mint wine

1.35kg (3 1b) blackcurrants, sprigged
8 sprigs of curled mint, 15cm (6in) long
1.35kg (3 1b) sugar
25g (1oz) sliced fresh ginger root
4.5 litres (8 pints) water
25g (1oz) fresh yeast

Put the prepared fruit, sugar, washed and torn herb, and sliced ginger into the fermenting bucket. Pour over the boiling water and leave to return to bloodheat. Then add the fresh yeast spread on newly made toast and float this on the top of the liquid, having given it a stir first. Cover and leave for 24 hours before removing the toast, being careful to squeeze the liquid back into the bucket. Cover again and stir twice daily for 3 days, as with the blackcurrant. Syphon or pour the strained wine into a prepared demi-john. Fit the bung and fermentation lock, label and store in a warm place until fermentation ceases. It may be bottled and ready to drink in less than a year.

After the currants have been picked and preserved in various ways, the damsons ripen on the trees to give another rich flavour. Damson, though powerful, can be tart and the slightly aniseed flavouring of the sweet cicely takes the edge from the tartness and complements the damsons. The resulting wine is delicious either drunk with desserts and included in them, or as a winter evening luxury.

Damson and sweet cicely

1.6kg (3½1b) of damsons
225g (½lb) of stalked elderberries
25g (1oz) fresh yeast
25g (1oz) of fresh, torn sweet cicely leaves
1.35kg (3 1b) sugar
4.5 litres (8 pints) water

Use only damsons in perfect condition and remove the stalks as you put them into a large preserving pan. Add the stalked elderberries, and torn sweet cicely (a little stem can be included with the leaves) and 1.7 litres (3 pints) water. Bring gently to the boil.

Remove from the heat and pour carefully over the sugar set ready in the fermentation bucket. Make up to 4.5 litres (8 pints) with boiling water. Allow to cool to blood heat and add the fresh yeast spread on a slice of slightly cooled toast. Leave covered for 24 hours. Remove the toast with a slotted slice and stir. Cover and leave for a further 5 days, stirring twice daily with a wooden spoon. Strain and pour or syphon into a prepared demi-john, taking care to wrap it with brown paper to keep out the light. Leave in a warm place until fermentation ceases and bottle.

The recipe below is my mother's own, named after the cottage in Shropshire where she made it for many years. It is rich, slightly spicy and excellent on cold winter nights, either taken as a nightcap, medicinally for coughs or colds, or simply enjoyed with no excuse at all.

"Pump Cottage" elderberry port

1.8kg (4lb) elderberries
1.35kg (3lb) sugar
4.5 litres (8 pints) water
25g (1oz) root ginger
25g (1oz) cinnamon stick
3 cloves
25g (1oz) fresh yeast
l00g (4oz) large raisins.

Boil the stalked elderberries gently for 20 minutes in a preserving pan with 550ml (1 pint) of water. Put the sugar, raisins and spices (cut the root ginger into pieces) into an earthenware crock or fermenting bucket. Strain the measured elderberry juice onto the dry ingredients and make up to 4.5 litres (8 pints) with boiling water.

When it has cooled to blood heat, float a slice of toast spread with the yeast on top. Leave, covered, for 24 hours. Remove the toast and stir. Leave, covered, stirring twice daily for 14 days, strain and pour into a demi-john fitted with a fermentation lock. Protect as for red wines.

When fermentation ceases, bottle.

Herbs in Liqueurs

LIQUEURS really are a luxury, in every sense of the word. The spirit base is flavoured with a distinctive selection of herbs - chosen for their medicinal potencies - as well as for their flavours. The sweetened and well matured result is unique. With wine-making, a certain amount of easy going leeway can be allowed in the ingredients and method, often producing an unexpectedly good result. Liqueurs, on the other hand, are for those who are exacting and absorbed by the fascination of careful experiment.

Before anyone begins to think about creating their own recipes, I advise them not only to gain experience with those already tried and tested, but to know their herb ingredients very well indeed. Being able to recognise the herbs and understand their various potencies is an important safety precaution.

Liqueurs can be made at any time of year, either with edible spring flowers, such as violets, as a main ingredient, or those of early summer - the clove pinks and roses. However, most of the potent roots, seeds and full-flavoured herbs mature in late summer and early autumn. It may be helpful then to follow an imaginary tour of the British liqueur garden in late summer.

Just outside my back door - almost hidden by the grasping honeysuckle, still flowering and attracting the bees - a huge bush of hyssop sprawls over the edge of the raised bed, its tall spires of blue and mauve flowers weighed down by the bees. The scent of this powerful digestive herb will only be developed to the full in poorish soil. It is included in Chartreuse and, in oil form, in absinthe. Both attractive and useful as a cautious flavouring, its bitterness is a warning to take care until you know the extent of the herb's dominance. In some medicinal uses, hyssop is similar to sage, being given for infections of the respiratory tract. It is, however, a herb to be avoided by epileptics and during pregnancy.

I find it helpful with other herbs in my winter cough cure of Honeyed rum liqueur. With a rum base, this mixture tends to encourage people to hang onto those last precious symptoms, just to take another bedtime dose.

Beside and behind the hyssop, towers the fairytale elf-dock (nowadays known as elecampane), blown back against the overhanging thatch by the first winds of autumn. The sunny yellow flowers which opened as inviting landing saucers for tortoiseshell butterflies a week or so ago, now provide even more attractive seedheads. Overflowing with fluffy down, they will soon release their seeds to reveal their elegant forms etched into the dried, golden brown seedheads; so perfect for winter arrangements. The huge, velvety leaves have begun to droop and soon the time will come to dig the roots. These are divided to replant in part, but also to use the excess for potpourri and to add a very distinctive violet flavour to liqueurs.

Elecampane is another herb that has treated chest complaints and asthma over the centuries. With this anti inflammatory role in mind it has been included in cordials and even steeped in white port with sugar and currants, which must have given an exceptionally sweet and rich drink. St. Paul's wine, made in Germany, was considered an antidote to the plague. Elecampane retains a place in a modern medicinal wine.

There is hardly room for the central **Rosa gallica** with its circle of protective garlic in this bed. Rose petals, particularly from this, the apothecary's rose, have long been included in tonics, wines, cordials and flower liqueurs. Rose hips from the wild dog rose are also a valued ingredient in spiced fruit liqueurs. Again, their tonic properties are the most important.

Nestled beneath the profusion of growth are the violets which will come to the fore after winter has bared the leafy stems which overhang them. Violet liqueur should be made from the sweet, **Viola odorata** flowers which will impart both rich, regal colour and their own distinctive flavour. Orris root or a little elecampane will strengthen this against the spices which traditionally accompany them. What could be more impressive than to produce your own bottle of violet liqueur from the cupboard on some future family celebration - especially if you have managed to keep it for at least two years before opening the bottle.

The medicinal effect of violets is directed towards bronchitis and infections, as it is antiseptic and a good expectorant. Where there are violets in my garden, primroses are never far away. I have found no record of these in liqueur recipes, although they have probably been included in some as they were so very popular in wines.

In neighbouring beds, huge clumps of rosemary are fast being overtaken by the junipers I have set close by. These trees, with their incredibly pretty appearance when frosted in winter, are charming to look at, but fearsome to touch should you catch their needle-like spines in the wrong direction. When fully grown they need space beyond the small circle required when young.

Juniper was cultivated by the Benedictine monks for the powerfully antiseptic berries, and often partnered with spices and spicy digestive seeds such as caraway, anise and coriander in aperitifs. Helpful for both rheumatism and cystitis, juniper berries should be avoided during pregnancy. We need only to be reminded that they are the main ingredient in gin to understand why. They have been exported from Scotland to Holland for gin-making.

To produce the berries, a male and a female tree must be grown close to each other. I have them planted in adjoining beds. Only *Juniperus communis* gives berries suitable for herbal use. The male flowers look rather like tiny catkins and the female bears cones which are fertilized to form the berries later. These can be used to flavour liqueurs when freshly picked or dried. They are blended to good effect with spices in brandy.

The rosemary has a similarly protective role against disease, being strongly antibacterial and having an equally powerful flavour. This is a herb to add in very cautious amounts. Always gather when flowering for the finest flavour and oil content. My largest rosemary bush, now over ten years old, is set beneath the thatch against a south-facing wall. In good years, this will flower from October through to the following June, giving an abundant harvest and much joy. The flowers of rosemary are so very beautiful; delicate, and yet with a strength of form. They are a haven for bees in the early spring when white dead nettles may be the only challenge for the insect's attention.

At one time, no celebration would have been complete without the presence of rosemary either in the decorations, food or wine - or all three. It could be just as popular today for it has so much to offer. If we are to believe its reputation, the herb is restorative for the old and young alike, enhancing all the senses as well as the memory. The most famous example of rosemary in this role was in the Hungary water invented for the ageing Queen of Hungary in 1235. The Queen, who suffered greatly from rheumatism, was over 70 years of age. It is written that she married soon afterwards, apparently restored to health with a youthful complexion.

The herb beside each rosemary - with an equal claim to being a recipe for long-life - is lemon balm. Where rosemary is powerful and strong in its action with a possibly irritant side effect, lemon balm is gentle and soothing in the extreme. The main ingredient in the famed elixir of life, sold by a medieval alchemist, Paracelsus, to many of the crowned heads of Europe, lemon balm is the supreme longevity herb. Several centenarians of the past attributed their great age to daily cups of melissa (lemon balm) tea. The powers of lemon balm were thought to include guarding against impotence and senility. It is certainly antiviral and has been shown to be helpful in some psychiatric disorders where a gentle sedative effect is needed.

The sweet, soft lemon fragrance and flavour in the leaves guides thoughts to a summer garden as it acts to regulate the heart and blood pressure. Its rapid growth habits can be kept in check by regular harvesting of the green leaves. You may not aspire to searching out recipes for the Eau de Melisse des Carmes, but a simple lemon balm liqueur will be very well received by friends eager to believe that enjoying a small tipple each day can actually lengthen their life.

My old-fashioned pinks and carnations provide a perfect contrast to the brightly variegated lemon balm. From early June, their array of flowers splash wondrous colours and whirls of pattern amongst the textured green of surrounding herbs through the summer months. The very old sops-in-wine is my pride and joy and makes a wonderful ingredient for liqueurs. Each head unfolds a fluffy, white flower with a circle of maroon close to the centre, and the spicy perfume from this mass of blooms is indescribable.

Fenbows nutmeg clove carnations are thriving in the next bed. Flowering later, these add the fascination of sports-flowers which are unlike all the others on the plant; some plain red, some striped, some half and half. Clove pinks have also long held a role as a herb to restore the spirits, bringing cheer where there was only melancholy. They are included, with over a hundred other ingredients, in Chartreuse. The Romans are thought to have been the first to spice wines with them.

Sage balances the playful pinks. Red or green sage can be added to liqueurs, the red sage having a stronger medicinal reputation. It is antibacterial, and thought by some to be as much of a restorative in old age as rosemary or lemon balm. The old saying, "Why should a man die when he grows sage in his garden?" tells us much of the herb's inner nature. Yet, like rosemary, it is powerful in effect and flavour and should be used with some caution.

A huge and amazing relative, the biennial clary sage, **Salvia sclarea,** towers in the larger bed alongside the cottage. Here it can gain all the moisture it needs for such lush growth. The huge, whorled leaves are the only clue to its membership of the sage family, being deeply textured and grey-green. The fairy-castle effect of the mass of delicate lilac/pink flowering stems, reaching over 1.2m (4ft) tall for the largest plants, has to be seen to be believed. The bracts which open like large petals beneath each pair of flowers are actually the colour we see and the perfume of the flowers is quite overwhelming.

This same perfume has a euphoric effect which is carried into wines and liqueurs. A little clary sage adds a lot of potency, so be warned. In past centuries, the aphrodisiac clary was included in varying strengths in order to render the drinker drunk, foolish drunk, mad drunk or - ominously - dead drunk. A herb to be respected. In modest quantities it has been included with elderflowers in Rhenish wines and may be recognized in some areas as muscatel sage.

The clary sage shares the rich soil of this bed with lovage, another herb with a lively reputation. Although the drink lovage, which is still available and blended traditionally with brandy, appears not to contain the herb nowadays, this is no reason not to include it in home recipes. Lovage seeds can be steeped in brandy to provide a helpful digestive to follow a heavy meal. Lovage grows to such a height - a mature plant can reach 3m (9ft) - that the seeds tend to be forgotten on their small cauliflower-like umbels high above your head. They have a strong, spicy aroma and can also be sprinkled on biscuits and breads.

One version of the origin of the name lovage is that girls hung bags of the dried leaves around their necks to attract the boys. In fact, lovage was one of the first deodorants and the herb appears in old elixir recipes for love potions. Deeply cleansing, being diuretic and antimicrobial, lovage also has some sedative effects. You will only ever need one plant of this giant, friendly herb, but I would never be without it.

In the shade of these spreading herbs grows sweet woodruff. Normally a woodland plant, it flowers with tiny white blooms on fine stems above the successive rosettes of spear-shaped leaves. The beauty of the herb is entirely in its form, for the colouring is plain, yet sweet woodruff could never be described as such. The herb has a special role in liqueurs as well as in wine cups, champagne cups and cordials. The crystallised, flowering stems can be seen preserved in some bottles of northern European liqueurs. The sweet scent of new-mown hay from the dried leaves once made it a popular strewing herb.

Further out into the sunlight, anise and marjoram have an annual role, each offering their own special qualities, both to the garden and to liqueur recipes. Anise needs a good season to come to fruition and produce the many tiny seeds which have such a powerful flavour and valuable digestive action. In fact, anise is particularly effective when steeped in alcohol. It then releases more medicinal properties than when infused in water.

It is a much-used ingredient and adds its liquorice taste to Pernod, ouzo and anisette amongst other liqueurs from Spain, Portugal, Greece, Cyprus and Turkey. The leaves can also be added with dill or fennel.

Sweet marjoram, too, needs a sunny position and a little protection from bad weather to give a good harvest. It is one herb I never seem to be able to grow sufficient of. The leaves or flowering herb can be added to liqueurs in small amounts.

Along the back wall of the house I have planted peppermint. Here, over centuries, the rain cascading from the thatch has worn away the soil, leaving almost a gravel bed in a line some 20cm (8in) away from the wall. With good compost regularly added to the peppermint roots behind this barrier, it grows in healthy profusion yet is naturally contained. Under the shade of the thatch, the leaves are not scorched by the summer sun and I have a plentiful supply to gather just before flowering, usually in June. Peppermint is, perhaps, the most loved of the digestive herbs. Taken medicinally for thousands of years, it has found a prominent place in liqueur recipes. Creme de menthe is well known and Benedictine and Chartreuse also contain peppermint. Another mint, familiar to liqueur makers, is curled mint, which has leaves curled into decorative ruffles about the stem. This has less energy than peppermint for spreading about the garden and is fine set amongst other herbs.

Still in the shade, where moisture is always available, my orris root, *Iris germanica,* provides a glorious show of elegant lilac flowers which open their buds with an impressive sound quite rivalling the popping broom buds later in the year. In many old recipes you will find a small addition of iris powder, which is the orris root better known as a fixative for pot-pourri. With a flavour of violets less powerful than that of elecampane, orris must be matured for a year before it is used and is therefore usually bought.

The last, large bed of herbs brings us to one of the most famous and well-loved plants, angelica. All parts of the herb have been valued medicinally and this was one of the most important herbs in monastery gardens. With the heady perfume and strong flavour of the stems and leaves, it is not surprising that angelica is also found in many liqueurs, as well as in gin and vermouth. The root and seeds are the most important parts of the herb in liqueur-making and angelica is included in Raspail, made by Bols since 1847, Chartreuse and Benedictine.

A large area of angelica is cultivated in southern France at Clermont Ferrand, both for candying and liqueurs. Angelica has also been included in English, German, Russian and Basque liqueurs. The wonder of its medicinal properties against the plague was said to have been revealed by an angel in a vision. What better recommendation for the *Archangelica officinalis.* The root oil is now thought to inhibit the growth of fungus and bacteria, which may support the claim of the vision. Interestingly, it has also been credited with the effect of giving regular angelica tea drinkers an aversion to alcohol. Angelica is not entirely harmless, however, for the juice can cause allergic reactions in some people. It is a sensible precaution not to rub your eyes when gathering angelica. The root should be harvested in early autumn from second-year plants.

Another herb that we tend to associate with sweets is liquorice. Rarely grown nowadays, it is an attractive plant, resembling a small, and later not so small, tree. It is unlikely you will want to harvest your own as the useful part of the root is the deepest underground. Eaten for many centuries and added as a flavouring to medicines as well as being a valuable anti-inflammatory herb in its own right, liquorice is an important ingredient.

A similar, if spicier flavouring growing nearby is caraway. When sown in autumn it seeds in the following season, rather than acting as a biennial. Caraway resembles both coriander and anise. It flowers early in the year, producing the long, striped seeds before summer is in full swing. An important digestive remedy for five thousand years, caraway is a popular flavouring in Austrian and German recipes. The Dutch Bolskummel was the earliest recorded European caraway liqueur, made in 1575, but caraway spiced wine was already popular in England in the reign of Henry VIII. It was cultivated in Essex and Kent.

Coriander, grown mainly in my kitchen garden, has similar small, white flowers and lacy foliage, but the round "cannonball" seeds are entirely different and ripen much later. Spicy in a different context, coriander is also a powerful digestive and the Chinese believed the plant could offer immortality. The seeds were an ingredient in the ancient drink, Hippocras, and were also grown commercially in Essex for gin distilleries. Helpful to the germination of anise, the plants should be set well away from fennel as they can hinder fennel seed formation.

Both the seeds from garden fennel and the bulbous root of its relative, Florence fennel, can be added to liqueurs. The digestive properties of fennel are well known; less celebrated has been the discovery that the tincture of fennel and a constituent of fennel oil reduce the toxic effects of alcohol on the body. Including fennel in a recipe will not, however, lower its alcohol content. Fennel root was once an ingredient of the popular Elizabethan drink, sack.

The feathery leaves of fennel and umbels of seeds are closely imitated in dill plants which are annual rather than perennial. Dill has slightly heavier and darker leaves with a spicier flavour. The seeds are tiny and flat in comparison. Dill seeds are often added with fennel and anise seeds and, in addition to their famous soothing, digestive properties, supposedly enliven the brain. Beware their pungent flavour.

Another herb to be used with caution is chamomile. In the same way that only a single plant of chamomile (often labelled "the plant nurse") aids surrounding herbs while several will not, so four or five flowers improve a liqueur, while more are soon overpowering. Either the flowers from *Anthemis nobilis* or those of the double-flowered chamomile are suitable.

With chamomile in the farthest sunny edge of the liqueur garden is a low hedge of thyme. The Romans, who enjoyed thyme in cheeses and other recipes, flavoured liqueurs with the leaves. The common thyme has the best flavour and antiseptic qualities, but lemon thyme should not be discounted. Gather either, when the flowers are just opening if possible, for the full flavour.

The chart below will help you to identify the relevant parts of each herb, their useful properties within the liqueur and their strength of flavour and action.

Summary of herb ingredients

Name	Latin	Action	Part used	Harvest	Strength
angelica	Archangelica officinalis	A	seeds root	summer autumn	** ***
anise	Pimpinella anisum	D	seeds	autumn	**
caraway	Carum carvi	D	seeds	summer	**
chamomile	Anthemis nobilis	R	flowers	summer	***
clary sage	Salva sclarea	R	flower tops	summer	***
clove pinks	Dianthus caryophyllus	R	flowers	summer	**
coriander	Coriandrum sativum	D	seeds	autumn	**
dill	Anethum graveolens	D	seeds	autumn	***
elecampane	Inula helenium	R	root	autumn	***
fennel	Foeniculum vulgare	D	seeds root	autumn autumn	** ***
hyssop	Hyssopus officinalis	A	leaves	summer	**
juniper	Juniperus communis	A	berries	autumn	**
lemon balm	Melissa officinalis	R	leaves	summer	*
liquorice	Glycyrrhiza glabra	D	root	autumn	***
lovage	Levisticum officinale	D	seeds root	summer autumn	*** ***
marjoram	Origanum majorana	A	leaves	summer	*
mint	Mentha piperita	D	leaves	summer	***
mint	Mentha crispa	D	leaves	summer	***
orris	Iris germanica	R	root	autumn	***
rose	Rosa gallica officinalis	R	flowers	summer	**
	Rosa arvensis	R	hips	autumn	**

Name	Latin	Action	Part used	Harvest	Strength
rosemary	Rosmarinus officinalis	R	flowers & leaves	spring	***
sage	Salvia officinalis	R	leaves	summer	***
sweet woodruff	Galium odoratum	R	flowers & leaves	summer	**
thyme	Thymus vulgaris	A	flowers & leaves	summer	***
violets	Viola odorata	A	flowers	spring	**

Note: Under ACTION - A = antiseptic, D = digestive, and R = restorative or tonic. In each case the action looked for in liqueur-making is designated. Some herbs, such as rosemary, are in fact antiseptic, digestive and restorative.

Before giving the method, it is useful to take a brief glance at the history of liqueur-making. The origins of the process are lost in the mists of time. The ancient Egyptians, Chinese, Greeks and Arabs have all been credited with discovering distilling, although some of these early methods almost certainly used powders rather than liquids.

The first written instructions we have, come from the Middle Ages. During this period, many doctors and alchemists gained knowledge from Arabic sources. Arnald de Villanova, both doctor and alchemist, distilled brandy - then known as aquae vitae - and expounded its virtues in prolonging life and preserving youth. He added herbs to the spirit for their medicinal properties and sweetened the resulting elixir simply to encourage his patients to drink the required dose.

The primary role of liqueurs was purely medicinal - for which purpose they were taken in very small quantities. We should remember that at this time a liqueur was far stronger than now, with a proof of around 50% rather than the 23% currently required. Their transformation into an after-dinner luxury came with the Renaissance. Catherine de Medici appears to have begun the fashion at the French Court and from there the practice spread.

After the Reformation, the famous liqueurs such as Chartreuse and Benedictine continued to be produced from highly complex and secret recipes in monasteries on the Continent. Liqueur distilleries did not open until the 18th century in France and England, although in Germany they were in existence somewhat earlier. At this time also liqueur distilling remained part of the syllabus for medical students at some Universities.

Many liqueurs, however, were made in the stillrooms of large households along with scented waters and all manner of herbal medicines, cosmetics and preserves. Housewives might compete to produce the finest recipes, some of which would most likely have been taken medicinally. While distilling liqueurs is now against the law, the skill and satisfaction of blending herbs in a base spirit to give unique flavours still offers a satisfying, if expensive, hobby.

Basic method

To produce a liqueur of high quality, as many of the herbal ingredients as possible should be freshly gathered and prepared. Roots should be dug in autumn from second-year plants, the main root scrubbed and sliced thickly, then chopped into cubes. Gather herb flowers, leaves and seeds on a dry day, when they are in peak condition. Wash leaves in cold water and dry on paper towel before chopping or tearing and adding immediately to the spirit. Flowers should also be washed and dried and the white heels removed from clove pinks or roses. All green parts should be removed from other flowers. Seeds must be free of insects.

The true flavour comes from these ingredients rather than from the base spirit. However, lighter flavoured liqueurs are better made in vodka or clear eau-de-vie rather than brandy. While experimenting with new flavours, one or two combinations of the same herbal ingredients steeped in different spirit bases will give an accurate guide to the range of possibilities. There is the inevitable problem of deciding exactly how much to make. While half a bottle of spirit may be all you feel you can afford for one recipe, if, in two or three years time this turns out to be magnificent, you will inevitably wish you had made a full bottle or more. The main problem being the long maturation time involved until the flavour is truly rounded. One to two years is the earliest recommended tasting time for a liqueur. The longer it can be left at the back of the cupboard, the better.

Jars used for storing the liquor while the herbs are macerating (steeping) in the spirit, must be absolutely clean. They may be sterilized as for wine-making and have airtight lids. Always label and date filled jars. Spices should be bought whole and pounded or ground. Try to obtain citrus fruits which have not been sprayed or treated with chemicals, so that prepared rind is as wholesome as possible.

Replace the jar lid between additions to the spirit and notice the difference each ingredient makes to the aroma of the liquid. Since it is difficult to memorize this information, keep a record book to note down your impression of the strength and sweet or sour qualities of each ingredient for future reference.

When the herbs and spices have been added to the spirit, set the airtight, labelled jar in a warm, dark place for about six weeks. In colder conditions, this stage may take slightly longer. Heat should not be applied. A kitchen cupboard is a useful storage area as the sight of the jar will remind you to give it a gentle shake daily to aid the release of the herb's properties. At the end of six weeks the liquor will have a powerful odour of the dominant herbs and should be filtered through either a fine coffee filter paper, or a nylon straining bag sold for wine-making.

The filtered liqueur is now ready for sweetening. Until this point your skill has almost been one of making pot-pourri, while bearing the medicinal properties of the individual herbs in mind. With the addition of white granulated sugar (sugar-candy is a luxury rather than a necessity) or, occasionally, honey, taste becomes the deciding factor rather than smell. The flavour at this time will inevitably be very raw compared to the matured liqueur. My recipes use considerably less sugar than commercial liqueurs, as I prefer them made in this way. You may wish to add more to your own taste.

Cautious experiment can lead to results that will be savoured and remembered for years to come. Many people remember home-made liqueurs they tasted ten and more years ago, they were so very special. Each, after all, can be unique. The recipes below offer a variety of flavours to provide early experience.

Angelica liqueur

1 bottle of vodka - 75cl (27 fl oz)
25g (1oz) angelica root
¼ teaspoon ground cinnamon
¼ teaspoon ground coriander seeds
¼ teaspoon saffron powder

Prepare the herbs as above, cubing the washed main angelica root, grinding the seeds and spice and pounding the saffron strands. Add these to the spirit in a clean jar, close the lid very tightly and label before placing it in a warm, dark cupboard. Remember to swirl or shake the jar from time to time for the following 6 or 7 weeks. Filter and sweeten with ½-¾ cup of white, granulated sugar, or to taste. Return to the original bottle, label and store for at least a year. After 2-3 years this makes a powerful and enjoyable drink at the end of a long day.

Peppermint liqueur

1 bottle of brandy - 70cl (1¼ pints)
1 cup of chopped peppermint leaves
1 tablespoon chopped lemon balm leaves
½ teaspoon dill seeds
½ teaspoon cinnamon

Wash and dry the herb leaves, discarding any damaged by insects, and tear or chop into the spirit. Pound the dill seeds in a mortar and grind the cinnamon stick to produce ½ teaspoon of powder. Add these to the blend. Store the labelled, tightly closed jar as before, not forgetting to swirl the contents during the weeks of steeping. Filter and sweeten to taste with approximately 1 cup of sugar. Bottle, label and store to mature. This is a good remedy for indigestion, or simply to enjoy after a rich meal.

Melissa liqueur

1 bottle vodka - 75cl (27 fl oz)
½ cup of lemon balm leaves
1 teaspoon cloves
1 teaspoon coriander seeds
½ teaspoon caraway seeds
2 teaspoons grated lemon rind
3 teaspoons marjoram leaves

Wash and chop the herb leaves, adding to the spirit with the pounded seeds and cloves and grated lemon rind. The cloves should be measured whole, but ground before adding. Leave to steep as before, swirling daily for 6-7 weeks. Filter and sweeten to taste with approximately ½-1 cup of sugar, before labelling in the original bottle and maturing. A soothing liqueur for troubled spirits.

Rosemary liqueur

1 bottle brandy - 70cl (1¼ pints)
1 tablespoon flowering rosemary
3 teaspoons lavender flowers
8 borage flowers
1 teaspoon chopped thyme leaves and flowers
½ teaspoon cloves
½ teaspoon cardamom seeds

The leaves must be stripped from the rosemary stems before washing, drying and pounding them to bring out the flavour. Strip the lavender flowers from their stems before adding and remove the green parts from the borage flowers. Once they have been measured, grind the cloves and cardamom seeds together and add to all the herbs already in the jar of brandy. Set the labelled and tightly sealed jar in a warm cupboard for 6 weeks. Try to remember to give the jar a "swirl" every so often and at the end of this time filter out the herbs, adding ½-1 cup of sugar to sweeten before bottling. Label again and store. After 3 or 4 years this liqueur is excellent.

Rejuvenator liqueur

1 bottle brandy- 70cl (1¼ pints)
3 teaspoons flowering thyme
3 heaped teaspoons lemon balm leaves
3 heaped teaspoons flowering rosemary tops
3 leaves purple sage
1 teaspoon aniseed
1 teaspoon coriander

Wash, dry and tear the herb leaves, pounding the rosemary to release the flavour. Measure the coriander and aniseed whole, but grind before adding. Steep as above in a labelled, airtight jar for 6-7 weeks in a warm, dark cupboard. Swirl daily if possible. Filter and sweeten before returning to a labelled bottle and storing for at least a year. (All the herbs in this recipe are associated with lengthening life or restoring youth).

Clove pink and rose liqueur

1 half bottle brandy - 35cl (12 fl oz)
36 clove pink flowers (Sops-in-wine are best)
4 red roses (heavily scented)
7 cloves

Cut the white heels from the lower edge of the clove pink and rose petals by laying each flower on a chopping board and slicing through close to the base of the flower. Wash the petals in cold water to remove insects and dry by patting gently with kitchen paper towel. Set the petals into the jar of brandy as they are ready. Pound or grind the cloves and add. Seal tightly and store in a warm dark place for about 6 weeks. At the end of this time the perfume of the liqueur will be quite lovely. Filter out the herb and add sugar to taste. Approximately ¾-1 cup. Keep for at least 2 years to mature. Perfect to cheer the melancholy.

Hawthorn flower liqueur

1 half bottle brandy - 35cl (12 fl oz)
hawthorn flowers
2 dessertspoons sugar

Pour a little brandy out of the bottle. Cutting away all of the stems, simply add hawthorn flowers until the bottle is almost filled. Then add the sugar using a funnel to direct it straight into the neck of the bottle. If you don't have a funnel, one is easily made by rolling greaseproof paper into a cone shape. Pour in a little more brandy to fill the bottle completely, seal the top and shake gently as the sugar dissolves. The bottle should now appear to be filled with flowers. Label and keep the bottle in a warm place, shaking from time to time, for 10 weeks. Filter and bottle. This delicate and easy liqueur was once used to flavour cakes. Mature for 2 years or more.

Honeyed rum liqueur

1 half bottle rum - 35cl (12 fl oz)
1 heaped teaspoon chopped hyssop
1 heaped teaspoon chopped, flowering thyme
1 dessertspoon chopped purple sage leaves
1 dessertspoon chopped peppermint
¾ teaspoon chopped horehound leaves
1 cup of clear honey

This liqueur makes a most acceptable cough remedy. Since I have always made it to be drunk as a medicine rather than purely for pleasure, I have included horehound with traditional liqueur herbs, in order to make it especially effective. The washed and chopped herbs are allowed to steep in the rum for ten days only. The spirit is then filtered and sweetened by adding clear honey. If possible the honey should come from local hives.

Spring liqueur

1 half bottle brandy - 35cl (12 fl oz)
1½ tablespoons chopped, flowering rosemary
1½ heaped tablespoons chopped lemon balm leaves
1 teaspoon chopped hyssop
½ teaspoon cloves (11)
½ teaspoon coriander seed
good pinch of saffron

Pour the brandy into a clean jar and cover. Wash, dry and chop the herbs, pounding the rosemary in a mortar, or simply with a rolling pin on a board. Add these to the brandy. Grind the cloves together with the coriander seed and add with the saffron. Seal the jar and label. Keep the liqueur in a warm dark place for 6 weeks, shaking it gently from time to time. Filter and bottle. Keep for at least 3 years. This liqueur makes a warming tonic for the first weeks of spring when returning to gardening after the winter may leave a few aching joints.

Sloe gin

1 bottle gin - 70cl (1¼ pints)
approximately (1lb) sloes
(8oz) sugar

Always pick the sloes after there has been a frost to sweeten them. Wash the fruit, drying it on kitchen paper towel. Then prick each sloe with a fork to release the juice, dropping it into a wide-necked jar as you do so. Spoon over the sugar and pour in the gin to fill the bottle. Seal and label. Shake the jar every day or so for the first week or two and then keep in a warm dry cupboard for 3 months. Strain and bottle, adding seven or eight blanched sweet almonds to the liquor. This may be ready for Christmas the same year, but is even better if kept for the following Christmas.

Herbs in Crafts

THE following section explores the possibilities of using herbs as raw materials or design sources for eight different crafts. It opens with flowercrafts, since, for many people this is where the role of herbs in crafts begins. For me, the connection sprang quite naturally from the desire to keep a record of unusual flowers - the sports of pinks, variations of violas, and so on. The thrill of finding whole specimen plants pressed between the blank end pages of an eighteenth century herbal reminded me of the origins of flower pressing in plant identification.

It was not until Victorian times, however, that pressed flower pictures became a decorative craft. Now, attractive frames, and even cards to hold needlework or pressed flower pictures enable us to show the delicacy of herb flowers and foliage in suitably elegant settings. The table of flower meanings on pages 94-95 may give inspiration as readily for pressed flower cards as for posies. Other thoughtful connections can be made, for instance, when decorating the top of a small pill-box, tiny flowers of medicinal herbs could be used. The forget-me-nots, once a pulmonary remedy, golden rod which treated gangrene and wounds, fennel for digestive and eye complaints, or lady's mantle for "lady's problems" are all suitable. Plentiful inspiration flows from larger foliage forms also, with the leaves of golden hop, variegated meadowsweet, silverweed, salad burnet, jasmine and many more to inspire both pressed flower and needlework designs.

As well as pressing herb specimens, anyone who gathers herbs will also hang them in bunches to dry. Whether they are to be used for cookery, pot-pourri or remedies, it is difficult not to see the potential in those colourful and fragrant bunches for making posies, garlands, swags and flower arrangements. While making these I stripped away the short flower sprigs on the lower stems and felt these too precious just to be discarded, so looked for an alternative. From that search came the notion of making miniature dried herb gardens. It proved the perfect way to use up scraps, while creating a new "art" at the same time.

The harvest of lavender for pot-pourri, leaves many wasted stems. These are lovely as fragrant firelighters, but again I looked for a decorative application. While thinking on this I read about corn dolly traditions and was side-tracked into a satisfying and enjoyable new pastime of using freshly-cut lavender to make favours and a fan to display the flowerheads. However, I soon found it was not the solution for using stems alone, as the lavender stems are not sufficiently hollow to be joined in the same way as corn.

The answer came in making stem baskets which - either have long-stemmed lavender woven around the sides, or just the top of a conventional basket framework - or can be made with bunches of stems tied against a simple frame to make up the sides themselves. In the second method lavender proved to be too smooth to grip on its own, but mixed with thyme, savory or rock hyssop, was both fragrant and strong. More combinations for stem baskets emerged from the first trials, including placing alternate bunches of silver and green foliage to form a pattern as in the basket illustrated on page xvi Stem baskets also provide charming containers for dried flower arrangements.

This is not to say that the ancient craft of basketry should be disregarded. In basketry too, herbs can provide a range of suitable materials. Making a basket means so much more when it is formed of a harvest from your own, or a friend's garden. In towns a shrubbery may offer as many opportunities as a country hedgerow, for it is only necessary to use the traditional willow for baskets needing great strength. Flower baskets, workbaskets for knitting or needlework, and miniature work can all be carried out using a range of herb stems and branches. Balsam poplar, red dogwood, lilac suckers, bramble, (preferably thornless) and snowberry offer stakes, while weavers come from honeysuckle, ivy, periwinkle, golden hop and more.

As you search your garden beds or hedges for suitable basketry stems you will also inevitably notice nature's own beautiful designs. One of my first delights in natural combinations of herbs was in a golden hop stem twining elegantly around a tall fennel plant. In the garden we are surrounded by natural arrangements and simple yet inspirational forms. Some of these may be captured in pressed flower and foliage pictures and these, in turn, can be traced and transferred to produce lasting designs in needlepoint or embroidery. This is an absorbing and satisfying area to explore in the winter months. Photographs or sketches from the summer can be transformed into colourful and decorative cushions, or embroidered motifs on scarves or tablecloths. A true joy in gardening and love of plants has long been expressed in needlework of all kinds. In this section I have sought simply to present a short history of herbs in needlework design describing sources previously used - from the illustrations in herbals to the garden itself, - give design ideas and practical ways of applying them - and patterns for small needlepoint cushions as a starting point.

For those who enjoy spinning, as I do, and find a use for the spun wools in needlepoint, weaving, crochet or knitting, the next craft of dyeing wool with herbs will be of especial interest. Many herbs can be used as dye sources and offer wonderful shades which cannot be matched by synthetic dyeing. They look naturally right side by side and will always attract interest in a finished article. Those which have a poor colour fastness when washed find the perfect application in needlepoint, while other, stronger hues may be saved for knitted or woven washable items. This aspect of the herb garden introduces many colourful plants otherwise thought of as "flowers" rather than herbs - including lupins, hollyhocks and sunflowers.

By happy chance these same plants, along with nettle and flax are also herbs which provide stem fibres for spinning into cloth. If you are a really keen spinner and wish to try spinning ready-prepared stricks of flax, or are even more ambitious and aspire to weave cloth from nettle - herb fibres for spinning is the section to study. It is a short introduction to an area in which I am still spending many happy hours on experiments. Spinning stem fibres is much harder than spinning wool, but the challenge is there and history tells us it has been done most successfully in previous centuries when nettle sheets were too familiar for us to expect to be stung by them!

Leaving this Herculean task to the experienced spinners, other readers may prefer to apply their prepared stem fibres to a much easier craft - that of paper-making. A simple kit, readily available, opens the door to hours of fun re-cycling used paper. This can be decorated by dyeing the finished sheets, including herb petals with the pulp, rolling pressed flower headings into single sheets of the wet paper, or by enclosing herbs between two sheets for an embossed effect. When all of these methods have been exhausted, making your own paper from herb stem fibres is a natural progression of skill. The resulting paper has not, in my experience, been suitable for writing paper, but offers fascinating background effects for displaying pressed flowers, or for lining gift boxes.

These same boxes could of course be made from herb woods. Although wood-turning and wood-carving are not skills I have practised, I do love to collect articles in herb woods. From the pale and lovely holly, through the wonderful contrasts in rich laburnum and yew to the trusted oak and delicate hawthorn, they each have their own beauty.

Whether your interest is in flower arranging, art, a range of needlework, paper-making, spinning fibres, dyeing wools, making baskets by traditional techniques or with bundles of herb stems, wood-turning or carving, - there is something here for you; either simply inspiration or practical instruction. The craft section links naturally with the later "20 Herbal Christmas Presents" and will, no doubt, offer notions for more gifts, projects and fun. For me, the crafts have seasons, with flowercrafts and stem baskets in spring and summer, dyeing wool carrying from summer into autumn, paper-making and basketry from autumn into winter, and spinning and needlework to fill the winter evenings. There is always something new and exciting to enjoy as a hobby.

Most of these activities entered my life many years ago when I was still using conventional materials. They were tried for a time, mastered, and then set aside after a year or so, in favour of a new craft. My discovery of herb uses and the possible partnership of the two then revived my interest in the discarded craftwork, bringing it new inspiration and fascination. The next pages, will, I hope, form a treasure store to dip into as fancy directs.

Flowercrafts

SITTING on the grass in the shade of the covered way, with its arching honeysuckle, roses, golden hop and white jasmine, on a hot July day, we can see into the "open knot" of herbs. Looking across the mass of blue hyssop flowers on their tall spikes, I watch fascinated as they are plundered by the butterflies; cabbage whites, a small heath and small tortoiseshells. The bees cluster around them, apparently happy to share in the abundance, and tiny hoverflies swoop and dive beside them both. Behind and above the hyssop rise the yellow and cream flowers of dyer's chamomile interplanted with wild yarrow. This sea of blooms has tall fennel, cupping umbels of tiny yellow florets heavenwards, as a backdrop. They lead my gaze on, along the line towards the rose-covered chamomile seat and the golden variegated sage which overflows across the gravel path beside it.

Close by me lady's mantle with petite, delicate, creamy flowers, is contrasted by the dark, velvety charm of purple sage. On the opposite side of the path, facing the line of hyssop, the lavender hedge seems to lean forward, vying for the attention of the bees. A few miniature lemon-coloured agrimony flowers remain on the tall stem above the seeds already forming below. They sway to touch the betony with its bright splash of deep lilac trumpets, encircled by clusters of white sneezewort. The dusky pink of a *Rosa gallica* edges the entrance to the medicinal beds, with elecampane just opening yellow "dishes" of petals, beckoning to yet more butterflies.

Looking around me from the elegant tracery of the golden hop against the trellis to graceful honeysuckle flowers, bright blue alkanet, rosemary and the sweet heartsease, I am tempted to set down my pen and walk amongst the herbs, harvesting. The flowering hyssop, lady's mantle, betony and sneezewort could be picked to dry for winter arrangements. Those flowers I leave could equally well be gathered later as seedheads to join the others. Poppy, teazle, foxglove, elecampane, St John's wort, fennel, horehound and marshmallow provide a wondrous variety of seedheads for floral art.

Walking out of the shade of the covered way towards the scented bank, I am greeted by a mass of spreading thymes amongst the chamomile. The tiny perfection of basil thyme will add romantic charm to any small arrangement. All the shades of thyme flowers are here, from the white, *alba,* through pink, lilac and deep mauve in the *Thymus serpyllum.* Dotted amongst them are a profusion of heartsease flowers for pressing and drying. At the foot of the bank, clumps of the finer-leaved red yarrow with clustered umbels of cerise-shaded flowerheads, beg me to rush for my flowerpress.

Further on between the banks we reach the serenity garden and the soothing formality of the closed knot in the centre. This is a reassuring reminder that all is in order, balanced by an abundance of wayward flowers in the outer border which separates the garden from the orchard beyond. Between the rigid lines of low herb hedges in the knot, softer forms are spread: "silver posy" and golden thymes, bearing fragrant, dark flowers, and a variety of old-fashioned pinks. The oldest of these is the "dark red", a medieval herb which is exactly as its name describes, with the rich quality of good velvet. Close by, the 17th century "sops-in-wine", double white with a maroon circle towards the heart of each flower, contrasts it beautifully. The smaller, petite blooms of "Queen of Sheba", with elaborate cream patterning on magenta, never fail to draw the fascinated interest of flower arrangers.

In the encircling border of taller herbs, the **Geums,** cultivated relatives of herb bennet, are flowering with yellow and red frilled petals. "Fenbows nutmeg clove", a brightly striped scarlet carnation, at times reminding onlookers of raspberry ripple, produces sports of entirely unique flowers. Some of these may be half pure scarlet and half striped, while others are almost completely a single colour. Fragrant "salmon flake" with its softer, pastel pinks graces the edge of the border, still flowering from June. Above and behind, amongst the variegated mints, the deep mauve and pink of oregano offers clusters of flowers perfect to hang-dry for so many winter projects. A darker shade again, and much larger, in almost imperial majesty, the purplish crowns of jagged bergamot flowers are best dried singly on nylon mesh in the airing cupboard.

In the silver garden, beyond the holly hedge, curry plant raises long, pale stems to support miniature brilliance in the form of startling golden buttons. Hung to dry, these later open slightly to reveal a white, papery edging.

Turning back towards the house, between the scented banks, I am surrounded by lavenders. To me, one of the greatest joys of summer is gathering lavender to weave into baskets, make lavender favours and fans, or simply dry for its perfect lasting fragrance. Dark purple "Imperial gem", lighter "Grappenhall" and "Munstead" and the pure white **Lavandula nana alba** are interplanted for variety. The fragrance and abundance of flower forms amongst a whole palette of colours in the herb garden draws many willing students to explore their own skills as much as the beauty of the herbs in flowercrafts.

Having glimpsed the July garden, let us search out herbs for particular projects. The most popular of these is the tussie-mussie. Tussie-mussie is a very early name, already used in the 15th century, for a posy of herbs and flowers carried to sweeten the air and keep sickness away. The original tussie-mussies were small, generally consisting of heavily aromatic and protective herbs, such as rue, rosemary, sage, southernwood and thyme, with either a pink or a rose at the centre. Later, hyssop, wallflowers, chamomile, marjoram and lemon balm were added, and nosegays, as they were also called, might be carried when walking through insanitary streets, or set close to judges and court officials to protect them from infectious diseases, and more, brought into court by prisoners. The wealthy also had their pews in churches strewn with these protective herbs.

The functional use of tussie-mussies gradually declined and they were revived with notions of romantic charm and the elaborate language of flowers in the Victorian age. Despite the vagaries of fashion which saw these posies ebb once more, to be revived at the present time, the tradition of presenting the Queen of England with a tussie-mussie at the annual Maundy Service has been retained without a break over the centuries.

The language of flowers, so popular with the Victorians, could be found in gardening and flower books, and centuries before, such symbolism appears many times in Shakespeare's plays. The best-known such quotation is "rosemary for remembrance". The earlier emblem books gave symbolic meanings for flowers both from religious and mythological sources. In the medieval period when few people could read, flowers in tapestries, carvings and paintings conveyed simple messages that everyone could understand.

Choosing herbs for a tussie-mussie then, can be as simple or complex as you like. You can pick flowering herbs in shades of a single colour together with green herbs to - complement the scheme, - make your posy vibrant with a riot of contrasts - or select those herbs which will convey a personal message. From the list of meanings you can soon appreciate the opportunities to make and give tussie-mussies which will share joy or sympathy with your friends at important moments in their lives. With this in mind I have suggested thoughtful combinations of herbs to celebrate a wedding, the birth of a baby or moving into a new home. There is also a posy for a sick friend and one to comfort the bereaved. These are simply my ideas. I feel sure you will have fun with your own adaptations.

Making a tussie-mussie

Generally, at the centre of a tussie-mussie, whether it consists of fresh or dried herbs, would be a pink or a rosebud. Modern alternatives are a helichrysum, a cluster of yarrow flowers (the deep cerise-coloured yarrow is the prettiest) or several lavender heads tied together.

Once you have decided upon your central flower, it is best while still inexperienced to walk around the flowerbeds placing other herbs next to it and seeing for yourself the kind of contrasts you can create. In this way pick sufficient of each herb to surround your last choice in a neat circle. How many are needed will vary with the nature of the herb chosen. Four, five or even seven different herbs can be included in a single posy. If you wish, a favourite may be used more than once. One of the most important features of a tussie-mussie is the last circle of herb leaves which encloses the others. These should be large and of a distinctive shape. Lady's mantle, the larger scented geranium leaves, avens, sweet cicely sprays or sprigs of purple, golden or green sage are all effective.

Once you are sure of the materials for your tussie-mussie, set these out on a table, together with strong thread or florist's wire, scissors, a doily, wide ribbon and foil or tissue paper.

Take the central stem, stripping it of the lower leaves. If it is a rose and the tussie-mussie is to be placed in water later, then break the lower stem to allow it to take up moisture. Before arranging the first circle of herbs - preferably a choice of green or silver foliage - around the rose, strip all their lower stems of leaves in the same way.

Tie this central posy together with green thread (I like to use crochet thread) or florist's wire, just below the foliage. Having prepared the stems of the next layer, again arrange these around the posy and tie in place. Continue in this way, alternating flowers and foliage with as much contrast of colour and texture as you can devise. With the last circle of herbs tied in place, cut the stems of the whole tussie-mussie if necessary to bring them to a slightly graded, uniform length. Enclose them in foil or tissue paper if the posy is not to be placed immediately in water. Insert the stems through a central hole cut in a paper doily or use a posy holder bought from a florist to add a thoughtful touch to your finished tussie-mussie. Finally, tie a length of wide ribbon just beneath the doily or holder.

Herbs for tussie-mussies

Foliage	Flowers	Silver
angelica	applemint	*Artemisias*
basil	betony	cotton lavender
bay	chamomile	horehound
eau-de-cologne mint	chives	silver posy thyme
germander	clary sage	tricolor sage
gingermint	cotton lavender	
golden marjoram	fennel	
golden sage	forget-me-nots	
green sage	honeysuckle	
lady's mantle	hyssop	
lemon balm	lavender	
lemon mint	oregano	
marjoram	pansies	
marshmallow	peppermint	
peppermint	pinks	
pineapplemint	primrose	
purple sage	rose	
rosemary	salad burnet	
savory	spearmint	
scented geranium	St. John's wort	
sweet cicely	sweet woodruff	
thymes	tansy	
	thrift	
	thymes	
	violet	
	yarrow	

The language of herbs and flowers

Herb	Meaning
agrimony	thanks
angelica	spiritual inspiration
balm	sympathy
basil	welcome, loving wishes
bay	all remains the same
betony	surprise
borage	courageous, straight talking
burnet	joy
chamomile	patience and stamina
red carnation	wounded heart
striped carnation	I am not interested
coriander	things are not so bad
cowslip	your charm can win through
fennel	I think you are special

forget-me-not	undying love
heartsease	I can't stop thinking of you
honeysuckle	bound in love
horehound	good health
hyssop	I would give everything for you
lavender	secrets, suspicions
marshmallow	I'm feeling generous
marjoram	shy happiness
mint	wisdom
motherwort	secret love
pansies	I think of you lovingly
peppermint	deep feelings
pinks, red	love
pink	take a chance
white	bright ideas
primrose	innocence
red rose	love
white	secrecy
yellow	suspicions of unfaithfulness
dog rose	sweetness and hurt
rosemary	memories
sage	homely comfort, wisdom, long life
St. John's wort	unhappiness
southernwood	joking
tansy	we are enemies
thyme	brave energy
violet	shyness
yarrow	good luck

A tussie-mussie to offer sympathy

A white rose surrounded by lemon balm to offer quiet sympathy and compassion, chamomile to give patience and stamina through difficult times, rosemary for happy memories, pansies with loving thoughts, all surrounded by sage to give comfort and a long life.

A tussie-mussie for a sick friend

Red rose is a good centre flower for love, with the added benefit of a soothing perfume. Lemon balm for sympathy (the variegated form is pretty), and chamomile to give patience and renewed energy, can be followed by heartsease or pansies to indicate loving thoughts and wishes. Coriander makes the optimistic suggestion that things will prove better than they seem and lady's mantle, if your friend is female, adds a protective blessing.

Tussie-mussies to welcome a new baby

Here you can indulge a little in the wishes of a fairy godmother.

For a boy – A white pink for original thoughts, tempered by the wisdom of mint (ginger or pineapplemint), thyme to give energy and fluffy southernwood to wish a sense of humour. The outer leaves could be of sage for a long life.

For a girl – A pink rose often symbolizes a young girl thought of lovingly, or a red rose for love may be preferred. Lemon balm will wish her sympathy for others, burnet – joy, and soft green marjoram adds shy happiness. Chamomile for patience as another virtue, or perhaps fennel to hope she will receive many compliments. A tricolor sage for long life or comfort, or the protection of lady's mantle leaves could enclose the posy.

The wishes above are traditional for boys and girls, today you may wish to mix them more as a "unisex" tussie-mussie.

A tussie-mussie to welcome friends into a new home

A central cluster of yarrow for seven year's good luck. Rosemary for happy memories to come, and betony to add surprises. Basil gives welcoming, loving wishes, fennel adds a special, flattering greeting and sage offers the hope for every comfort.

A wedding tussie-mussie

Red rose for love, white yarrow for good luck, rosemary for happy memories, marjoram (preferably flowering) for happiness, burnet leaves and flowers for joy, and honeysuckle as a symbol the couple are bound together by love.

If the wedding is that of a close friend or relative you may wish to give them the joy of confetti made from the dried herbal flowers from your garden. When making it in quantity this is a time-consuming task, but very rewarding. The confetti may also be mixed over a period of weeks, simply adding new ingredients as they are ready. If the dried flowers are sealed and away from the light, they will keep both their colour and fragrance.

When I was first asked by a friend to make up confetti, I turned for inspiration both to the table of flower meanings above and to wedding traditions. Those herbs associated with weddings over centuries are the rose, myrtle, orange blossom, fennel or dill and yarrow. All of these provide flowers which can be dried and, where necessary, cut into smaller fragments with sharp scissors. The rose remains a favourite in bridal bouquets, with its message of love. Do remember however, that yellow roses may hint at infidelity. Red roses, myrtle and orange blossom speak only of true love. Fennel or dill can wish both luck and compliments to the bride and groom, while yarrow was once carried by the bride to give the happy couple 7 years of good fortune. The bridesmaids also carried sprigs of yarrow to ensure they would find a husband within 7 years.

Other herbs can be added to the recipe if they are available. Rosemary was always carried at weddings for protection against evil and to wish happy memories. When adding the leaves and flowers do remember that the flowers are fine as they are, but the leaves should be cut into shorter lengths. The scent can overpower other delicate fragrances in the blend and so only use a little. Sage is also a strongly scented herb, but again may be added in a small amount to wish comfort and a long life.

Weld

(Top right)
Soapwort

(Right) *Bramble*

Madder

(Below right) *Sorrel*

Herb cultivation

Snowberry

(Top left) *Cardoon*

Alecost

(Bottom left)
Golden rod

(Left) *Guelder rose*

Wines and liqueurs

Wine and liqueur garden.

Liqueurs steeping.

Wines and liqueurs

Liqueur ingredients.

Herbs in crafts

Spinning ramie, dyed wools and crewelwork.

Flowercraft

Swag of dried herbs.

Seed head and helichrysum garland.   *Fresh tussie-mussie.*

Flowercraft

(Top left) *Flower press.*

Flowers in craft.

(Top right) *Pressed flower cards.*

Fan and favours.

xiv

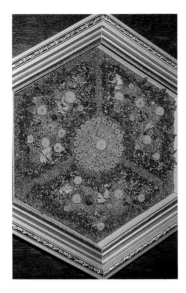

Swag or flower rope.

(Top left) *Knot garden in miniature.*

Dried flower casket garden.

Stem baskets

Finishing a stem basket with lace.

Large stem basket displaying dried flowers.

A little mint - perhaps eau-de-cologne or pineapplemint - will add soothing fragrance. Mint flowers are a lovely way of adding a touch of the herb without greenery. Violets might be added to confetti for a spring wedding with their quiet contribution of modesty. Forget-me-nots add delicate colour and have long been linked with love and lovers. Marjoram adds wishes for happiness in a new home and at the same time helps to blend the fragrances of other, dominant herbs. Sweet basil has always been a herb associated with love potions and offers good wishes to the bride and groom. Vervain is more unusual and almost ethereal in nature with the tiniest of flowers on fragile stems; not surprisingly it adds a note of enchantment to the occasion.

Both honeysuckle and lime flowers give honeyed sweetness. Honeysuckle represents the bonds of love and lime flowers were once strewn before newly-wed couples to wish them handsome children. As lovely as honeysuckle and alive with bright colour, pansies will give the perfect touch with their offering of loving thoughts.

As you will see, there is plenty of choice from a modest garden and friends are always happy to contribute flowers for such a special project. If the wedding is in winter or early spring and has caught you without a store of dried herb flowers from the previous year - remember marjoram, yarrow, sweet basil and lime flowers can all be bought by the ounce from wholefood shops and added to dried roses from a florist. For extra colour at this time add bright statice and Tudor immortelle petals which are also sold for dried flower arrangements. The symbolism in their case, is one of everlasting love.

Those herbs which can be used in large amounts are rose petals, pansies, orange blossom, violets, honeysuckle, statice and Tudor immortelles. In lesser amounts, add yarrow, myrtle, sweet basil, marjoram, lime flowers, fennel and dill flowers, mint and vervain. Herbs to add very cautiously are rosemary and sage.

When estimating how much confetti you will need, make sufficient for - each guest in the family party - or every guest - to partly fill the palm of their hand with the chopped petals. Either use your own palm as a standard measure or allow about two heaped tablespoonsful per person. The confetti looks beautiful set ready in a large wooden or china bowl on a table near the outer door of the reception area. If this is at the bride's home then a banner may be hung on the wall above the bowl bearing the names of the herbs and their meanings, - so that all the guests taking part understand the symbolism used as well as enjoying the fragrances and colour.

Pressed flowers

Making pressed-flower creations is an art-form in its own right. There is not the space in this book to give the preparation and creative use of pressed flowers and leaves the attention they deserve, so instead I will suggest a few easy experiments with the herbs listed below. They can add unusual and delicate touches to any pressed flowercraft you have already developed, or possibly bring you to a lasting interest in the subject. My own earliest desire to explore the art of pressed flowers came from the wish to record the exact forms and colours of the herbs. My greatest interest was in the flowers which cross and give entirely new and exciting shades and patterns; mainly the *Violas, Primulas* and *Dianthus.* When planning new garden beds during the winter, it can be helpful and add fun to the project to bring out pressed flowers and leaves, consulting these for inspiration in your design.

I soon realized that the beauty I had captured was worthy of display and began making small pressed-flower pictures for cards and bookmarks. They serve also as a basis for needlepoint and embroidery design; the flower stems and foliage in their pressed state being arranged and re-arranged until satisfied. Once fixed in place with glue, the outline can be traced and used as the initial stage of your work.

No expensive equipment need be bought to press flowers. For many generations they have been pressed between sheets of blotting paper inside a large, heavy book, with more volumes piled above to add weight. Some flowers will actually be better treated in this way than in a conventional flower press. Others, however, will need a press to give really good results. Flower presses are readily available at little cost, or can be made using two squares of wood with holes bored about 1.25cm (½in), from each corner to take the nuts and bolts which apply the necessary pressure. Layers of absorbent paper and cardboard can then be cut to fit. There should be both absorbent paper and then cardboard on either side of each layer of herbs.

To press flowers and foliage

Pick the herbs on a warm, dry day, preferably when the air is still if you are hoping to arrange them in the press while remaining in the garden. Each petal and leaf should be in perfect condition and laid carefully on the absorbent paper without touching the others. As you arrange them remember that their form will be fixed exactly as the upper layer of absorbent paper leaves them. You must imagine any petals still raised from the surface, pressed flat against the others.

Each layer is best kept to a particular flower or leaf so that they are all of uniform thickness. Avoid flowers with a pronounced three-dimensional effect, such as borage, at first. These can only be pressed successfully either by taking them apart and then restoring the pressed petals to their original form, or by using deep layers of absorbent paper with depressions specially cut to accommodate the flowers. Small rosebuds can be successfully pressed by slicing them in half to reduce their bulk. This method may also be used with avens and marshmallow flowers.

Care and patience are the two qualities most needed in pressing flowers, both as they are placed in the press and when removing and assembling them into a design. You may find it best to do this with tweezers. Leave the herbs in the press for about three weeks to be sure the thicker foliage is completely dry. You can then enjoy the excitement of finding out exactly how successful your efforts have been. Remove the pressed flowers and leaves with care and place them between layers of tissue paper in an old telephone book or storage box with layers of card keeping the pressed flowers flat. This must then be kept in a dry, warm place. Each layer should be neatly labelled. (The telephone book offers a ready-made alphabetical filing system.) With a box, a small sachet of silica gel crystals inside will ensure your flowers remain dry.

When you are ready to use your pressed material in a design, you will be able to arrange and re-arrange the flowers and leaves before applying tiny drops of clear glue with a cocktail stick to fix the finished work.

Herbs which press well

In a flower press	In a book
agrimony	**Artemisia** (leaves)
broom	avens
clary sage (bracts and flowers)	carnation (petals)
annual clary sage	heartsease
chive flowers	honeysuckle
cowslip	parsley
dill and fennel (small sprays)	pinks
forget-me-not	St. John's wort
gingermint	small flowering thymes
golden hop	
golden meadowsweet	
golden rod	
hyssop	
lady's mantle	
lungwort	
marshmallow	
meadowsweet	
motherwort	
oregano	
pineapplemint	
primrose	
rosemary (flowers)	
rose petals (leaves and buds)	
sage (all kinds)	
salad burnet (leaves)	
scented geranium flowers	
silver tansy	
silverweed	
sweet cicely (leaves)	
sweet woodruff	
tricolor sage (leaves)	
variegated lemon balm	
variegated meadowsweet	
variegated rue (leaves)	
variegated tansy	
white honesty leaves	
white jasmine (leaves)	
woad (flowers)	
wormwood (silver warrior)	
yarrow (especially cerise flowered)	

Drying herbs

Herbs can also be preserved by drying for arrangements, garlands, tussie-mussies and miniature herb gardens. Most herbs will dry best tied in small bunches with stems about 25cm (10in) long and hung from lines in an airy room, away from direct sunlight. A spare bedroom will serve well, with one or more curtains partly closed to keep out bright sunlight. If you have an airy loft, this too can be used. Places to avoid are rooms with large windows and kitchens, which are regularly made humid by steam. Small amounts of herbs can be hung from the racks in an airing cupboard to dry quickly, if you have the space for them. Some flowers, such as roses, may dry better in this way.

In good conditions, the herbs will usually be crisp and ready to store in 5 to 10 days. They can then be cut down and laid in cardboard boxes with a sprinkling of silica gel crystals in the bottom, or left hung in large brown paper bags in a cupboard.

Herbs to hang dry

applemint (flowering)	lady's mantle
bergamot	lavender
betony	oregano
chamomile	peppermint (flowering)
chives (flowering)	pineapplemint
clary sage	rosebuds
cotton lavender	sneezewort
curry plant	tansy
germander	thymes
helichrysum	winter savory
horehound	yarrow
hyssop	

Dried herbs in tussie-mussies can be supplemented with dried seedheads, those below will give a variety of forms and textures

angelica	Jerusalem sage
cardoon	poppy
dill	salad burnet
elecampane	sea holly
fennel	sorrel
golden rod	St. John's wort
hop	teazle
horehound	thrift

Note: All umbelliferous heads and golden rod need to be sprayed to hold their seeds.

Garlands

Small garlands can be set around candlesticks, or used as central table decorations. Historically, they were more usually hung over doors, or from house beams to protect all who lived there from ghosts, witches and evil - including sickness. Times of celebration gave an opportunity to place emphasis on the role of herbs as protectors. As the folklore of herbs records, the most common time of year to make garlands was on St. John's Eve or St. John's Day, at midsummer, since the healing power of the sun had then been absorbed to the greatest degree by the plants. Fennel and flowering St. John's wort were favourite protectors at this time. Yarrow, which can give red, pink, white or yellow flowers, and one of the green-leaved *Artemisias,* mugwort, were much in favour.

A garland can be made of any flowering herbs to hand, the foliage of the *Artemisias* – whether southernwood, wormwood, "silver queen", "silver warrior", or mugwort - is invaluable. Bay, thymes and lavender keep well, with dried rosebuds, oregano, peppermint and bergamot as colourful additions.

A small base of wet oasis will keep fresh herbs alive, or a larger wreath can be made by inserting the stems into damp sphagnum moss, or wet oasis, wired to a frame. This frame could be made from two coat hangers bent into shape and bound together. It should be remembered that water adds weight and these garlands cannot be made too large. They are better laid in a dish on a table, rather than hung damp, against a wall.

Dried herb garlands are much easier to handle and a variety of bases can be made for these. Honeysuckle is my favourite vine, although others in the garden can be cut for garlands. Either strip the leaves and twine the longest tendrils you can find into a circle of the desired size, or strip the stems of leaves and lay in a damp, shady place in the garden until they are pliable (about three weeks). Stems needed in a hurry can also be soaked before working. Make sure all the ends are neatly tucked in and catch in shorter lengths with one long one to finish. For a large garland this base should be 7.5 - 10cm (3 to 4in) across, all the way round. Smaller garlands may only need to support a small spray of herbs and ribbon, in which case they can be lighter. Other bases could be made up of bundles of long lavender stems, plaited raffia or seagrass.

Small bunches of dried herbs, seedheads, lengths of cinnamon stick and spices, florist's wire or strong crochet thread, ribbons or lace, and a little ingenuity are all that is needed to make an impressive garland for a special occasion. As soon as you begin experimenting, all kinds of new ideas will come to mind.

Lavender fans and favours

Every year the harvest of lavender provides inspiration for experiment. Corn dolly patterns are easily reproduced in lavender as long as it is worked within 20 minutes of picking. It is unfortunately not possible to join the stems in the same way as corn and so the lavender items are restricted to those which can be made with single-length stems. Even so, pretty, small favours are quickly made and the fans which would spread the ears of corn to best effect are even more impressive when made with lavender. Favours can be worn as fragrant brooches while the fan can be hung on your bedroom wall, or wrapped in fine lawn and laid with clothes in a drawer.

Choice of lavender is important. Only lavender with long, supple stems will give good results. Most lavenders grow long enough to make favours but the fans require extra length. Some miniature lavender bushes only a few inches high can send up very long stems which are perfect. The tallest stem I have cut was 84cm (33in), long enough for a much larger dolly. Here I will detail the popular lavender patterns for which most lavender bushes will provide the materials.

Lavender favours

Cut 5 stems of lavender, searching out those with a shorter, rather than long, flowerhead. They should each have one or two flowers already open. Try to find stems which are all about the same length, at least 25cm (10in). Soft, rounded stems are best if these are available. Munstead is a good lavender to use.

Strip the flowers and small leaves below the main flowerhead. Tie the lavender stems together just below the flowerheads with fine crochet thread. Cut the ends to neaten. Gently bend each of the stems outwards into a star shape, curving them slowly by bouncing them against your thumb with your forefinger. Be especially careful of the weak joint where you have already removed the tiny flowers and leaves.

Keeping the star shape by holding the fingers of your right hand lightly over the outstretched stems, take stem number one as in the diagram over two stems, to point to the right. If this should break you can easily cut the tie holding the lavender heads together and begin again.

All being well, take the second stem, now lying beneath it, over stem number one and the stem next to it, so that it is pointing away from you. Continue in this way, turning the "Star" clockwise as you work and taking care not to crush the flower heads. As you reach the point on each stem where the weak joint might split, try to avoid bending it in exactly that place. Keeping the stems forming a tight square pattern, work until you are within 2.5cm (1in) of the ends of the shortest stems.

Bring the ends around behind the flowerheads to form a loop of worked stems. Tie again just beneath the flowerheads, holding the worked stems in place. Cut the ends to neaten. Tie a bow of narrow lavender-coloured ribbon to cover the crochet thread ties. If the favour is to be worn as a brooch, insert a small pin into the back of the favour. Clip any fragments of stem which may have split away as you were working. Hang from a hook or thread for 24 hours to dry out.

If there is a partial break in the stem at any point, you can continue as long as it does not break altogether. The weakness will be supported by the following stems and any stray ends can be clipped away when the favour is finished.

L. nana alba is a dwarf lavender with short stems mostly unsuitable for favours, but some of the longer ones can be used, giving the advantage for the beginner of having their weak flower join further down the stems, where it is easier to cope with.

Lavender fan

Cut 19 stems of lavender with good flowerheads, preferably with the longest stems and flowerheads you can find. An extra 2 or 3 are a good idea as a reserve of replacements in case they should be needed. Remove any flowers and leaves below

Lavender favours and fan

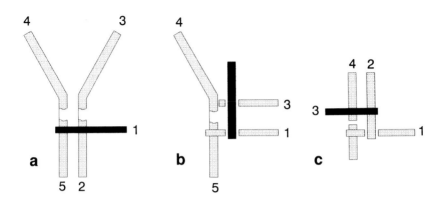

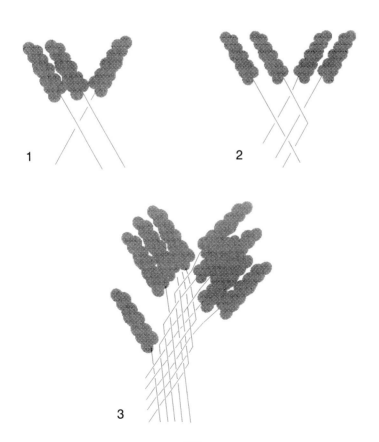

the main flowerhead on all the stems. Sort the lavender by grading the length and appeal of the flowerheads. The longest which are most appealing should be used first. Select 3 stems and begin by tying these together with fine thread, just below the flowerheads. Lay them down on a flat surface, with 2 heads facing to the left and 1 beneath them to the right. These are stems, 1, 2 and 3 (see diagram). Insert stem number 4 under the outer stem of the pair, and over the next 2, to lie parallel with the single stem, number 3. Bend the stem now on the outside, towards the left and pass it under the next to lock in place (see diagram).

Working on the opposite side of the fan, insert a 5th stem, under the outer and over the next 2 stems and lock in place in the same way. Continue joining stems on alternate sides, making sure they are as evenly spaced as possible.

When 11 stems have been worked, an extra locking movement is introduced between joining in new stems. This helps to avoid crowding the lavender heads on the outer edge of the fan.

Continue, locking each new stem in place with 2 successive outer stems (see diagram), until all 19 stems have been used.

Work 4 more "locks" on either side of the fan to complete, and tie the ends on the left and on the right with narrow bows of ribbon.

Miniature herb gardens

These can be made with the small fragments left over from dried herbs in floral arrangements, or tussie-mussies. Since they are painstaking to make, and also very fragile, you will want to give them the best possible protection. This is done by framing the completed miniature herb garden in a deep, display frame which can then be hung on the wall as a picture. Such frames are obtainable in craft centres, and some florists. If you wish to make a garden which gives you the opportunity to enjoy the perfume of the herbs and to re-arrange or renew them at intervals, a box or glass casket can be used to contain it.

The fragments of herb foliage and flowers are set into a dry oasis base, with each stem inserted individually. Tall grass can be imitated by using dried moss, or paths made with a variety of seeds. These are glued in place before the herbs are added. Many fascinating textures can be created. Aniseed will give the effect of fallen leaves or sticks, celery seeds appear as small gravel, while dill is one of my favourites for larger stones. Horehound seedheads make ideal bushes, with thrift seedheads a close second. Short lengths of cinnamon stick can be glued down as fallen logs, small pieces of root ginger add realistic rocks, and tiny pine cones and nut shells are fun to arrange.

The first step is to cut a base of dry oasis to fit your frame, both in area and thickness. A frame with an inner, smaller frame, which can be inserted behind the glass while already holding the garden, is best. The thickness of the oasis is critical, as it must be thick enough to hold the stems, but allow sufficient space for the herbs beneath the glass, without crushing them. Experiment with a few herbs before you begin the design proper, to be sure your measurements are accurate.

Having cut the oasis, decide upon your design. This could be a formal knot of herb foliage hedges, filled with colourful flowers, or a natural garden relying on colours and textures for effect. Either can be stunning. The table of suitable herbs will give you some idea of the possibilities. The joy of oasis is that you can experiment with a few sprigs of herb, removing these and replacing with others until you achieve the desired result.

If a knot garden is chosen it is best to mark out the lines on the oasis first. A ruler and pencil can be used for this. For circles, diamonds and other shapes, press egg-cups, glasses or biscuit cutters lightly into the oasis.

With the layout marked into the oasis, glue the surface for any "grass" or "paths", a little at a time. Apply the seeds or dried moss to cover, shaking any loose particles away to be sure there will be no gaps later.

Now the paths are set, work from the centre of the garden out towards the edges. In this way you should avoid risking damaging herbs as you work. Make sure you have sufficient of each of them at the planning stage and prepare the stems by cutting them to 1.5cm (½in) in length. I like to hold the herb stems between my fingers to insert them into the oasis, but tweezers can be used. Push each stem gently into place, making a hole first with a stronger stem if you find a particular herb too soft. Curry plant can be a problem, but the extra work is worthwhile for the good results.

At the edge of the oasis take especial care to leave enough space to slot the finished garden into the frame without crushing the herbs. There is no substitute here for experiment in the early stages. You may prefer to work with the garden already slotted into the first frame as this stops the edges crumbling and gives you a better grip.

Set your finished garden into the larger frame behind the glass and hang away from direct sunlight for a long life.

I have included a list of herbs that will give a variety of colours to include in your garden designs, followed by some suggestions for different types of miniature gardens. With experience, planning new designs and working with the flowers will become quicker and easier. Making gardens can be a relaxing and satisfying pastime in summer or winter. They can record a garden you have enjoyed, show possible plans for a new one, or simply pass on to others a glimpse of the beauty of a herb garden.

Herbs for miniature gardens

Yellow flowers	Blue flowers	Pink-purple flowers
cotton lavender	hyssop	bergamot
curry plant	lavender	chives
lady's mantle		eau-de-cologne mint
tansy		germander
cultivated yarrow		hyssop
		lavender
		oregano
White flowers	**Foliage**	peppermint
lavender	germander	thyme
sneezewort	hyssop	Tudor immortelles
thyme	thyme	yarrow
winter savory	winter savory	

Framed garden

To make an 18cm (7in) hexagonal garden, you will need:
a block of dry oasis
clear glue
scissors
celery seed
2 or 3 heads of flowering oregano
dill weed
3 heads of tansy
1 head of white statice
approximately 15 heads of cotton lavender
a bunch of dried germander
8 to 10 heads of peppermint flowers
approximately 20 lavender heads dried on the stem
a few tiny white rosebuds or Tudor Immortelles.

Following the instructions in the introduction, mark out the shapes on the oasis which has been cut to fit the frame exactly (see diagram). If necessary two pieces of oasis can each be cut to fill half of the base of the frame and then wedged tightly together to achieve the full width. Working a short length at a time, glue down the celery seeds on the paths and dill weed inside the beds. Be careful to shake off any excess to reveal bare patches that still need to be covered.

Beginning with the central head of cotton lavender, work outwards, setting the circle of tansy heads to edge the bed next. A single lavender stem can, with some varieties, give several smaller, complete flowerheads if it is cut carefully. The head can be cut at intervals, peeling away sufficient flowers to give a short length of stem only 1.25cm (½in) to push into the oasis.

In a similar way, germander can be cut at intervals to give numerous lengths for hedging with two or three leaves or flowers on each. It is best to fill dishes of the prepared leaves and flowerhead before you begin. With the inner outlines of the beds and lavender path edgings inserted, place the rows of peppermint next to the lavender, to be followed by random placings of the flower "bushes" in the beds. Lastly, push each sprig of germander gently into the oasis to mark the outer hedges. Set the oasis into the frame, being careful to remove any loose fragments of herb inside before sealing it.

Your framed garden can now be set on a table or hung on the wall away from direct sunlight. In this way its colourful beauty can be preserved.

The box garden

To make an 11.5cm (4½in) hexagonal box garden, you will need:
oasis
clear glue
scissors
approximately 26 cotton lavender heads
6 spikes of hyssop
approximately 6 stems of flowering oregano
celery seed

The casket garden

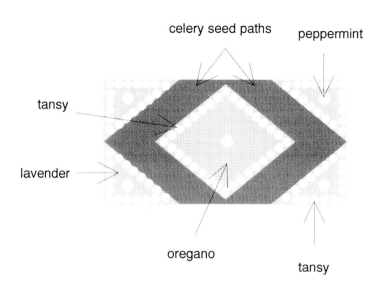

celery seed paths

peppermint

tansy

lavender

oregano

tansy

The Box garden

thrift

hyssop

oregano

tansy

celery seed paths

hyssop

celery seed paths

Framed garden

dill weed

cotton lavender

tansy

celery seed paths

germander

dill weed

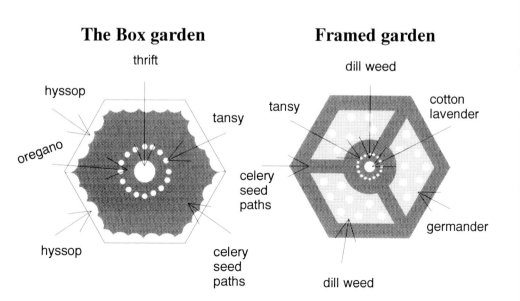

The box lid can be used to press into the oasis to cut a shape which fits exactly. Mark out the shapes for the central bed on the oasis (see diagram) and glue celery seed onto the path. Push the oasis into the box, leaving the required depth for the herbs beneath the lid. Begin with the central cotton lavender heads and outer circle of cotton lavender. Fill the space between them with oregano. Lastly, glue down the flowering spikes of hyssop at the edges of the garden.

The casket garden

To make a garden to fill a casket, 12cm (4¾in) long, 5cm (2in) deep and 8cm (3¼in) wide, you will need:
oasis
clear glue
scissors
cocktail sticks
3 or 4 heads of tansy flowers
approximately 8 to 10 heads of flowering oregano
3 flowering tops of peppermint
10 to 12 heads of lavender dried on the stem
several sprigs of savory

First, mark out the shapes into the oasis and glue down the celery seed paths (see diagram). Because of the varying heights of the herbs within the casket, the approach is slightly different. The tiny tansy flowers are set in place first, marking triangles and chevrons of bright colour. Between these are set individual heads of lavender which will then stand above them. The taller, central peppermint heads can now be added in each yellow triangle and at the centre of the garden. Fill the remainder of the space with oregano.

Since the side edges of the oasis will be visible in the casket, cover these thinly with glue and dab on tiny sprigs of savory or small seeds.

Lower the garden carefully into the casket using two cocktail sticks set into the oasis between tansy heads at either end. These can be removed with gentle pressure on the tansy if necessary.

No doubt ideas for more gardens will spring to mind as these are completed. They may even inspire you to new garden planting and growing and enjoying a wider range of herbs and herb recipes.

Herb stem baskets

FOR those who wish to make small, attractive baskets without the complication of soaking the stakes and longer stems for weaving, this hobby is the perfect answer. There is also the added advantage of being able to grow the materials for numerous baskets in a comparatively small garden bed. Planting a knot of herb hedges can provide a focal point for the garden that is attractive in all seasons and trimming it regularly will give the harvest you need. The stems are light and pliable and a little practice will soon reveal the knack of securing the bunches of herbs in place without undue strain on the fingers. The finished effect is suitably delicate and fragrant.

Thyme is the easiest herb for the beginner to use, as the stems tend to be rough, with tiny sideshoots, and these cling to each other as the bunch is brought together. Lavender with squared stems is preferable to varieties with a smooth, rounded outer layer. For small baskets, the rock hyssop *Hyssopus aristatus* is also more suitable than the taller *Hyssopus officinalis* as the aristatus has rougher stems bearing closely spaced leaves for their full height, enabling these to be incorporated into the basket.

Although I prefer to use one of these three herbs for the main part of the basket, both for their lasting fragrance and ease of use, others can be substituted. Mints, when allowed to grow tall in order to gather the flowers, will yield thin stems of young growth which can be incorporated in baskets of thyme or hyssop. Bergamot, very young fennel, chamomile, winter savory or cotton lavender could equally well be brought together with any of the three basic herbs to give a pot-pourri of fragrance "on the stem".

Certain herb stems will give colouring for simple patterns. St. John's wort, black peppermint or hop stems offering shades of brown-red, and curry plant or cotton lavender for grey-silver effects. As with all herb crafts, more ideas will come if you take a little time to look around the herb garden with an open mind.

Gathering the herbs

Low hedges of thyme, lavender, rock hyssop, curry plant or cotton lavender, including the green *Santolina viridis,* are the perfect sources of herb stems for baskets. Thyme can be harvested twice in the year. The first harvest is taken as the flowers open and the second at the beginning of autumn, generally producing stems long enough to make a basket 7-12cm (3 to 5in) in height. The same applies to the *Santolinas* and curry plant. Since rock hyssop does not flower until later in the summer, and is slow growing, I generally take only one harvest with the flowers (which can be included).

Lavender should be harvested as the first flowers are opening, cutting it to the previous year's growth in order to maintain the health of the plant. Lavender flowers can then be stripped from the dried stems before use, or left, as desired. If all of the flowers are removed, extra fragrance can be held with the stems by not stripping their leaves. Lavender with smooth stems should be mixed with a little thyme or hyssop for easier working as otherwise it tends to slip. Mints, of course, are best gathered late in the season and also need to be mixed with thyme, savory or hyssop. St. John's wort and hops give single autumn harvests.

With the exception of St. John's wort and hop stalks, all other herbs should be cut with future growth safeguarded. That is, never cut more than two-thirds of the growth of the plant. Always use strong scissors or secateurs, depending on the thickness of the stems, so that clean cuts are made without tearing the plant. Herbs will contain the maximum essential oil if gathered when the dew has dried and before the sun has been full on them to draw out their goodness.

When cutting chamomile flowers with their whole stems for basketry it should be remembered that this will considerably reduce further flower production for the plant. You may prefer to leave such a harvest until the last flowers of the season. By contrast, only very young fennel plants will have sufficiently slender stems, but these can be gathered when weeding out excess seedlings in both spring and autumn.

The herbs should be dried as before, away from direct sunlight and in a warm, dry, airy atmosphere. Where bunches of a single herb are to be used in basket-making, these can be tied in the correct size bunches in readiness and hung from strings across an airing cupboard or loft to dry. Tie them decoratively with green crochet cotton rather than string if you wish to leave these ties on when the basket is made. Once the leaves and stems are completely dried they can be attached to the basket sides just as they are. Mixed bundles are better made up with the ready-dried herbs.

Preparing the base

Since the stems do not have the strength to make a base without considerable support, it is best to use a shaped piece of wood. Bought basketry bases may be the answer if you do not wish to prepare the base yourself. The method is, however, simple. Trim the wood which must be at least 1¼cm (½in) thick, to the desired shape. This can be round, oblong, oval or square. More ambitious hexagons, heart shapes, etc are best left for the largest projects. Use sandpaper to remove any sharp points around the edges. The base can be stained if liked. Two rows of gimp or panel pins are now hammered into place around the edges of the base to hold the raffia bindings (see individual basket instructions).

Preparing the rim

A larger basket, particularly one intended for dried floral arrangements, will need a strong edge which can be provided by lengths of stick gathered on a walk, or thin dowelling, nailed together. For smaller rims, a supple stem of honeysuckle, ivy or thornless bramble will have sufficient strength. These natural materials, together with the alternatives of bunches of broom or periwinkle shoots, will need to be bound around a "former" and secured when first gathered, then left to dry out in shape. The initial base can be used as a former for a straight basket. Any shaping in the design will, however, need a larger former. A dish of the right size in relation to the wooden base will do as well as wood.

Preparing handles

These may match the rim of the basket or be made of a contrasting material. Thicker stems will need to be faded by leaving them laid under a garden hedge in damp conditions for 2-3 weeks until they are sufficiently pliant. They can then be soaked further if necessary and ties bound from one side of the handle to the other in order to create the desired shape. These must be left on overnight before the handle is attached to the basket and the ties released.

Having decided on the base, natural materials and design of your basket it is pleasant to work on it out of doors where the inevitable debris of trimmed stems and fragments of herb can be allowed to fall in an area where they will not be a problem. If autumn or winter is already upon you by the time you come to use the dried stem bunches, then there is the opportunity to recreate the fragrance and memories of your summer herb garden as you work by the fireside. Do, in this case, set an old sheet or newspaper on the floor around you to catch stem fragments as these can be damaging to your vacuum cleaner.

A large flower basket

You will need:
wooden base 28 x 10cm (11 x 4in)
2 sticks – thick lilac suckers or thornless bramble could be used, approx. 10cm (4in) long
2 more approx. 28cm (11in) long
gimp or panel pins
a hammer
a saw
strong scissors or secateurs
bunches of dried thyme or thyme and cotton lavender stems
garden raffia (preferably green or buff)
a large-eyed needle or bodkin

To make
Hammer the gimp pins around the sides of the base at 2½cm (1in) intervals, setting one row of pins below and slightly to the left of the other as in diagram 1a. Lay sufficient ready-prepared bunches of dried herb to complete at least one side of the basket before you start working. Try to include some flowering stems in each bundle and make sure there is some dried foliage from a little way up the stems to avoid bare patches on the side of the basket. Cut the prepared stem bundles (which must fit between the gimp pins) to 14cm (5½in) long.

Take a length of raffia and tie this firmly around a gimp pin in the top row, calling this no. 1. Lay the first bunch of stems between this pin and the next, with the stems protruding just beyond the under side of the base. The bundle should give a thick covering. If necessary lay two bundles together. Holding the stems down firmly with one hand, take the raffia tightly across them in a diagonal line, looping it around the lower gimp pin of the next pair, no. 2. See diagram 1b. Keeping the tension on the raffia, pull it up towards the gimp pin above, and loop the raffia around it. This pin is no. 3. You will now have made a figure of eight with the raffia, with the free length ready to take diagonally over the next bunch of herbs.

In this way the raffia is taken over itself with the loop holding the lower length from slipping over the pin. Pulling the loop tight and keeping the raffia taut, lay the next bunch of herb alongside. Continue binding the herbs in place while maintaining the tension. Should you need to set the work down, even for a moment, you must knot the securing raffia around the next gimp pin before letting go.

Stem baskets

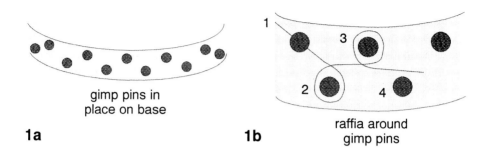

gimp pins in
place on base

1a

raffia around
gimp pins

1b

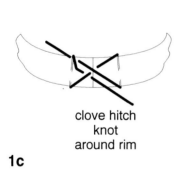

clove hitch
knot
around rim

1c

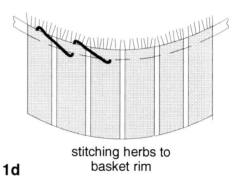

stitching herbs to
basket rim

1d

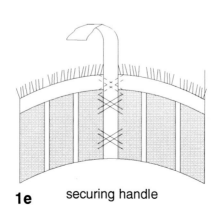

1e   securing handle

When you have finished the first long side of the basket, set the rim about 2cm (¾in) below the top edge of the herb bunches, with the side of the basket leant firmly against a cushion or table. Knot one end of a long length of raffia around the rim using a clove-hitch knot (see diagram 1c) and thread the other end through a large-eyed needle. To oversew the herbs to the rim, bring the raffia around the edge of the first bunch of herbs and take it back through to the inside at the centre of the second bunch. Your needle should emerge on the inside of the basket, below the rim. See diagram 1d. Bring the raffia back over the rim and out to make the next "stitch".

As you reach the half way point set the prepared handle amongst the stem bundles (see diagram 1e). The handle is included in the stitching to secure it to the basket. Several figure of eight movements are made with the raffia thread at the height of the rim and further down the basket around the adjacent stem bundle as in diagram 1e.

With the whole side stitched to the rim, push the threaded needle between the stem bunches until you need it again, so that it will not prick you as you continue down the next side tying bunches to the base.

Continue in this way until the herb bunches completely cover the basket sides. Finish the basket by clipping the stems neatly, leaving them so that the rim and base are both hidden.

Round pot-pourri basket
You will need:
wooden base with a diameter of 7½cm (3in)
2 lengths of pliant honeysuckle or ivy for the rim and handle
gimp or panel pins
hammer
scissors
dried lavender or savory stems, rock hyssop and thyme
green or cream crochet cotton no 20.
approx. 2m (2yds) of 1½cm (½in) lace
a large-eyed needle
small pearl button
fragment of cheesecloth or net.

To make
Hammer the gimp pins around the wooden base at 1½cm (½in) intervals, setting one row of pins below and slightly to the left of the other. Gather the dried herb stems in bunches which will fit between these pins and cut them to 15cm (6in) long. Check to ensure you have sufficient bunches to encircle the basket before beginning.

Take a length of crochet cotton and tie this firmly around a gimp pin in the top row, calling this no. 1. Lay the first bunch of stems between this pin and the next, with the stems projecting just beyond the under side of the base. The covering with this basket need not be thick since you will later weave lace in and out of the bunches. Holding the first bunch down with one hand, take the crochet cotton across the stems in a tight, diagonal line, looping it around the lower gimp pin of the next pair, no. 2.

113

(see diagram 1b). Keeping the crochet cotton taut, pull it up towards the gimp pin above, and loop it around the pin, calling this no. 3 (see diagram 1c). You will now have made a figure of eight with the crochet thread and have the leading thread ready to place diagonally over the next bunch of herbs. Pulling the loop tight and keeping the crochet thread taut, lay the next bunch of herb stems alongside. Continue in this way, leaving slight gaps between the bunches for the lace weaving. Again, do not set the work down without first securing the thread tightly.

When you have attached all the bunches to the base, thread a large-eyed needle with crochet cotton. With so small a basket it is easiest to attach the handle to the honeysuckle or ivy rim with firm ties of crochet cotton before stitching through the basket sides. Do this and then insert the rim and handle together on the inside of the stem bunches with the rim 2cm (¾in) below the flowering tops of the herbs. Tie one end of a long length of crochet cotton to the rim, and begin oversewing it in place. Take every stitch in through the centre of a herb bunch, beneath the basket rim and back out above it, ready for the next "stitch".

The tops of the stems can now be trimmed to give the effect of a fan shape at the back of the basket, or scalloped round for decoration. The narrow band of lace is woven in and out of the bunches, beginning at the bottom of the basket. As each round is completed simply take the lace on above the last row until the top is reached. Both ends of the lace are left on the inside and stitched to the nearest herb bunch to secure. A delicate lid can be made to keep light from the pot-pourri by stitching the slightly gathered lace in spiral fashion onto a circle of cheesecloth or net. A small pearl button in the centre will give you a "handle" to lift the lace easily, while adding decoration at the same time.

Having practised making both a large and a small basket, the technique will be sufficiently familiar to plan more baskets for particular uses. Decoration of the baskets may be achieved by using various combinations of different herbs, as suggested at the beginning when discussing stem colours. You will soon find which herbs you prefer to work with, for each has its own characteristics and is correspondingly "kind" or "harsh" to your fingers. A further variation might be to stitch a pattern over the herb bunches using freshly gathered wild strawberry runners or coloured raffia, just as the mood takes you.

Basketry

MAKING baskets is a relaxing craft which I have enjoyed over many years. When natural cane became steadily replaced by a synthetic substitute, however, I found much of the pleasure was lost for me. Willow baskets seemed the only alternative and willow was hard to obtain, so I began searching my garden and the hedgerows for suitable natural materials.

In the garden, autumn pruning and clearing provides many valuable stakes and longer, thinner stems for weaving, which can be harvested with satisfaction rather than burnt, shredded or laid on the compost heap. Beginning at the end of September or early October, harvesting continues throughout the winter months until the sap rises again, usually in March. Basketry with red dogwood, snowberry, lilac, thornless bramble, ivy, hop, rose and honeysuckle fills some of the time left available when the garden lies dormant. Summer baskets can be made of softer stems, cut at the peak of their growth, and used immediately, while still supple. Long-stemmed lavender can also be woven amongst the periwinkle, broom, honeysuckle and ivy into small, soft, fragrant baskets.

For thick honeysuckle stems, thicker ivy which creeps along the ground, thornless bramble, balsam poplar, dogroses or rambling roses, snowberry, dogwood, elder, lilac suckers and home-grown willow (which can be cut from ornamental weeping willows) a week or so of "fading" will be necessary before they can be soaked and woven.

This process is simple and requires little attention. Having cut the longest stems in autumn - choosing those which are either of a constant thickness, or neatly tapering - remove the leaves from the tip of the stem back towards the root end. Any thorns must also be removed, wearing stout gloves and using a sharp knife, or by pulling the bramble through a tightly fitting circular hole in a piece of metal. Growing thornless varieties of roses or bramble will, of course, save this chore.

Lay the stripped stems, tied in a bundle for neatness, beneath a hedge or other shade, where they will remain damp and away from sunlight. Water them occasionally in very dry weather to ensure they do not dry out. The thinnest of these stems will require two to three weeks before they feel leathery and pliable to touch and will not snap if curled around your hand. Thick stems saved for handles and stakes may need up to three months. Experience with the thinner stems will soon give you guidance on the texture that should be sought. Testing all the stakes regularly will increase your awareness of the subtle changes that take place during fading.

Taking the stems in for use on a damp day will give a better result than when the atmosphere is dry. Further soaking will then be necessary before weaving. Thinner weavers will be ready after 20 to 45 minutes in cold water. Thick stakes and handles may need a whole morning, or benefit from soaking overnight, after which patience will be rewarded with easier weaving. Once the stems are removed from the water bath, wrap them in a damp towel until they are used.

When planning a basket design consider the materials available and the purpose of the finished basket. If the materials cannot meet the purpose, then a few offers to prune suitable bushes for your friends at the right point of the year may be welcomed, or you may find some materials in wild hedgerows. If this is the case, always make sure your pruning does not leave a gap in the hedge that may allow livestock to escape, or damage the hedgerow. If gathering in any quantity, permission should be sought from the landowner.

If, on the other hand, you have a choice of available materials you may wish to cut with decoration in mind. For the stakes, red dogwood and balsam poplar give attractive deep colours. Thinner stems of red dogwood can add colour in a stripe or band amongst brown snowberry or pale, stripped ivy. The bright green of broom and periwinkle will fade in time unfortunately, but the lovely tan of golden hop lasts for years.

The bark of ivy or honeysuckle may be left on for a rustic effect, or stripped by dipping the lengths in boiling water and peeling to leave them more uniform in shade and thickness for a basket with a clean image. Red or white willows can also offer contrasts. Weavers can be dyed, a practice more associated with "less civilised" parts of the world where, it should be remembered, skill in basketry is at its height. The Hopi Indians in America used the purple dye from sunflower seeds to decorate their baskets. In Britain, we might substitute elderberry or bramble juices or the stain from walnuts, which are in keeping with a natural look basket. Brighter dyes from *Coreopsis*, dahlia, *Tagetes*, golden rod, tansy and so on can be prepared as for wool.

These dyes will need the basketry weavers to be prepared with a mordant for a good colour to be obtained. Elizabeth Jensen, in her book **Baskets from Nature's Bounty**, gives instructions for mordanting the weavers overnight in an alum solution, then simmering them in the dyebath, which has been prepared as for wool, and leaving them to soak in the dye afterwards for long periods. All manner of original patterns are possible with imaginative variations on traditional weaves with added colours.

To judge whether you have sufficient materials for your basket design, allow 25cm (10in) plus the height of your basket for each stake. This allows for a length below the base of the basket to work the "foot-trac" which will need to be approximately 10cm (4in), and a further length beyond the top of the basket for the border. Elaborate borders will require more than this allowance. Handle lengths should take account of the depth the ends must reach down into the weaving to give strength, as well as the height of the handle above the border. The height of handles tends to increase according to the overall size of the basket, although, depending upon the function of the finished basket, this may not always be so. Weavers are best around 70-100cm (2 to 3ft) long or more, for a basket of any size. Remember three weavers will be needed at the same time for those areas of a large basket which require extra strength - that is, the base of the side, half way up the side or, in a tall basket, at several stages in the sides, and just underneath the rim. Usually two or three rounds are worked with these extra weavers at these points. Elsewhere, a single weaver will be taken around or across the shape.

The chart shows the possible uses of a variety of materials within a basket. The term soft baskets is used here to apply to small baskets which contain the softer weavers such as periwinkle, broom or, in miniature work, wild strawberry runners, with the lightweight stems of snowberry.

116

| Herb | Hard baskets | | | Soft baskets | | |
	Weaver	Stakes	Handle	Weaver	Stakes	Handle
balsam poplar		*	*			
bramble		*	*			
broom	*			*		*
dogwood	*	*	*		*	*
elder			*			
honeysuckle	*		*		*	*
hop	*		*			
ivy	*	*	*		*	*
jasmine	*				*	*
lilac		*	*			
periwinkle	*			*		
rose	*	*	*		*	
snowberry		*	*	*	*	*
wild strawberry				*		
willow	*	*	*		*	*

Harvesting natural materials

If you wish to weave with freshly cut stems, harvesting is best done on a damp day, or at least straight after a heavy dew. With climbers such as golden hop, jasmine, rambling roses and honeysuckle (if trained through a trellis), this consideration is especially important as the stems need to be at their most supple as you unthread their progress to release them from other plants, hedging or fencing of any kind. Always cut branches of shrubs with the welfare of the shrub's continued growth in mind. Remember you are shaping it for the future and will probably wish to return to it at a later date for more harvesting. Use secateurs that are in good condition, or branch pruners for the balsam poplar, willow and lilac, leaving clean cuts which should be sealed if necessary.

Balsam poplar This tree, which produces fragrant, sticky leafbuds in the spring and a considerable incense-like perfume in the garden on hot days later in the year, is prolific in its growth. My own tree - which, because of its golden leaves in early summer, is included in the treasure garden - gives numerous young branches for basketry in spring. Since I have no wish for it to grow to any great height, I keep it almost pollarded, although in a rather attractive curve of growth, to control such enthusiasm. These young branches have early, tight buds when they are cut which can be stripped and dried to add to pot-pourri. The branches are then laid under the hedge for a few weeks in preparation for weaving. When supple, they mix well with thicker dogwood stakes. Do take care when soaking them, however, as the resin is liable to stain the container used. Balsam poplar also has a strong odour, which remains with the basket for a time, becoming stronger when it is near a source of heat.

Bramble The two thornless brambles in my garden have put an end to my former problems of removing the thorns from the branches of wild bushes. However, for those who are still trying, I have come across numerous ideas over the years as to how to de-thorn brambles. Anyone who has tried seems to have their own method to recommend. These range from pulling the stem through an old woollen jumper which protects your hands while at the same time removing the thorns; to drilling a round hole through both ends or both sides of an empty tin and pulling the bramble stem through the holes. Perhaps I like to do things the hard way occasionally, but I always used a sharp knife and sliced the thorns off, being careful to angle the knife blade away from me.

Growing brambles in your own garden, whether thornless or not, can also overcome the usual problem when harvesting – that of the apparent affinity of brambles and nettles. The best stems always seem to require one to be stung in reaching them. On occasion I have harvested as many as 5 lengths each 3m (9ft) long from my cultivated bramble. However, if you wish to encourage more bushes, it is wiser to curl the long stems down, weighting them and piling earth over the top at strategic points to encourage fresh roots to grow. It is exceedingly unlikely that you will be wanting stakes of more than 1m (3ft) in length and the shoots from the new root will be more supple in their new growth than a very long stem. Prepare as for the balsam poplar by leaving the cut lengths, with leaves and any thorns removed, in shade for several weeks before soaking and weaving.

Broom The best time to cut broom for basketry is just after the bush has flowered. The growth is still quite young and flexible and it will save the herb from using energy in producing seed pods. Of course, if you are gathering the flowers for dyeing or wine, the basket harvest can be done at the same time. Broom is really best if worked immediately however, and there is the question of taking on too many things at once. If the weather is damp then broom will keep in good condition left out in the shade for a day or so, but longer than that and it will dry out and be of little use. Since most lengths of broom are comparatively short, it is really only suitable for small baskets. The bright green is most effective for a time but does fade eventually.

Dogwood Red dogwood is the most attractive of the dogwoods, but others can be used as readily. These may be pruned in autumn, through the winter, or in spring. I have even taken a little in early summer when I found I needed a few more stakes for a project. It is a shrub which grows quickly and seems eager to replace your stock of materials as soon as possible. Give thought to the future growth of the shrub when pruning, for it can be most effective in a large bed, especially in spring. Long branches of young growth make excellent stakes and handles, while the thin twigs that grow from them will supply handles for small, delicate baskets, or stakes for miniatures.

Elder At first glance the common elder, which I have seen grow from a cutting to a large tree in just 5 years, seems to be an ideal source of basketry material. Its use is limited, however, by the hollow nature of the stem growth. I have tried elders for handles, but nothing requiring a great deal of flexibility. Also cutting the trees back is best done immediately after the berries have been harvested or the promise of the following year's flowers will be removed at the same time.

118

Honeysuckle Healthy honeysuckle bushes will soon give rampant growth when set in good soil and a little shade. Cut back three or four times a year when the reaching tendrils are beginning to give the rounded bushes the look of a Medusa's head. Often several of the free-ranging stems will find each other and twine together so that they seem to beg to be cut as a single length and wired end to end to form a garland. Cut each one at the point where the thicker, and usually paler growth changes to darker, pliable stem. Honeysuckle will weave more easily if you can identify the root and tip ends and always begin with the root and work towards the tip. To assist this identification, do not be tempted to trim both ends in order to have a uniform weaver. Honeysuckle may be used immediately, or within 2 or 3 days if the weather is consistently damp, without soaking. Or, it can be faded for a week or two and then woven after soaking. This will give a tighter basket than freshly woven stems.

Hop The rich colouring of golden hop stems makes them the perfect basketry material. By autumn, the rather rough surface of the stems earlier in the year will have softened a little to make them a pleasure to work with. Care should be taken to gather them before the frost, however, as this can leave them soggy and unpleasant and generally of very little use. The common hop is just as good from the weaving point of view, but not as ornamental in the finished basket. I prefer to weave with my hops almost immediately, rather than fading and soaking them. If cut and stripped of their leaves on a damp, mellow morning when there is sun but also a heavy dew, they will be a joy to weave in late morning and early afternoon as the sun lifts the temperature sufficiently for you to sit in the garden as you work. Very long weavers can be obtained which makes hop a good choice for a large basket. The good colour is retained in the finished work and could be used to advantage alongside stripped ivy to make bands of tan and cream, or panels of colour within a basket.

Ivy This makes a good material for the beginner, being quite pliable and flexible and, in many places, easily gathered from the wild. Do be careful to gather the trailing stems of ivy that cover the ground in some woodlands and leave the ivy stems, however interesting they appear to be, which are wrapped around tree trunks. This, older ivy has suckers set along the stems which draw sustenance from the tree bark and make the stems unsuitable for weaving or stakes. There is usually plenty of more useful growth to be found.

Take time to examine a few lengths of ivy around the area, to determine the longest available, before harvesting. If you have some distance to carry them, ivy stems are best coiled together to form a large hoop which can be carried over your shoulder. Should you wish to be more discreet, it is possible to persuade quite a large quantity of tightly coiled ivy into a sizeable carrier bag without damaging the stems. Once home, strip the leaves, always working from the tip of the stem back down towards the root. Lay the stripped ivy in the shade for fading, or use within two or three days if the weather is damp. For best results, ivy may be gathered from early October through to March - or April in a late spring.

Jasmine Either summer or winter jasmine may be gathered for basketry when the bushes are pruned for their better growth. Winter jasmine can be cut hard back after flowering in the spring and the stems used as stakes for small baskets. The fragrant *Jasminum grandiflorum* which flowers at the end of the summer can provide longer, slender stems for weavers in autumn after flowering. Winter jasmine has an altogether tougher nature and may benefit from fading and soaking rather than being used straight away; unfortunately the lovely green colour which it sports at first will lighten and vanish quite quickly. Summer jasmine can be used immediately.

Lilac Anyone who has lilac in their garden and is plagued with suckers appearing in nearby flower-beds will, I think, be glad to find a use for them. However, you will need to allow the suckers to grow to a useful height of some 1m (3ft) in order to cut them at ground level for stakes, which may be seen as a disadvantage. Shorter lengths can be used for handles of baskets, or possibly for support rims in stem baskets, see page 110. Since in this case you are not concerned about future growth patterns, the only factor to consider is whether the lilac itself will be at its best for basketry. Between autumn and spring is a better time to cut the suckers than in summer when they are full of sap, but for handles this is not too critical and so the appearance of the area where the suckers are unwelcome can be allowed to be the first priority.

Periwinkle This lovely herb, which flowers in the spring and then on into the summer, seems to be as busy spreading by sending out long runners as it is in producing flowers. The stems can be cut almost throughout the year and used immediately to make soft baskets. They contrast well with snowberry stakes, especially when still bright green. Simply cut the longest lengths you can find, close to the plant itself, and strip the leaves back from the tips of the stems.

Rose Clearly climbing roses are referred to here, dog-roses being one of the best for harvests. These often clamber over whole trees in the wild and can spare long stems without leaving the area bare. Do take thought when removing such glory and always leave part of each bush unless you are deliberately stripping them back in your own garden. They are best gathered in autumn or winter, de-thorned and faded before use. Garden climbers may also give a harvest at the normal pruning time.

Snowberry A hedge of snowberry can be a perfect source of basketry materials and dye together. I have enjoyed cutting the thin branches which are laden with berries in late autumn and early winter and, having put the berries to soak for dyeing, using the stems for a small project. Snowberry has a pliable nature but will almost certainly require fading and soaking if the stems have achieved any real substance. Thick branches make good stakes when soaked, while thin twigs may be torn from them as part of their preparation and used immediately in miniature baskets; again as stakes or handles. The pretty pale tan colouring will often make them a first choice as soon as you have worked with them.

Wild strawberries These are a great joy in my garden and show their zest for life by sending out long runners to establish new plants. In late spring they are plentiful and can be harvested easily by cutting with a pair of scissors, close to the parent plant. Some will have tiny roots forming part of the way along their length which may, occasionally, be removed without damaging the stem, but will probably determine a break in the length at some stage. They are at their best when cut immediately before use for miniature baskets. It is a good idea to have the stakes and base ready-prepared and weave them straight in. The basket must be tiny in form as they are too frail to give real support to the sides. They may also be used for decorative stitching into a soft basket or a stem basket.

Willow You are unlikely to be able to grow willow osiers in your garden, unless you live alongside a watercourse, but weeping willows and even large willow trees can provide young branches for use. A willow tree growing in a damp place may well sprout many useful shoots after the main trunk has been cut down. I have also seen slender willow wands growing from a fallen tree laid along the ground.

Commercially, osier willows are supplied in 3 grades for basketry. Brown rods are those which have been cut during the winter and stored. Rods of 1-1.3m (3 to 4ft) in length will need an hour or so soaking in cold water and are then wrapped in a wet towel for a further hour or so, before use. Longer rods will need a longer soaking time. I have always found these quite hard work to persuade into shape. White rods have been cut as the sap is rising and are peeled. Although they must also be soaked and carefully prepared, they are slightly easier to use. Green rods are not always available and are not as good for making baskets as the other two.

Basketry projects
Ivy and cane basket
My first experiment with basketry materials from the garden was to try using ivy stems as weavers within a conventional framework of cane. For anyone who is already experienced in basketwork but feels they would like to approach home-gathered materials cautiously, I would recommend this small basket, or a similar project as an easy introduction to handling freshly gathered stems.

You will need
a semi-circular wooden basketry base 10 x 12.5cm (4 x 5in)
No. 5 cane to supply 19 stakes (or one for each hole in the base) each 36cm (14in)
3 lengths of No. 5 cane for "upsetting" (see fig. 2)
several lengths of thin, pliable ivy for weaving
secateurs
a knitting needle or bodkin

Unless real cane is used rather than the synthetic that is generally available, soaking the stakes will not be necessary. If, however, you have a source of cane or slender willow, soak the cut stakes and the three weavers for the upsetting in cold water for at least 20 minutes. If your source of ivy is in your garden, or close by, you might like

121

to gather this while the other material is in preparation. In autumn, winter and early spring, ivy is generally easier to weave when freshly cut than when it has been faded.

Cut a plentiful bundle of stems so that any which split as you are learning to handle them can be discarded. Leave the ivy laid in the shade with the leaves still on the stems until you are ready to use it. First, thread the prepared stakes into the holes around the wooden base with about 10cm (4in) on the underside, and work the foot-trac to secure them. Hold the base so that the shorter lengths of cane are upwards. Begin the foot-trac by taking any stake and, calling it no. 1., lay it in front of stake no. 2 (to the right), behind stakes 3 and 4 and in pointing towards the centre of the basket base (see diagram 1). Then take stake no. 2 and do the same, putting it in front of stake no. 3, behind stakes 4 and 5 and in to the centre. Continue in this way until the last 3 stakes are left. Using a knitting needle or bodkin, gently lever the first stakes a little away from the base, in order to thread these last stakes between them to complete the pattern. That is, take the next stake between the original stakes no. 1 and 2, behind nos. 2 and 3 and in towards the centre. With the next stake left upright, take this between the original stakes nos. 2 and 3, behind nos. 3 and 4 and thread it in towards the centre. The last stake is taken between stakes 3 and 4 and emerges in the only space left to complete the pattern, between nos, 5 and 6. Check back against the previous pattern made by the foot-trac if you have any doubts.

With the foot-trac made, firm the stakes in an upright position above the base, giving each a slight tug to see that the foot-trac is tight against the base. You are now ready for the upsetting or setting up a strong base for the side of your basket. Place the first of the three prepared cane or willow weavers between any two stakes above the base, with a short length pointing inwards towards the centre of the basket. Holding this in place, set the next weaver between the next two stakes in the same way and follow this with the third between the next two stakes. Now bring the first weaver in front of two stakes and behind one and out. This will hold the other two weavers down (see diagram 2). Repeat with the second weaver and the third and continue in this way until 3 rounds have been worked. Leave the ends pointing inwards and trim just past the next stake.

With this substantial foundation made for your basket, choose a length of ivy which feels really supple and is not too long to manage. Test it by gently forming it into a loop. When satisfied, hold it in one hand right at the tip. Close the fingers of your other hand tightly around the stem and sweep them downwards stripping away the leaves in a long, smooth movement. Longer lengths will take a couple of sweeps. The leaves should come away easily if you remember to work towards the root end of the stem.

Set the ivy, with the root end pointing towards the inside of the basket, between two stakes about half way round from the ends of the earlier weavers which you left pointing inwards. Take this ivy weaver in front of the next stake, calling this no. 1 and behind stake no. 2, in front of stake no. 3 and behind stake no. 4. Continue in this way in front of one, behind one, in a simple weave called randing (see diagram 3). A steady pressure on the ivy with each weave should keep a good shape to the basket.

When the basket side is approximately 7.5cm (3in) deep, leave the end of the ivy weaver pointing inwards and trim it to lay behind the next stake. If you have worked continuously without problems, natural stakes will probably still be sufficiently damp

Basketry

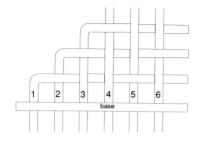

1. foot-trac

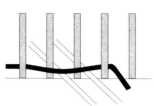

2. waling

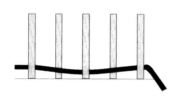

3. randing

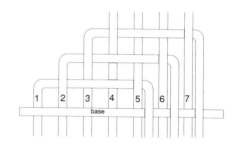

4. border

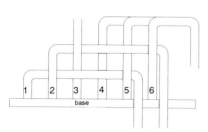

5. finishing border

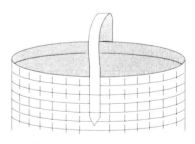

6. inserting handle

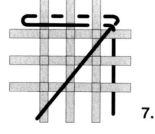

7. posy basket base

to work the top border of the basket without resoaking them. To test whether this will be necessary, bend one stake along behind the next, gradually easing the point of pressure back towards the place where the stake emerges from the top row of weaving. Bounce the stake lightly with your finger to coax it to lay flat. With synthetic cane you will be able to omit this stage and start the border immediately. If natural material seems likely to split under the strain, resoak by setting the basket upside down in a bucket of water for another half an hour.

To work the border take your trial stake behind the next, no. 2 in front of the following 2 stakes nos. 3 and 4, behind no. 5 and out (see diagram 4). Continue around the top border until there are only 3 stakes left standing upright. As with the foot-trac, use a knitting needle or bodkin to lift the stems already folded down and complete the pattern by threading the last three through, under and between them (see diagram 5). Keep checking the appearance of this piece of the border with that immediately before it. Trim the ends neatly just beneath the border.

Miniature basket

This pretty little basket might be made for a child's doll, or to sit on a shelf, filled with a small, dried flower decoration. Making it will extend your basketry skill in natural materials, while not involving coping with tough stakes that can be difficult to handle.

You will need

8 slender snowberry stems 60cm (2ft) long for stakes
3 good lengths of thin snowberry for upsetting
lengths of broom, freshly cut, green and supple
strong scissors or secateurs
a fine knitting needle

Remove the leaves from the snowberry stems and test by bending them over your knee. If they are not sufficiently pliable to work as they are, soak these in cold water for 30-60 minutes. When the stakes are ready, lay them in a cross-shape of 2 groups of 2 pointing away from you and 2 groups of 2 laid horizontally across them at the centre point. Take the longest and most supple broom stem and fold the end diagonally across the centre where the pairs of snowberry stems meet. Hold this in place between your thumb and forefinger, and with the other hand, take the stem under two pairs of snowberry stems and over the next two. Repeat this for 2 rounds to make a square, then begin opening out the pairs by taking the broom under one pair and over the next. Because you have used both ends of the stakes for the basket you will have an even number, this means that after the first round your weave would come behind and in front of the same stakes in every row. To counter this, when you reach the end of the first round, set a second length of broom between the next two stakes and weave until you reach the first weaver. Continue for 4 rounds, weaving first with one weaver and then the other in alternate rounds. This is called pairing. These rounds will establish the size of the base of the basket. For a slightly larger base, simply work more rounds.

Next, bring the ends of the stakes together and tie them to make the sides of the basket upright. Take the soaked 3 lengths of snowberry and set the first between any 2 stakes, pointing inwards. Holding this in place, set the second weaver between the next 2 and do the same with the third. As for the upsetting in the first basket, take the first weaver in front of 2 stakes behind 1 and out. This will hold the other two down (see diagram 2). Repeat with the second and third weavers and continue for 3 rounds of the basket to make a solid base for the sides. Leaving the trimmed ends pointing inside the basket, change back to weaving with broom. Begin half-way around the basket from the trimmed ends, and work rounds with pairing as in the base. One round with the first weaver and then a round with the second, and so on, until the basket is the required depth of approximately 5-8cm (2 to 3in). Soak the stakes again if necessary by immersing the basket upside down in a tall container of water. Work a simple border by taking each pair of stakes as one, in front of the next stake to the right, behind the following stake and out. As before, the last 3 pairs of stakes will need to be threaded under and between the following stakes in order to complete the pattern. Use a slender knitting needle or crochet hook to ease them through.

Make the handle by inserting a length of snowberry, which is slightly thicker than the stakes, down through the border alongside a pair of stakes, and into the side of the basket to the snowberry upsetting. Push the other end down into the opposite side (see diagram 6). The height of the handle must be in proportion to the depth, but is a matter of personal choice. One of the great joys of hedgerow basketry is that the materials are not uniform and offer so much variation in colour and texture that each design becomes a unique project which stimulates the imagination as you work.

Posy basket

This attractive basket will give you experience in shaping stronger materials to produce a durable and useful container. While the methods used are similar to those in the miniature basket, the actual shaping is achieved largely by pressing the basket around your knee at frequent intervals, while working it.

You will need
a length of elder, bramble or willow for the handle
6 stakes of willow or red dogwood approximately 1.2m (4ft) long
9 lengths of willow or red dogwood approximately 60-90cm (2 to 3ft) long for weaving
approximately 8 or 10 lengths of ivy for weavers
secateurs
knitting needle or bodkin
a craft knife

Take 3 soaked stakes and lay these down pointing away from you. Lay the remaining 3 stakes horizontally across them at the centre. Find the most supple length of ivy and carefully bend the stem into a smooth curve at the half-way point. Loop this around the three stakes pointing away from you, above the bar made by the 3 horizontal stakes (see diagram 7). Hold the cross of stakes firmly in place with one hand while taking the left-hand weaver in front of the 3 stakes pointing away from you, over the other half of its length, now known as the right-hand weaver, and behind the next 3 horizontal stakes. As with the base of the miniature basket, continue taking the weaver over and under, but this time with groups of 3 stakes instead of 2. Because the basket is so much larger, you will need to turn the cross to the left as you work. At the end of the first round, again take the left-hand weaver over the right, so changing weavers. This is called pairing. After 2 rounds, begin opening out the stakes into a star shape, still pairing the weavers, as you take them behind and in front of alternate stakes.

Having worked 6 rounds, begin forming the shape of the sides, bringing 2 opposite groups of three stakes into an upright position, while the ends of the basket are left at a lower, more gradual, angle. Join in extra lengths of ivy for weaving as you need them by leaving the cut end supported behind the next stake and pointing into the basket, to the right, and laying the new end over it with a short length pointing into the basket and to the left. Work by pairing until the basket has reached a depth of 6cm (2½in). Leave the ends of the ivy weavers trimmed and facing into the basket, and begin at another point to avoid placing all the ends of weavers in the same part of the basket. Place the first willow or dogwood weaver between any 2 stakes, and pointing in towards the centre of the basket. Holding this steady, place the second weaver between the next 2 stakes to the right and repeat with the third weaver. Take the first weaver over the others, in front of 2 stakes to the right, behind 1 and out towards you. This will hold the second and third weavers down. Repeat with the second and third weavers and continue, always taking the left-hand weaver in front of 2 stakes and behind 1, until you have worked a full round. When this pattern is worked higher in the basket than immediately above a base, it is called waling.

Return to the ivy weavers and pair these for 5 rounds. Remember to keep shaping the basket as you go. With another 3 willow rods or lengths of red dogwood, work 1 round of waling as before, to give the top of the basket strength and confirm the shaping you have given so far. With a sharp knife whittle each end of the pre-soaked handle length to form a point. Push the ends down through the weaving into each of the upright sides of the basket, as far as the lower row of waling.

Work the border (after soaking the upper basket stakes again if necessary) by taking each stake behind the next, calling this no. 1, in front of stake no. 2 and behind no. 3, with the end pointing out from the basket. As before, use a knitting needle or bodkin to raise the first stakes to thread the last 3 stakes through, under and between them to complete the pattern. Trim the ends.

Rustic wool basket

Inspiration for the next basket came originally from the notion of using herbs which are sources both of dyes and basketry materials to make a basket for my bobbins and balls of home-dyed wools. A tray shape seemed the most practical to allow me to find the right colour without tangling the balls. When developing basketry skills it is interesting to make a square or rectangular base which then needs to receive the stakes.

As sources of dyes, golden hop and thornless bramble were an easy choice of contrasting colour materials for the base. Snowberry could also have provided side stakes, but my hedge was too young to give sufficiently strong growth. I therefore turned to the red dogwood and balsam poplar for their attractive colourings. The balsam poplar has the added advantage of fragrancing the basket over a long period, whenever it is left in the sun or in a warm room. Weavers for the sides could be of ivy as a dye herb, but I have used honeysuckle in the basket illustrated on page xvii, as the colour combination works well.

The joy of this basket is that since your availability of materials will decide the size of the base, the number of stakes and amount of side weavers can be adjusted accordingly. If you do alter the instructions below, remember that the basket needs the strength given by side stakes placed between each pair of base stakes at the ends, but you can be far more flexible about placing side stakes along the longer sides. This is particularly helpful if you need to use one or two rather thicker and less flexible side stakes - as the extra space between them will require less strain in sudden bends around the next stake for the foot-trac and border. Smaller versions of the basket will require the side stakes to be placed as closely along the long sides of the basket as at the ends.

For a basket 41 x 25cm (16 x 10in) **You will need**
sufficient thornless or de-thorned bramble for 12 base stakes, each 45cm (18in) long
approximately 10 full lengths of golden hop (depending upon their growth)
38 stakes in any combination of red dogwood, balsam poplar, supple thornless bramble, or snowberry, each 45cm (18in) long
approximately 12 to 15 lengths of ivy or honeysuckle for side weavers
secateurs
knitting needle or bodkin

The base stakes must first be kept in place, evenly spaced from one another. This may be achieved by setting them in a clamp, firming them in position in hard packed earth in the garden, or pushing them into a thick layer of very firm dough or plasticine. An alternative method is to pierce 12 holes in thick card set 2cm (¾in) apart, with a second card prepared in the same way for the other ends of the base stakes. Thread either end of the base stakes through the holes.

With the 12 stakes secured firmly, begin weaving with freshly gathered and stripped golden hop stems. Taking a long, pliable stem, fold it almost in half and loop it around the edge stake to the left of your row of stakes. You will now use the two ends of this weaver as if they were separate weavers and weave by pairing. Unlike the pairing in previous baskets, where the weavers were changed at the end of each round, in this case, weave the lengths alternately, changing after each movement - in front of 1 stake, behind 1. At the edges the weavers are looped around the edge stake in turn, changing the pattern so that you have a double row of weavers in front of the same stake, followed by a double row behind it (see illustration on page xvii). Continue weaving to within 5cm (2in) of the ends of the base stakes and finish with both weavers neatly tucked in to the weaving.

The base made, choose the 22 most flexible side stakes (which should have been soaked for several hours, or overnight) and set these to one side. These will be used at the ends of the basket. Beginning half way along either long side, push the stakes through between the pairs of weavers, at intervals of every other pair or, possibly, every three pairs, depending upon the frequency of rows of weaving. Pull the stakes carefully through to leave about 10cm (4in) of stake below the base. When you reach the corner of the basket, stop and go back to work the foot-trac with the first stakes placed. Do this as before by taking stake no. 1 in front of stake no. 2, to the right of it, behind stakes 3 and 4 and in front of stake 5 to lay against the base pointing towards the centre (see diagram 1) Continue until you need the end stakes to be inserted. Place these between each of the pairs of base stake ends sticking out from the edge of the basket. Loop a short length of golden hop around the end base stake on the left-hand edge and weave this quickly around the stake ends to hold the side stakes in place. Push the ends neatly down into the base weaving to secure them.

Continue weaving the foot-trac across the end, and then, having added more side stakes, work the second side and finish as with the first. To finish the last 3 side stakes in the foot-trac, the knitting needle or bodkin should be used, as before, to open the way to thread them under and between the stakes already laid down. Care should be taken to begin and end with 3 supple stakes as these will take more strain than the others.

Having made sure the foot-trac is holding the stakes firmly against the base of the basket, set either a pre-soaked or freshly cut, long weaver of ivy or honeysuckle, root end first, between any two side stakes with the end pointing into the basket. Weave the sides in simple, in front of 1 stake, behind 1 stake randing, as in diagram 3. Continue, joining in new lengths as necessary, leaving the new end pointing to the left behind a stake and laid over the old end which is pointing to the right. If you have an even number of stakes you will need to pair 2 weavers as before, changing from one to the other as you reach the end of each round. With an odd number of stakes, simple randing with one weaver can be worked.

When the basket is approximately 7.5-9cm (3 to 3½in) deep, trim the weaver end and test the side stakes for flexibility. If they have retained this while you have been working, continue straight away with the border. If they seem likely to split under pressure, soak the basket sides again. Starting half way along one of the long sides of the basket, take any stake, behind the next, and out. Continue laying down each stake with the ends pointing downwards and away from the basket. Very firm pressure needs to be applied at this point in order to keep a good shape and strong top to the finished basket. Trim the ends.

Herbs in needlework design

MY very first interest in herbs came about through writing a novel set in the Elizabethan period. In order to do it, I had to know about herbs at an intimate level, for they were so much a part of everyday life at that time. Ladies who ran large households had, of necessity, to be efficient in making remedies for those who depended upon their skills. Often they distilled sweet waters, made fragrant blends of herbs, sweetmeats and, after the monasteries were dissolved, liqueurs. It is hardly surprising then, that after working to capture the essence of herbal beauty in recipes, her hands and clothes still fresh with their fragrance, a lady planning to embroider a set of bedcurtains or a cushion, might choose herbs for her design.

After twenty five years of studying herbs I decided my knowledge of the subject was sufficient to re-write the long-discarded novel. As part of my more recent research I went to the Victoria and Albert Museum in London to look at needlework of the period. Fascinated by the rich quality of the designs and stitching, I found myself longing to take needle and thread and make my own "Elizabethan style" sampler. I wondered how there was so much wonderful talent in an age when, contrary to popular belief, life was busier than now. Later I realised that that was the key - the many tasks and skills of the Elizabethan housewife involving herbs, gave her a love and understanding of the plants which showed through in the embroidery. The skills with herbs I already possessed, the question of repeating their standard of needlework, might, of course, be another matter.

Herbs had been very much a feature of everyday life before Elizabeth I came to the throne and I decided to look a little further back into history to compare medieval needlework with that from Tudor and Stuart times.

Medieval needlework

A similar flowering of needlework appears, co-incidentally or not, I found, with more settled times and the consequent introduction of gardens as we know them. The flowered meadow was surrounded by banks of earth, often covered by chamomile to make seats, and became a grassy, flower-speckled mead. The petite perfection of the flowers which grow amongst the shorter grasses, appear as a fascinating, almost solid background on tapestries.

Several elements of the medieval garden found their way into stitchery of various kinds. The rose-covered trellis which enclosed chamomile seats or parts of the garden, the chamomile banks themselves and the small "tuffets" of raised flowers amongst the grasses - with gillyflowers (pinks), lilies of the valley, heartsease, violets, wild strawberry plants, daisies and forget-me-nots. In some paintings of the period we see ladies out in the garden working at their embroidery and may imagine a talented needlewoman portraying a herb flower exactly as she saw it in the afternoon sunshine.

We know that the wealthy wore embroidered clothes. On reading Geoffrey Chaucer, writing in **The Canterbury Tales** in the second half of the 14th century, I found him describing the handsome young squire:- "Embroudue was . . . as it were a meede / Al ful of fresshe floures, whyte and reede." Even gold threads decorated bed hangings as well as church vestments; in Chaucer's writings we find: "I woll gyve him a featherbed / Rayed with golde and ryght well cled".

At this time herb and flower motifs would have been embroidered on a separate background and then cut out to apply to silk or velvet. Wool needlework continued through the Middle Ages. The term embroidery was used to refer to working on silks, while needlework might be applied to decorative stitches on a much wider range of materials, involving various techniques.

Any elaborate work was expensive and associated either with the Queen and her ladies at court, or professional embroiderers who were well paid in comparison to other craftsmen. **The Canterbury Tales** again gives us clues as Chaucer writes of the haberdashers, dyers and weavers as wealthy merchants. The designs of medieval embroideries show elements of the manuscript illuminations of the period, which is not surprising, since the same artists supplied the embroidery patterns. As far as church embroidery is concerned, appreciation of herbs seems to have been extremely small. Perhaps this was partly because the design and stitching was carried out by professional men rather than women with knowledge of household affairs and herbal use.

The heyday of English embroidery with much beautiful work being exported and embroiderers taking commissions overseas came to an end with the Black Death in the 14th century. The flowing circles and tree of life designs were replaced by strapwork, split stitching by stem stitch, and the English flair set aside in favour of European fashions. However, all was not lost, and in the following century we find the wealthy owning magnificent bed-hangings decorated with gold roses or swans and bright flowers portrayed together. The wealthy lady practised her needlework in the garden as well as in the house and although she might employ a man to paint the design, her love of flowering herbs could emerge as she selected the subject matter. For furnishings, a linen canvas was used and embroidered with tent stitch to give a durable as well as attractive material.

Elizabethan needlework

When I returned to researching the Tudor period, I was reminded that this was when embroidery truly came into its own. For the wealthy, almost every article of clothing, together with cushions, chest-tops, wall hangings, bed·hangings, coverlets, chair seat covers, jewellery boxes and so on, were covered in fine embroidery. The earliest English needlework carpet known was worked about 1550, but of course carpets covered tables and chests long before they were set on the floor. The range of mediums, with silk embroidery, tent stitch motifs appliqued onto velvet, crewelwork, blackwork, goldwork and stumpwork, was equally exciting. Young girls were expected to work samplers as they learnt needlework, taking several herb subjects and working them in each medium to explore the possibilities for their later projects. I spent happy days studying more beautiful samples of needlework. To my joy these abounded with herbs - roses, gillyflowers, heartsease or pansies, violets, borage, lilies, strawberries and woodbine (honeysuckle) were the most popular choice. Primroses, jessamine (jasmine), lavender, foxgloves, daffodils, bluebells, cornflowers, periwinkle, peony, rue, rosemary, cyclamen and germander are some less familiar subjects.

As a luxurious item of clothing, often given as a present, detachable sleeves were heavily embroidered and occasionally covered in a fine lawn to soften the effect of stark blackwork, sometimes outlined with gold. Blackwork also appeared on collars and pillowberes (pillowcases), as it needed a white fabric background for full effect. We see more of the scrolling tendrils enclosing realistic flowers in this work than the herb "slips", which dominate the tent stitch motifs applied to a velvet ground. Inspired, I began to plan my own embroidery and looked at the smaller items. Gloves were embroidered and scented and even a Bible, or perhaps, a herbal, might have an embroidered velvet cover or bag to protect it. Again, this was decorated with roses - a favourite of great importance in the stillrooms - or other herbs, worked in tent stitch on linen and then appliqued onto the rich background. The idea of embroidering a book-cover attracted me as it would also supply a suitable protection for my oldest herbal.

Design sources

When planning this project I looked at design sources and learnt that a herbal was as likely to have been the origin of the design as the garden itself. The invention of printing in the mid-15th century had led to the first embroidery pattern books, but herbals offered many suitable illustrations for the herbwise housewife to follow. I had seen many embroidered slips of herbs. Slips were cuttings, and if we look in the illustrations of **Culpeper's Complete Herbal,** which was a favourite design source for needleworkers, we will find many herbs shown in this way. I hoped that as the love of herbs and great familiarity with their uses, strengths, folklore, leaf texture and flower forms show through in the exceptional work surviving from this period, I might capture some of the same spirit in my humble offering.

Transferring the design seemed the next hurdle and again I looked to history. In 1586 a book appeared offering illustrations of animals, birds, herbs and fruits. This was called **La Clef des Champs,** and was dedicated to all craftsmen who could "pounce" the illustrated patterns to copy them. Pouncing involves pricking the outlines of the design on the paper with a fine needle before laying the cloth beneath and dusting charcoal powder through the holes to transfer the design.

Looking in **Gerard's Herbal** for more illustrations, my fancy was taken by his description of the sunflower (then known as the marigold of Peru). He wrote of it as having a great flower like a chamomile with a border of leaves that he likened to those of lilies and a centre :- "as it were of unshorn velvet, or some curious cloath wrought with the needle". Who could resist such an invitation to embroider a herb? I was reminded of the intense interest taken by Elizabethans in plant introductions from the New World. This, I realised had shown in their embroidery with sunflowers, tulips and nasturtiums (then known as yellow lark's heels).

Symbolism was of great importance when planning a design, and symbol or emblem books were consulted. These I did not have to hand, but rosemary for remembrance, pansies for love-in-idleness and the wild strawberry as a symbol of purity I already knew. I also remembered that as early as the medieval period thyme had been embroidered with a bee hovering above the flowers, to signify a combination of activity and strength with a quiet, patient nature. I was surprised that borage continued with its earlier identity as a herb to give courage, from the ancient verse, "I borage bring alwaies courage". Whereas the Elizabethans - from their own use of the flowers in tarts, salads and wines, as Gerard writes, to "make the minde glad" – might have rechristened it a symbol of happiness. The many herbs, mostly white-flowered, which were associated with the Virgin Mary, such as the lily, I knew represented innocence. The references in Shakespeare's plays to flower meanings tells us they were widely understood at the time and have ensured our own knowledge.

Flights of fancy

A stumpwork box is another project which fascinates me. The heights of creativity were reached with stumpwork which often covered caskets and mirror frames, or provided a picture in its own right. In this raised work, figures, birds, animals, insects and elaborate gardens were brought into 3-D with the clever use of silks, seed pearls, wools, metal threads, and hands and faces bought ready-carved in wood or ivory. Leaf forms were imitated by couching thin wire bound with silk, and whole strawberries might be padded out with wool or horsehair to give the appearance of luscious fruit. The favourite gillyflowers, roses, borage etc often have a butterfly, ladybird, snail or bee close by.

In the 16th century, stumpwork, which could be bought in kit-form, offered only controlled flights of fancy. Yet it illustrates a design feature not unusual at that period. The proportion of insect to plant, plant to animal and so on was often completely ignored. I took comfort – when faced with design problems - in the success of their fanciful results. Particular favourites such as pansies might be enlarged out of all proportion to their true appearance – in those days, pansies were still a similar size to heartsease, with the giant pansies yet to be introduced. Occasionally the same herb might be shown in varying sizes in different parts of the embroidery for special effects, and, in embroidery design since, I have enjoyed imitating this freedom.

In more conventional embroidery another perennial favourite, the honeysuckle, had progressed from the elegantly twined border to spread over the material in scrolling tendrils, enclosing a variety of other herb flowers – irises, pansies, gillyflowers, roses, wild strawberries, borage and pot marigolds being the more popular. A modern interpretation of the scrolling pattern might include a dormouse peeping from within the coiling tendrils, since the dormouse weaves its nest from honeysuckle bark.

When studying embroideries I was delighted to find that in Tudor work small insects and birds accompany the herb flowers, just as they might in a real garden. Scale is once again ignored since butterflies are portrayed as larger than flowers, while a beetle half the size of a leopard and snails huge enough to horrify any gardener accompany some herbs, together with equally dominant, but more friendly ladybirds. Perhaps the same sense of fun which encouraged the fashion of trick fountains in Elizabethan gardens which squirted water at unsuspecting guests, is appearing here. Although even the insect life had a symbolic meaning within the embroidery. Moths referred to the swift passing of life, often cut short by sudden illness or injury, silkworms might signify an industrious nature, while snails were seen as the epitome of laziness, and the peacock became a symbol of Christ.

132

Later needlework

My interest continued and later I looked at fashions in needlework in the Stuart period to discover dramatic changes. Honeysuckle shrank back to the borders, joining ivy and periwinkle once more. Wild strawberries, lilies of the valley and the tiny flowers of the meadow fade into insignificance as an era of bright colours and bold designs opened. Changing perceptions of the world at large and ideas coming from abroad, along with imported materials and embroideries, show clearly. The Oriental influence is evident in plants with fantastic rather than realistic flowers and exotic foliage. I saw much of this turn of emphasis in crewelwork hangings.

Needlework in home dyed wools, applied to homespun twill combines the crafts of spinning, dyeing and needlework. This was often achieved with the talent of the housewife who also knew her herbs well. It is strange that the dye herbs of weld, madder, tansy, alkanet and meadowsweet rarely, if ever, appear. The first two are hardly inspirational, but the others could be most effective. Perhaps the dominance of blue-green or blue and brown in early crewelwork may provide an answer.

My search in later needlework for the joyous celebration of usefulness coupled with beauty in herb designs, was doomed to failure. The twining herbs so suitable for borders remained popular - ivy, honeysuckle, periwinkle, nasturtiums, wild roses, jasmine and even the humble convolvulus. Garden roses have never lost their attraction, but they are seen in a different light. In the 19th century a Berlin printer made considerable changes to needlepoint design by printing coloured charts which could be studied to enable the stitches to be counted out on the canvas. The influence of these was such that needlepoint became known as "Berlin Work". At this point the inspirational influence was completely divorced from the needleworker's experience and I realise from my own childhood efforts with kits, possibly as far away from true needlework as painting by numbers is from art.

Needlework today

However, in this century fashions in needlework of all kinds have changed and seen new developments. Talent thrives and is encouraged both by official Embroiderer's Guild sources and the independent spirit of the second "Elizabethan" era which drives us to seek ways of producing our own patterns and adding the personal touches of once more seeking inspiration in our immediate surroundings.

The interest in conservation in recent years has perhaps supported the appearance of wild poppies, daisies and the ever-perennial wild strawberry, so beloved in the far past, in contemporary designs. With the return of the herb garden and knowledge of herbal qualities and characteristics, it is once again possible for the ordinary person to express a love and knowledge of particular herbs in stitchery of all kinds. We no longer need to be able to spin and dye the wools or silks, but the opportunity is there for the adventurous who have the time. The range of shades in wools and silks has increased dramatically with synthetic dyes, but often the most sympathetic colours are natural. Both home-produced and commercial embroidery wools have their advantages. It is extremely difficult to produce the right purple for violets, for instance, with natural dyes, and the blues and reds are comparatively limited. On the other hand, naturally obtained shades are rarely garish and almost always look right alongside each other in a way certain synthetic dye colours most definitely do not.

Herbs in your own needlework design

If you do wish to experiment with natural dyeing to enhance your original design, then there is sufficient information in the dyes for wool in pages 143-155 to offer suitable hues for a range of herb foliage and flowers. You may even go to the lengths of spinning and weaving your own linen on which to embroider.

As for inspiration for the subject of your embroidery, we have a considerable advantage over the needlewomen and men of the past in that we can capture a herb at its best in a moment - in a photograph. We do not need the talent to paint its delicate beauty in order to record the exact colourings, since colour photography gives us a record which lasts even longer than pressing the flowers and leaves themselves. Do experiment with black-and-white photography as well, which seems to make the outlines stand out in quite a spectacular way. Pressed herbs, instructions for which can be found on pages 97-99, can be a wonderful design tool. Not only do these give us the relationships of size of one herb to another, their colour and forms, but we can place them against different coloured backgrounds and arrange and re-arrange them until we are satisfied with our design.

Designs may be formed with the aid of photographs or a tour of your own garden, and taken from deliberate or chance companion plantings within flower beds and even in wild situations. The first natural combination to inspire me was the sight of a tall stand of fennel, bejewelled with dew and embraced by a coiling, exploratory tendril of golden hop which twined elegantly around it. Stately bushes of salad burnet with the outer stems curved into candelabra shapes, heartsease peeping cheekily out from amongst the stems of St. John's wort, the majesty of a biennial clary sage in flower, bright blue stars of borage and the delicacy of pinks have also fascinated me.

If individual herbs inspire you, then you may wish to portray these as part of a posy, in a garland with other herb flowers or foliage, or standing alone. In the last instance a herbal illustration may be as helpful as a photograph when deciding how best to show the flowers and leaves. You can use part of a herbal illustration by tracing exactly what you need and omitting the root, or some of the leaves and stems, rather than copying it in entirety. **The Craftsman's Plant Book,** written by Richard Hatton and first published in 1909, shows many herbal illustrations and plants ranging from monkshood to salad burnet and the rowan tree to artichokes (Dover Books republished this work in 1960 under the new title of **The Handbook of Plant and Floral Ornament).** Richard Hatton, in addressing the would-be designer, discusses the ideal approach to the work. He feels that conquering and understanding geometrical forms is a necessary starting point and warns that it is a mistake to ignore normal plant growth by twisting stems into unnatural shapes and positions. In his view one of the chief errors is not really caring about the plant, and he goes on to make clear what anyone may see from looking at the varying portrayals of herbs in needlework over the centuries a love and knowledge of the plant itself is an important factor in design. He writes of creating a "portrait of the plant", but at the same time retaining a sense of "architectural fitness" and "rhythm".

It would be easy, having read his words and derogative statements about "mere still-life rendering", to feel totally unfitted for the task, yet if love of the herb is there, as we see in many historical samples, it is possible to find other charms than a perfect plant structure which can bring an embroidery almost to life. He recommends studying Kate Greenaway's floral designs before beginning on one's own.

Thomasina Beck in her lovely work, **The Embroiderer's Garden,** gives plenty of support and encouragement for the beginner, with advice on choosing viewpoints, framing what you see, choice of stitches for special effects, including quilting and applique in your embroidery, and portraying walls, hedges, paths and garden ornaments to complement your choice of flowers and foliage.

Reading her book may inspire you further to explore your choice of herb or herbs in a collage of different threads and background fabrics. One flowering plant might be embroidered in silks, another version worked in wools, another with beads and pearls added - with the stitches chosen changing to suit the medium. Bright orange pot marigolds, blue borage and a variety of pinks might be shown in patchwork effect, just as working Elizabethan samplers presented many possibilities and developed the embroiderer's skills before she applied them on larger works. Thomasina Beck also returns our attention to the Elizabethan habit of using herbal illustrations for inspiration.

Using herbals today

With a set of small curtains in mind, I decided to imitate Jacobean crewelwork on these to put my homespun and dyed wools to good use. Almost inevitably, I soon found the irrepressible wild strawberry, heartsease, honeysuckle, pot marigold and borage emerging in my initial ideas. Not being an artist I enlisted my mother's help in providing me with small paintings of the herbs based on illustrations in old herbals for the curtain designs. We then photocopied these onto transparent film, producing copies at three different sizes to give the possibility of placing smaller versions of the herb in a border, or to appear in the background of the larger plant. I have experimented both with transferring the designs onto the fabric using dressmaker's carbon and a tracing wheel, and cutting out stencils of the designs which, I find, can give a clearer outline. Other methods are available with a variety of transfer pencils and dyes. Tracing the design onto soft tissue and embroidering through both this and the fabric tacked below is another approach you may prefer. The tissue is then carefully torn away when you have finished working. There are, of course other ways of approaching your design.

Using photography

Even the smallest herb garden may offer inspiration, if not an entire planting, perhaps in a single flower, or bush of variegated foliage. When I am planning a new garden area, I like to take the camera and simply use the viewfinder as a means of focussing my attention even before many of the herbs are planted. Taking photographs in your garden also helps to identify the best angles in portraying the herb. You are at once aware of its good side if it has one, of a clutter of stems which may point to cutting some before taking the shot, and, inevitably of that weed that so often seems to have sprung from nowhere as soon as a photograph is required.

Through recording herbs with photographs year after year I have built up a store of pictorial ideas including those which have a bee, butterfly, ladybird, toad or bird in the frame. One of the toads in my garden can often be seen basking in the sun in the low, sheltered circles of hedge provided by my closed knot. I have even known this large toad remain in the knot for a full hour as I am clipping the hedges, steadily moving round the circle just ahead of me, while keeping a baleful eye on my unwelcome disturbance. Knot gardens are a wonderful source of inspiration with the possibilities of imitating the variegated foliage of silver and golden thymes or golden box. Silver can also be introduced with cotton lavender, while variations of shiny and dull foliage can be interpreted with matt or shiny threads as well as using tiny or more open stitches. Tufted stitches, reminiscent of the Victorian plush stitch, give wonderful three-dimensional effects to knot hedges. Within the knot, brightly coloured flowers might appear as French knots to accentuate the different growth pattern of these herbs.

The possibilities opened by taking individual herbs and using them in a repeated pattern are also promising. Having chosen your main herb and settled upon its appropriate design form, each copy of this might be nestled within an Elizabethan scrolling curve (perhaps presented as honeysuckle) to separate one from another, or within strictly geometrical divisions which might be worked as lines of chain stitch. The ladder-like formation of salad burnet or stems and leaves of Jacob's ladder are perfect in this situation. You might even arrange a diamond shape of four leafy salad burnet stems about a single flowerhead, with its tassel-like male flowers suspended as an elegant fringe and just a tiny length of stem shown.

Pressed flowers
Although I have previously described only such curling tendrils of growth as honeysuckle, periwinkle, ivy, wild roses, nasturtium and so on as suitable for borders, those herb flowers that are naturally found in the front of garden beds can also be charmingly adapted in simplified form to repeated border patterns. Forget-me-nots, primroses, cowslips, violets, basil, chives and thrift are pretty depicted as clumps, while the individual flowers of violets, primroses, lungwort and cowslips can be strung together by a creeping wild strawberry runner. This is where pressed flowers can be of most assistance in the planning and designing stage, for you may have a stock of similar flowers which can be tried with different spacings on a prepared background. You will soon see whether the repetition of the one herb will work, or whether you need to alternate two or three different herbs, possibly within a uniform framework in order to achieve the desired effect.

The other advantage of a pressed flower is that the very act of pressing it has simplified the design shape for you in the transformation from a three-dimensional plant to a two-dimensional form. A herb that presses well generally also embroiders easily. The herb leaves which I now find a preference for are the salad burnet already mentioned, sweet woodruff with its wonderful spiky rosettes of leaves and tiny white flowers which seem perfect to be worked in cross-stitch, variegated meadowsweet which also adapts well to needlepoint since the variegation tends to follow angular rather than curving lines, golden hop with similarly stepped leaf edges – and jasmine.

Pressed flower designs can also be worked in an exact copy by glueing down the herb flowers and foliage on a card background and tracing over this to give a pattern. For needlepoint designs, it is possible to buy a squared graph tracing paper produced specially for needleworkers and with the same number of squares per inch as the tapestry canvas. You can then colour or code the squares of the graph accordingly and use it as a counted chart to work to, or tape it behind your canvas and stitch through both as with the soft tissue in embroidery.

It is fun to make small cushions with needlepoint squares backed with plain velvet and fill these with fragrant dried herbs. The same design might be repeated and applied to the centre of a cushion or framed and hung on the wall. The once-popular design of a bee hovering over thyme can be enlivened by introducing lurex thread into the wings of the bee. This small project, or that of the pinks, may open your thoughts to many more elaborate designs from your favourite herbs. The forms of the more difficult - but exceedingly attractive - bergamot, hyssop, water avens, mullein, *Iris germanica,* biennial clary sage and betony would also make exceptional subjects for embroidery or needlepoint.

The variegated leaves that abound in my Treasure garden with thymes, elder, holly, box, meadowsweet, tricolor and golden sage, rue and tansy may be used to great effect in designs so avoiding large patches of greenery and adding the stamp of originality to your work.

Thyme for honey

A bee hovering over thyme was embroidered on scarves centuries ago. Ladies then gave them as favours to be worn by knights of their choice at the jousts. The embroidery tradition is commemorated in this design.

You will need:

1 hank of crewel or homespun wool in each of the following

colours –	D.M.C.	Appletons crewel wool
cream	7579	841
green	7346	833
light brown	7463	122
yellow	7786	552
lilac	7241	451
white	blanc	991b
black	noir	991
dark brown	7238	186

1 reel or card of gold lurex thread
tapestry canvas, 14 threads to the inch. ½ metre (½yd) will be sufficient for three squares.

The finished square measures 13 x 13cm (5¼ x 5¼in)

Look closely at the graph on the pattern sheet before stitching and note the special features. Emphasis is given to the movement of the bee by working the body and one wing with the stitches slanting from top left to bottom right. The remainder of the central panel is in conventional tent stitch. A single gold thread is added over the needlepoint to outline the bee's wings, lending the effect of sunlight.

Stitching the design

Begin by marking the central vertical and horizontal lines of your needlepoint panel onto the canvas with tacking stitches. Next, carefully mark the diagonal lines from the centre of the panel in the same way.

Thread the needle with crewel wool and work the yellow outline of the inner square in tent stitch (see diagram 1a). Complete the panel, following the graph and referring to the illustration on page xviii if necessary. With the exception of the central line of stitching, which includes the stem of the flowerbud, repeat this pattern to form the border. Each flower has only one stem, see illustration.

The border is worked in a vertical variation of long stitch, (see diagram 1b) covering first 2, then 4, 6, 8 and 10 threads, before reducing to 8, 6, 4, and 2 threads, forming a diamond pattern. A double row of tent stitch surrounds the border edge.

The finishing touches

As a picture – Cut a piece of strong card to the exact size of the panel and stretch the needlepoint over this, pinning along the edges to secure. Stitch the edges together as in diagram 1c to hold the needlepoint tightly in place. Remove the pins. Place the needlepoint in the centre of a card mount, inside the picture frame. Or set it into a frame which is the exact size. In either case, non-reflective glass is recommended to show the picture to best advantage.

As a fragrant cushion – Cut a square of velvet or close-weave fabric 15cm (6in) square. Lay the finished picture face down onto the right side of the fabric. Stitch three sides of the square, keeping the line of stitching very close to the outer border of the needlepoint. Turn right side out. Fill with a cheesecloth or fine mesh sachet of fragrant herbs. Stitch the final edge closed.

To decorate a larger cushion – Stretch the front of the cushion in an embroidery or tapestry frame and measure carefully to find the exact centre. Mark the central vertical and horizontal lines with tacking. Pin the needlepoint in the centre with the edges turned neatly underneath. Pin and tack. Remove earlier tacking stitches. Using a large-eyed needle attach the panel, taking each stitch up through the cushion fabric and back through the edge stitches of the needlepoint. This will cover any tapestry canvas showing. It is most important to maintain a straight line with these stitches. Remove tacking and make up as a plain cushion cover.

In the pink

This pattern was inspired by the sports or occasional unique flowers on the herb shown with the small cushion in the illustration on page xviii.

You will need:

l hank each of crewel or homespun wool in the following

colours –	D.M.C.	Appletons crewel wool
dark red	7209	149
light green	7335	641
dark green	7348	646
pink	7760	224
white		9916

tapestry canvas 14 threads to the inch. ½ metre (½yd) will be sufficient for three squares.

The finished square measures 13 x 13cm (5¼ x 5¼in)

Stitching the design

Begin by marking the central vertical and horizontal lines of your needlepoint panel onto the canvas with tacking stitches. Next, carefully mark the diagonal lines from the centre of the panel in the same way. Thread the tapestry needle with dark red wool and outline the inner square with tent stitch (see diagram 1a). The whole of the inner design is worked in this stitch. Refer to the graph for details of colour.

To complete the border, work the dark green lines first in straight stitch (see diagram 2a). Next, add a row of backstitching down the diagonal line as the straight stitches meet (see diagram 2b). The horizontal straight stitches over two threads in light green should be completed before the white areas. Smaller straight stitches over a single thread are worked alternately at the top and bottom of the white stitching to complete the pattern. The illustration on page xviii should be consulted carefully as these are worked. Again a double row of tent stitch encloses the border. For the finishing touches refer to the instructions already given for the thyme for honey square.

Stitch diagrams

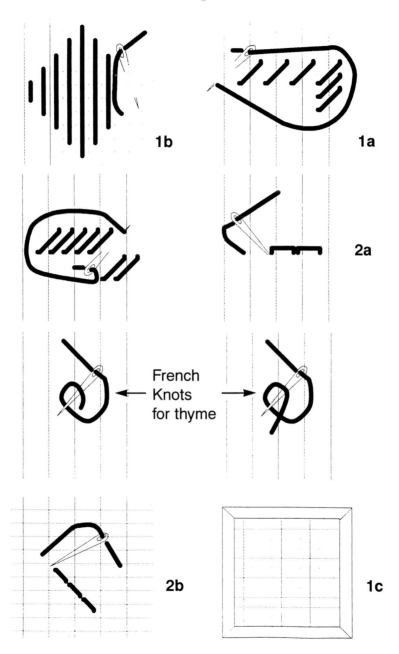

1b

1a

2a

French
Knots
for thyme

2b

1c

Thyme for honey – Centre square

```
YYYYYYYYYYYYYYYYYYYYYYYYYYYYYYYYYYYYYYYYYYYY
Y                                          Y
Y                                          Y
Y                                          Y
Y                                          Y
Y                                          Y
Y                                          Y
Y        YY      W                         Y
Y        DDDD    W                         Y
Y        DDDDDWWW                          Y
Y      WWWDDDYYYWWW                        Y
Y      WWWYYYYDDWWW                        Y
Y      WWWWDDDDDWWW         L              Y
Y       WWWDDDDDWW         LLL             Y
Y        WWWWYYY          LLLLL            Y
Y         DDWW         G LLL   G           Y
Y         DWD            G B GG            Y
Y                        GGBGG             Y
Y             L          B       LL        Y
Y            LL         GBG     LL         Y
Y            LLL      G B G   GLLL         Y
Y           G B        GBG     LL          Y
Y           GBG      G B G   G BGGG        Y
Y          G B G G    GBG      BG          Y
Y          GBBBG      B G GB               Y
Y            B  G   BG   B GG              Y
Y          G GBGG  GB G BG                 Y
Y          GGBBB G BG   B                  Y
Y             BG  B  BGG                   Y
Y          GGGBBBB  BG                     Y
Y                  B B                     Y
Y                  BB                      Y
Y           BBBB      B                    Y
Y      BB      B   BBBBB                   Y
Y      B BBBBBB                            Y
Y      B  B B                              Y
Y        B                                 Y
Y                                          Y
YYYYYYYYYYYYYYYYYYYYYYYYYYYYYYYYYYYYYYYYYYYY
```

```
Y = yellow
G = green
B = light brown
L - lilac
W = white
D = dark brown
```

All of the background is in cream

141

In the pink – Centre square

```
DDDDDDDDDDDDDDDDDDDDDDDDDDDDDDDDDDDDDDDDDDDD
D                                          D
D                                          D
D                                          D
D                        G                 D
D       DDDD             G                 D
D     DDDPPDDD          g G                 D
D    DPPDPPPDD D        gGGg                D
D DDDPP   DDPDDDD        Ggg                D
D DDPPDDDPDPPPDDD        Gg                 D
D DDDDPDPPPD PPD      gg Gg       P P   P P D
D  DDDP   PPD PDDD    gGgg       PPPDP DP P D
D DPPDPPDPPPPDPPD      GG        PPDP DPPP  D
D DPPPDDPPDDP PDD      g         DDDDDPDPP  D
D  DP PDDD  DPPD gG  GG           GDGDDP    D
D  DPPDGDPPPPDDD  gGGg            GGG       D
D  DDDGGGDPDD      gg              G        D
D    GGGDD        GgG         G   G         D
D    G           Ggg          G G          D
D   G           Gg G          Ggg          D
D   G           Gg  g         Ggg          D
D  GG           Gg  G          Ggg  g      D
D   GG          GgG  g         GGGgGG       D
D   GG        Gg    gg       GggGGGgg       D
D   G    GgG       ggGGgggGgG               D
D   G  Gg          gg     GG                D
D   GGGg                   g                D
D    gG G                 GG                D
D    Gg                  gG  GGG            D
D    gG                  GgGG   G           D
D    g                   GG       GG        D
D    GG                  g         G        D
D  GG  ggG              gG         G        D
D  GGgGG  g            G                    D
D   GGGGgGGGGgGgGGgG                        D
D           Gg                              D
D                                          D
D                                          D
D                                          D
DDDDDDDDDDDDDDDDDDDDDDDDDDDDDDDDDDDDDDDDDDDD
```

```
D = dark red
P = pink
G = dark green
g = pale green
```

All of the background is in white

Dyes for wool

ALTHOUGH many spinners dye their own homespun wool, either in the fleece, or when the wool has been spun and plyed, it is not necessary to be a spinner to enjoy this craft. Plain wool can be bought and dyed at home to produce a rainbow of soft, natural shades to delight weavers, knitters and needleworkers alike.

In all of these crafts it is a joy to produce combinations of unique colours which are soft on the eye and blend well. This is not to say that no plants yield vivid colours, simply that these are the more unusual. The range of yellows, greens, browns, blues, reds, pinks, purples, oranges, tans and blacks are obtained from leaves, stems, flowers, roots, seeds, bark, fruits or nuts.

There is always a measure of unpredictability in the resulting shade as the mineral content and ph level of the soil surrounding the plant, the maturity of the harvest, which mordant has been added to the wool, the softness or hardness of the water and its temperature in the dyebath can all affect the final result. Even using an aluminium or copper pan rather than stainless steel can add mordant, so changing the colour. Similarly, afterbaths of salt or vinegar, or sprinkling a little iron into the dyepan for the last few minutes of simmering, can change the colour completely.

Natural dyeing, then, is a constant experiment, and for this reason one should, ideally, dye the total amount of wool needed for a whole project in one batch in order to achieve the same shade. For many, however, a large measure of the fun is in the ever-present possibility of producing a surprising and excellent batch of a shade never achieved by the dyer before. No elaborate equipment is required, simply, measures, a large pan which takes at least 4.5 litres (8 pints) of water, old wooden spoons or a glass rod, rubber gloves and time.

A general guide to the colours and shades that may be achieved with particular combinations of herb and mordant is given in this section. Also some details for the more useful dyes, taken from my own record book. Do not be disappointed if your experience is different because of variations in any of the factors above. Sometimes the very best results happen when a different colour is expected.

Do keep a record book of your own, noting which herb is used, where it was gathered from and when, its maturity, the amount of herb in the dyebath, time simmered to produce the colour, and the mordant added and time simmered with the wool entered. A small sample of dyed wool attached to the page will complete your guide for future experiments.

Natural dyes have a very long history which can be traced back through all manner of written records and archaeological finds over thousands of years. The ancient Egyptians valued saffron and indigo. The use of woad as a bodypaint by the ancient Britons is well known, thanks to Roman records. Those herbs we find harvested on a commercial scale in later centuries – woad, madder, weld, saffron, indigo, etc - are superior to many others in their fastness during washing or exposure to sunlight. Many plant dyes tend to fade a little but often stabilise with an even more attractive shade. Heirlooms of dyed materials which have been handed down over centuries often still retain pleasant and, occasionally, bright colours.

With a project that will need frequent washing, it is advisable to keep some dyed wool aside to make up first as a sample, washing it a few times and noting the results against the original shade. Dyed wool dried in the sun will give an early indication of fastness to light.

Mordants are used to increase the fastness of the colour and are needed with most, though not all, dye herbs. Whether a mordant is to be used or not, the wool must first be well washed in soapy water, rinsed and then soaked for an hour or so to expand the fibres so that they will absorb mordant and dye, or dye alone, thoroughly. Warm water rather than very hot is recommended. When bringing wool to simmering point for mordanting or dyeing, it is best to do so slowly - over a period of about 45 minutes in order not to damage the wool fibres. The wool and mordant are simmered on for another 30-45 minutes, and left to cool. The wool can then be taken out of the mordant and the excess liquid pressed, rather than wrung out of it, before drying to store ready for dyeing or entering into a prepared dyebath. With both mordants and dyes there should be sufficient space in the pan for the wool to move about in the solution; correct dilution is also important to results and so a pan to contain 4.5 litres (8 pints) of water is the smallest used for 50g (2oz) wool. Choice of mordant depends on the particular colour and brightness required. When the wool has been prepared by washing and soaking, it can be entered into the pan with the mordant already dissolved into the water at a hand-hot temperature.

The one exception is **iron** – also listed in old recipes as green vitriol or copperas, and in modern as ferrous sulphate – which is added for the last 15 minutes of the dyebath to deepen or "sadden" the effect of the dye. It is mostly used where grey-black, green or sometimes brown is wanted. When the dye being used is weld, iron can also turn the yellow already achieved to green (see the following recipes). A very small amount of iron is added; for example when dyeing 50g (2oz) wool in 4.5 litres (8 pints) of water, I have used only a rounded ½ teaspoon. One teaspoon of cream of tartar can be added at the same time.

By contrast, chrome and tin, both toxic materials, will brighten colours and are associated with reds, gold and bronze dyes. In general, such toxic mordants are only available from specialist suppliers (see appendix). **Chrome,** or bichromate of potash, is light sensitive which means taking extra time and trouble to exclude light from the wool, both while mordanting and when the wool is in the dyebath. If the mordanted wool is stored before dyeing, it should also be kept in the dark until the process has been completed. Chrome is added to the pan as the water reaches hand-heat and should be stirred in with a glass rod. A generous ¼ teaspoon is added to water for 50g (2oz) wool, but with chrome simmering should be continued for the full time with the wool entered. Rubber gloves should be worn when using toxic mordants and care taken to avoid inhaling the fumes. Using an outside source of heat, keeping an extractor fan running, or windows open, are sensible precautions. Some instructions add protective glasses to the list. Of course the most important precaution is to transfer mordants to screwtop jars as soon as you have opened them or even before. Label these clearly with a toxic reminder and keep them well out of the reach of children.

I have little experience of **tin** (stannous chloride), preferring other mordants since tin tends to make the wool brittle. As with chrome, add a ½ teaspoon to water for 50g (2oz) wool, also the same of cream of tartar to help to soften the action on the wool fibres.

Basketry

A selection of baskets – *Showing the posy basket (top), the rustic work basket, base of golden hop and bramble sides of honeysuckle. Ivy and cane baskets next to stems of red dogwood, ivy and balsam poplar. The miniature snowberry and broom basket in the making.*
(Right) *Shows the double row of weavers around the edge stakes forming the base of the rustic wool basket.*

Herbs in needlepoint

Pressed flower designs.

(Left) *Pinks, 'Dye' Tagetes.*

(Below) *'Lazy thymes' – cushion.*

Herbs in needlepoint

Pattern making.

(Below right) *Pot marigold patterns.*

Embroidery and crewel work.

Dyes

Herb dyes and mordants.

(Left) Wools for spinning.

(Below left) from
Top left clockwise
*Meadow sweet,
angelica, coreopsis,
tagetes.*

Dye records.

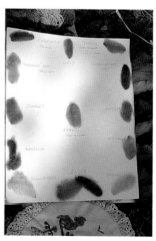

Fibre spinning

(Right) *Flax, ramie, sunflower and mallow stems.*

Woven nettle and flax.

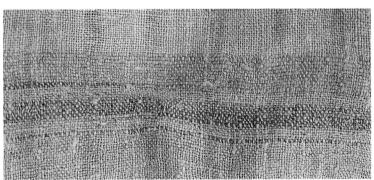

Paper making

Elderberry dyed paper and ink.

Dyed paper.

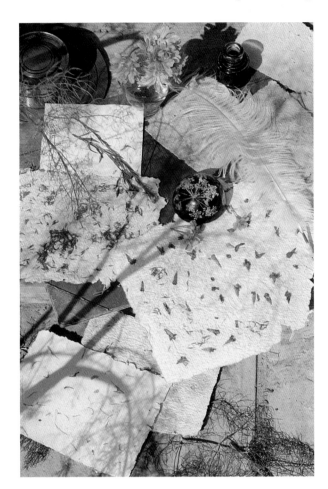

Paper with added dye petals, sunflower paper.

(Below) *Fennel paper.*

Woodcrafts

(Top left) *Turned herbal woods.*

Oak thrush.

Mordanting with **copper sulphate,** in old recipes sometimes listed as verdigris, is useful for blues and greens, although other colours can be achieved with this mordant. It may occasionally be added after the dye, as with iron; otherwise it is mostly partnered with cream of tartar, the two being dissolved in boiling water and then added to the pan before the wool. One teaspoon to 50g (2oz) wool is sufficient with a ½ teaspoon of cream of tartar.

The best non-toxic mordant is **alum (aluminium sulphate),** and this is also often assisted with cream of tartar. For 50g (2oz) of wool, dissolve 12g (½oz) of alum and ½ teaspoon of cream of tartar in a little hot water and add to the pan of water; enter the wool when the solution is hand-hot, simmering for a full hour.

Other substances that affect colourings are acids or alkalis in the form of vinegar or salt, yeast to ferment some dyes, malt, tannic acid, oxalic acid, washing soda, woodash, lemon juice and ammonia, which may be bought at the chemists or provided by urine which has been stored for a week – not everyone's choice! Afterbaths of vinegar will turn elderberry dye to a pretty pink, while an afterbath of salt can bring out blue shades. With some plants their acid or alkali content will change the colour effect of the mordant and dye together. Also, more than one colour can be obtained from certain herbs. By first fixing the yellow from weld with an alum mordant, the wool may be lifted out and while half is rinsed and dried, the other half can be returned to the dyepan after adding a little iron. The remaining yellow wool will turn green within a few minutes of further simmering.

Opportunities for different combinations of plant material and mordants are limited only by the dyer's source of supply and imagination. In the past, cottagers dyed their own homespun wool and linen with numerous herbs; some gathered in the wild and others grown in the garden. Although commercial production required more stable results, we can imagine many a housewife over the centuries experimenting with bright flowers and fruits or dark roots. A glance at the tables of plants and colours yielded shows that even a modest garden with comparatively few herbs can give a good selection for dye experiments. Should you wish to gather dye herbs from the wild, always make sure you are not seeking to gather a protected plant and ask permission before digging roots or harvesting in quantity.

In the recipes for the more useful dyes I have not included poisonous plants that are likely to affect you in dyeing use; please note, however, that snowberry and *Tagetes* are not recommended for consumption. Should you grow and use more powerfully poisonous herbs, or pick them in the wild, it is worth noting that some may affect you not only from handling, or through inhaling fumes as the plant material is simmering on the stove, but also from breathing in tiny particles from the wool as you card and spin. It is, therefore, safer to use these dyes on readyspun and plyed wool with plenty of fresh air while the dyeing process is taking place. Some plants can also produce allergic reactions on the skin; angelica is the only herb I have listed which may do this as you prepare it. Wearing rubber gloves when dyeing is a good idea for more than one reason.

In general, twice the quantity of herb to wool will be needed. Exceptions to this rule are the flowers of *Coreopsis, Tagetes* and dahlia which will each dye their own weight or more, very successfully. The herb leaves and stems, or flowers, are simmered very gently for up to one hour to extract the colour before entering the wool. Dahlias or *Tagetes* will give up their colour in 20 minutes or a little longer, while other herb flowers, such as tansy or *Coreopsis tinctoria,* require 50-60 minutes. As ever, let experiment be your guide.

Bark and roots need longer soaking and should be left at least overnight. The heartwood of yew needs even longer. Fruits, such as elderberries, ready-stalked and with a little added vinegar, can also be stood overnight to encourage the juice to flow.

A dye garden

AFTER a few successful experiments with herbs you are already growing, you may wish to plan a full dye garden. Your first consideration when doing this should be how large an area you are willing or able to give to each herb concerned, which also poses the question of how many different colours you will want to gather from your plot. If your total area is small then unless you are happy to dye only 50g (2oz) of wool in each colour per year, you should make a point of rejecting those herbs which take up a large area for a small harvest and particularly those which need to be grown for 2 or 3 years before harvesting, such as madder. Such a herb will take up three times the area of an annual, since you will always want to be bringing more plants on in readiness for harvest. Of course, it is possible to "cheat" a little with biennial plants by buying them in their second spring rather than growing them from seed.

With a small area, multi-value dyes should be a priority, along with annuals. In the first category, weld will give yellow and green and a thornless bramble might be trained along a fence or wall to give grey-black, pinks-purple and green. Annuals to add colour in the garden as well as your dyebath include *Coreopsis tinctoria* to give bright orange and red, and the tiny *Tagetes,* tangerine or lemon gem which will give bright yellows and tan-orange.

Suitability of the herbs to your soil is another factor; some herb roots, such as lady's bedstraw, can be satisfactorily harvested only from sandy soil. A large tub filled with an appropriate sandy mix could be used if the garden is of heavy clay.

If you have the space to grow a selection of dyes, but are not setting out to make a comprehensive collection, the following table shows those I have found most useful. Your own experiments may add more to this list, that is part of the fun. Refer to the herb cultivation section for each herb's soil, sun/shade requirements.

Selected Dyes

Yellow
dyer's chamomile
oregano
snowberry
tansy
weld

Orange
Coreopsis tinctoria
dahlia
dyer's chamomile
tangerine gem *Tagetes*

Red
alkanet root (best bought)
Coreopsis tinctoria
madder root

Pink-purple
bramble
elderberry
hop stalks

Blue	Green
elderberry	angelica
indigo (readily bought)	comfrey
woad	nettle
	sage

Tan-brown	Grey-black
fennel	bramble
gypsywort	gypsywort
tansy	meadowsweet root

For Yellows

Dyer's chamomile - This is a very easy herb to grow and makes a pleasing evergreen addition to the garden behind lower annuals, with a succession of bright flowers over some six to eight weeks of summer. The flowers can be gathered and dried for dyeing as well as being used fresh. Six plants give me ample harvest for my needs in July and August, although a weaver might want more. With alum mordanted wool and twice the quantity of newly opened bright yellow flowers which had been pre-simmered for one hour, I have obtained a pleasing, quite bright yellow.

Oregano – A herb that brings the pleasure of butterflies to the garden as well as a certain challenge as a multi-colour dye. I have oregano plants in almost every area of my garden as it is such a versatile herb; if restricted to a dye garden you might wish to grow a whole bed. I have obtained a bright, mustard yellow from harvesting in July or August and simmering the flowering tops for one hour, removing these - then adding wool mordanted with alum and cream of tartar and simmering for a further hour. Several years ago I found a mention of a purple dye obtained in medieval times using oregano tops and crab apple. I presumed the bark to be needed. Not having a ready source of crab apple bark, the experiment went into my "interesting" list and was half forgotten. Recently I found a recipe in Su Grierson's book, **The Colour Cauldron** which involved drying the flowering tops first and using crab apple leaves, fermenting the mixture with malt and yeast. Here is a new way for me to experiment.

Snowberry – These berries have given me some of my most delightful bright yellows, although they can give deeper, even khaki shades with slightly different preparation. I have always used a relatively large quantity of berries to wool and have now planted a snowberry hedge for a plentiful supply. Harvest time is October. Around 5 or 6 times the weight of wool gives a brilliant result, and simultaneous dyeing is best. I simmer the berries (which have been soaked overnight), held in a muslin bag to prevent them from tangling in the wool, giving them plenty of room to move in the dyebath for about an hour and then allow the liquor to cool. When it is only hand-hot I add the wool mordanted with alum and cream of tartar and simmer it for a further three-quarters of an hour, this has resulted in a lovely cowslip yellow. On one occasion, experimenting for khaki to green, I soaked the white berries overnight first, before heating them in the steeping water for one hour. Again adding the pre-mordanted wool with the berries still in the dyepan. This time the mordant was ferrous sulphate but instead of the expected khaki I obtained a gingery yellow. This may have been partly due to the light frost which had already touched the berries.

Tansy – A dominant herb, it gives a good harvest of flowers and leaves and spreads with such vigour that if you start with only one plant, you will soon have sufficient for dye experiments. It is really best contained, or grown in a bed on its own. In late summer the tall stems may need support since the heavy flowerheads pull the stems down in high winds. Gather the flowers as soon as they open, for in wet weather they readily become soaked and spoil. I simmer twice the weight of flowers to wool for about one hour, obtaining a good yellow with alum mordanted wool. The green leaves and top stems can be included with a different mordant for a tan colour.

Weld – This is one dye herb I would definitely not be without. While it is not a particularly attractive plant in the garden, a few bright flowers around it will add colour. Always keep some young plants coming on with seed each year, remembering that it is the second year plants that are harvested. I pick mine generally in July or August when the flowers are just opening. The whole plant can be used and I add double the weight of plant (weld has quite a heavy stem) to wool. Having simmered the weld for about one hour, I add the wool pre-mordanted with alum and cream of tartar and simmer again for some three-quarters of an hour. By this time the wool can be a beautiful, rich yellow. Lifting the wool out of the dyebath over a wooden spoon handle, I add a half teaspoon of iron and stir this in before returning half of the wool to the pan. While this simmers, I then rinse the yellow wool in first warm and then cold water and set it to dry. The second half of the batch is ready in a further 15 minutes to be taken off the stove and this I leave in the liquor to cool before rinsing it to reveal leaf green.

For Orange

Coreopsis tinctoria - The decorative plants are readily grown from seed and planted out in May to give colourful flowers by the end of June or July. These flowers can be dried for future use or the fresh flowers simmered for up to one hour to give a rich, red liquor. Both the yellow and red flowers will yield the same shades because the dye pigment is at the red heart of each flower. An equal weight of flowers to wool offers a good result when simmered for almost an hour. As an experiment, I tried a mix of fresh and dried flowers, allowing that the dried would have a stronger dyeing capacity. With the two together I obtained a deep red liquor in about an hour and having strained out the flowers, added the wool which had been pre-mordanted with chrome. A further hour of simmering gave a deep, reddish orange.

Dahlia – I have found it necessary to be careful as to which dahlias I use for dyeing. The size and form of the flowerhead will also determine how many will be needed to dye 25g (1oz) of wool. I have known one very large dahlia head dye this amount, whereas the smaller pompom dahlias generally require more. Red or bronze flowered dahlias have given the best results in my experience, while purple has done very little without yellow flowers to assist the dye and then the result is a gingerish yellow. For a bright orange dye, I have put 3 medium and 4 small red dahlia heads into 4.5 litres (8 pints) of water and simmered these for 15 minutes. This gave a brightly coloured liquor and left the petals colourless to the point of transparency. With the heads strained out I entered 100g (2oz) of wool pre-mordanted with chrome and simmered this for a further 20 to 30 minutes. I then left the wool to cool in the liquor, before rinsing and drying to obtain an attractive ginger-orange.

Dyer's chamomile – This has already been detailed as a yellow dye. For orange shades which are more towards tan than the brighter colours above, I pre-mordant the wool with chrome and simmer the flowers for about an hour as before. Having strained out the flowerheads, I enter the wool and simmer again for half an hour.

Tangerine gem Tagetes – These flowers are a delight to pick and use. Only half the weight of the wool in the tiny, bright flowers simmered for about 20 minutes will produce a good dye liquor. After straining the liquor, I enter chrome mordanted wool and simmer for a further 45 minutes. This produced a good ginger-orange.

For Reds

Alkanet – This herb has been an important dye in the past and might seem an essential in the dye garden, however the seeds or plants of *Alkanna tinctoria,* which offers the best dye source, are difficult to come by. My own experiments with closely related members of the alkanet family, all of which are supposed to contain some dye, have been disappointing, therefore I recommend buying prepared root and following the supplier's instructions which gives good results.

Coreopsis tinctoria – This is a dye already given under the orange shades - and may be deepened to brick red by adding a little washing soda to the dyebath. Chalcones, found in *Coreopsis* are ph sensitive pigments, and so various experiments may be tried with that in mind. The more I use *Coreopsis,* the more impressed I am by the number of flowers per plant, which seem to increase the more you pick them, and the consistently good results. A packet of seeds will more than likely give you between 20 and 30 plants, which will dye at least a pound of wool.

Madder – A herb that requires time and space in the garden and is probably only grown by keen dyers with fairly large gardens. A good area is needed as the plant must be left to mature for three years before digging the root in autumn. Clean it well and either chop into small pieces and pound for immediate use, or dry and grind in an electric grinder, storing the root powder. Having soaked the prepared root overnight, I heat it very carefully in water for an hour and a half, to reach the simmering point at which the wool should be entered. Boiling madder must be avoided or the yellow pigment will be released from the root instead of the red alizarin. A temperature of below 60°C has given the best results for me, but this is difficult to hold on an electric hob. I simmer the alum mordanted wool in the dye liquor for a further 45 minutes, before leaving it to cool in the dyebath, rinsing and drying. This gives me a strong, bright red.

For Pink-purple

Brambles – These are a ready source of dye and a pleasure to pick on a late summer walk in the country, or from your own garden. I have found little to be gained by leaving the brambles in a bowl overnight but have left them for an hour or so after picking before simmering them for the dye liquor. Brambles can also be used from the freezer and it is sometimes more convenient to freeze them for later use when there are so many preserves to be made at that time of year. Simmering for 45-60 minutes will give the dye liquor, and at this point I strain out the berries and enter alum mordanted wool. The result was paler than I had hoped, but deepened by an afterbath of vinegar.

Elderberries – Years ago, when living in a town, I was fortunate enough to have a friend with an elder tree which gave far more berries than she needed. Now I have grown my own elders and having picked the berries leave them to stand overnight in a large bowl to encourage the juice to flow before dyeing. A little vinegar can also be added to deepen the shade. For a small amount of wool, some 50g (2oz), I simmer 700g (1½lbs) of berries for 45 minutes in 2.25 litres (4 pints) of water. I then strain the liquor and dilute it with a further 2.25 litres (4 pints) of water before entering the wool, which has been pre-mordanted with alum, and simmer for a further 45 minutes. Elderberry dyes, although lovely at first even without a mordant, can fade quite quickly, both with light and washing. An afterbath of salt can alter an unsatisfactory pink to a bluish purple.

Hops – In my garden, they are grown primarily as a basketry material, but there are always lots of short ends of stalk which are discarded either as I unthread the long stems from the trellis which has supported them, or later on trim the finished baskets. Having chosen those from the golden hop with a deeper red in their stems, I chop them into 4-8cm (2 to 3in) lengths and soak these for an hour or so before simmering for almost an hour. I then strain out the stems which leave a rich, burgundy coloured liquor. I enter unmordanted wool and after a further hour of simmering this achieves a soft, but very definite pink. More experiments with mordants seem indicated to try to obtain darker shades.

For Blue

Elderberry – As just related under pinks, the elderberries should be picked and stalked, leaving them to stand overnight in a bowl to encourage more juice. As yet I have only succeeded in gaining a really satisfactory blue when dyeing paper with elderberry juice - rather than wool, and then used alum and salt (see papermaking section). It is reputedly possible to achieve blue with wool also, have fun experimenting!

Indigo – For several years, I have tried to grow indigo with little success, since the sudden bursts of cold weather which often happen in Britain after we hope spring is well on will kill the young plants. I have, therefore, found it easier to buy indigo for dyeing. It is obtainable with full instructions as a dye kit and this is the best way to start, as the details of temperature when making up the dye solution and then using it, keeping oxygen out of the dyebath and then dipping and exposing the wool to the air repeatedly are vital, and there is little space for such length here. Indigo can produce wonderful shades from pale blue through to deep hues and is well worth the trouble needed for the results.

Woad – This is another dye which is complex in its preparation, but in this case easy to grow in a temperate climate. In fact, woad is also linked historically to indigo; when indigo replaced it as a commercial dye, woad continued to be added to the indigo vats to aid fermentation. Woad does not require a mordant but does need to be kept at around 40-60°C for up to 12 hours in a sealed container before adding ammonia and then steeping the wool in the mix with air kept excluded. Bran and lime may be added. For home-grown woad and easy dyeing - Jill Goodwin gives good instructions in her book, A **Dyer's Manual.** Otherwise buy a woad dye kit which comes with full details. Pink, greys and green can also be obtained from woad.

For Green

Comfrey – The leaves may be harvested through into late summer for dyeing. Clearly it is best always to gather fairly young leaves in good condition. By pre-mordanting the wool with copper sulphate and cream of tartar, and simmering double its weight of comfrey leaves for almost an hour before adding the wool, I have obtained a particularly lovely, deep leaf-green. As the wool simmers in the dye liquor for a further hour, there is the additional benefit of the comfrey herb softening the wool in the process. The comfrey leaves were left in the dyepan when the wool was added (keep them enclosed in a muslin bag).

Angelica – My first harvest of angelica leaves and stems in spring is for rhubarb and angelica wine, but the next harvest of the stems for crystallising, in June, offers the bonus of the discarded leaves for dyeing a small amount of wool. I have also gathered them as late as September, collecting all that was left after the angelica syrup was made and before the frost destroyed them. At this point of the year I mordant 50g (2oz) of wool with copper sulphate and cream of tartar and simmer 125g (4oz) of angelica leaves in an aluminium pan for an hour. I then strain the liquid and simmer the wool for a further three-quarters of an hour. At the end of this time, I was disappointed to find that although the liquor was a good green, the wool remained a pale beige. I therefore lifted it out over a wooden spoon handle and stirred in a quarter of a teaspoon of iron. A quarter of an hour later the wool had achieved a deep green which was later much admired. The wool was left to cool in the dyebath before rinsing and drying.

Sage – So far I have not tried dyeing with green sage, having gathered purple sage first and found this most satisfactory. I gather the leaves and tops at their best, in July, before flowering. Using double the quantity of herb to wool, I simmer the leaves for almost an hour, giving a strong-smelling, deeply coloured green liquor. After straining this I enter the wool which has been pre-mordanted with chrome. Simmering for a further hour produces only a greenish yellow which after rinsing proves more grey than green. However, once the wool has been spun the deeper sage-green shows clearly with a very pleasing result.

Weld – The joy of weld, is of course, that it is a true multicolour dye. With an alum mordant and cream of tartar, the pigment luteolin, which is also present in dyer's broom, gives a brilliant yellow, rivalled only by snowberry at its best. I have achieved this colour by simmering the weld for an hour to make the liquor and then added the pre-mordanted wool for a further 45-60 minutes until the desired shade was reached. When dyeing wool for crewelwork I like to remove half the wool at this stage, to rinse and dry; I then stir in a small amount of iron before returning the remainder to the pan for the last 15 minutes of simmering and leaving to soak in the cooling liquor to give a soft, yet strong, green.

Nettles – These need to be gathered at the beginning of the year for the best results. In the later months I have ensured young growth only is harvested. Having pre-mordanted the wool with alum and cream of tartar I have always used the simultaneous method, putting the nettles into a muslin bag and bringing to simmer before adding the wool. I have taken care to swish the bag of herb in the water a little from time to time to spread the dye evenly. The greens I have obtained from both tops and roots with this method have proved rather pale, fading quickly, Further experiment, perhaps with a copper sulphate mordant seems indicated.

Grey-Black

Bramble – One experiment I have not yet tried, but which seems well recommended, is to simmer the young spring shoots of the bramble to give a dye colour. With iron as a mordant this can give a grey. A possibly deeper colour may be obtained by soaking the berries overnight with some vinegar, before following the dye recipe given above under pink-purple. This apparently can also give grey-black.

Gypsywort – Although trying to achieve a brown at the time, I discovered a good grey-black in gypsywort. I had left harvesting rather late as the herb was already flowering and harvest for brown should take place before the flowers open. However, I decided to try 125g (4oz) of chopped tops simmered in 3.5 litres (6 pints) of water for an hour. At the end of this time I strained the liquor, adding the wool. The dye liquor was rather pale and after three-quarters of an hour the wool was similarly poor in colour, being more fawn than anything. However, I lifted the wool out and added a little iron, stirring it well in before returning the wool to simmer for another quarter of an hour. When the wool had cooled in the dyebath the rinsed wool was grey.

Meadowsweet - The soft, frothing flowerheads may be gathered as the flowers first open and twice the weight of the wool put into the dyebath with it, kept separate by a muslin bag. The wool should already have been mordanted with alum. A full hour of simmering them gives yellow, but it is rather pale and elusive and so in recent years I have turned to using the roots only to dye from soft grey through to almost black. The roots may be dug in autumn or spring, with a single plant root giving about 50-125g (2 to 4oz), sufficient to dye 50g (2oz) of wool. I clean the root, chop it finely and then soak it in water overnight, or sometimes for 48 hours, before simmering for 1-2 hours. This has produced a reddish dye liquor that should be strained before entering the wool which may be pre-mordanted with alum. Using unmordanted wool I have simmered this for a further hour. Next I added iron and cream of tartar that gave a distinctive grey after a further quarter of an hour of simmering, and being left to cool in the liquor.

Dye herbs by colour

Yellow

Dye herb	parts used	mordant
agrimony	tops & leaves	alum
broom	flowering tops	"
Calendula	flowers	"
Coreopsis	flowers	"
dahlia	yellow flowers	"
dandelion	flowers	"
day lily	flowers	"
dyer's chamomile	flowers	"
golden rod	flowers	"
saffron	stigmas	"
St. John's wort	flowers	"
snowberry	berries	"
sorrel	tops	chrome
sunflower	flowers	alum
sweet gale	leaves	alum
tansy	flowering tops	alum
weld	tops & stalks	alum

N.B. cream of tartar is generally indicated to be included with the alum.

Orange

Dye herb	parts used	mordant
Coreopsis tinctoria	flowers	chrome
dahlia	flowers	"
dandelion	flowers	"
dyer's chamomile	flowers	"
sunflower	flowers	"
Tagetes	flowers	"

The best dahlia flowers for orange are either red or bronze.
The *Tagetes* to use are the tangerine gem.

Red

Dye herb	parts used	mordant
alkanet	root	alum+acid
Coreopsis	flowers	chrome
dyer's woodruff	roots	chrome
lady's bedstraw	roots	chrome
madder	roots	alum
yew	heartwood	acid

Yew heartwood can be obtained as sawdust from woodturners, or from a supplier who will also provide madder and alkanet roots.

Pink-Purple

Dye herb	parts used	mordant
bramble	leaves & berries	alum
elder	berries	vinegar
hops	stalks	–
oregano	flowering tops	see below
sloe	berries	alum
sorrel	tops	vinegar
woad	leaves	alum

The flowering tops of oregano should be used and crab apple leaves, malt and yeast. See Su Grierson's **The Colour Cauldron** for full instructions.

Blue

Dye herb	parts used	mordant
bearberry	berries	vinegar
bramble	berries	alum+salt
day lily	flowers	copper
elder	berries	alum+salt
elecampane	root	see below
indigo	tops & leaves	fermented
sunflower	seeds	copper+ chrome
woad	leaves (lst year)	alkalis

I have yet to achieve the desired result with elecampane root, but steeping the pounded root in ammonia, using copper sulphate as a mordant and adding logwood chips to the dyebath may help the process. Happy experimenting.

Green

Dye herb	parts used	mordant
agrimony	tops & leaves	copper
angelica	leaves & stems	copper
bramble	young shoots	iron
cardoon	tops & leaves	copper
comfrey	leaves	copper
day lily	flowers	copper
elder	leaves	copper
fennel	tops	copper
feverfew	flowering tops	iron
lily of the valley	leaves	copper
mullein	tops	copper
nettle	leaves	alum+iron later
sage	tops & leaves	copper

snowberry	leaves	copper
sorrel	tops	copper
tansy	leaves	copper+iron
weld	tops & stalks	alum+iron
yarrow	flowering tops	iron

N.B. If a good result is not achieved with copper sulphate alone, it is always worth trying adding a little iron towards the end of the dyeing.

Tan-brown

Dye herb	parts used	mordant
burdock	tops & leaves	copper+iron
fennel	tops	copper
gypsywort	tops & leaves	iron+ammonia
hop	stalks	
juniper	berries	alum
madder	root	iron
sorrel	tops	copper+ ammonia

Grey-black

Dye herb	parts used	mordant
bearberry	leaves	iron
bramble	berries	iron
yellow flag iris	root	iron
ivy	berries	iron
meadowsweet	root	iron
mugwort	flowering tops	alum+ copper & iron later
woad	leaves	

Cultivation details for the herbs above are given either in this, or my previous book, **Herbwise Naturally.** There are of course, even more dyeplants to be discovered. Most of those listed here are dyes which I have used – a few remain interesting experiments for the future.

Spinning herb fibres

MY ambitions to spin herb fibres began twenty years ago when my husband first bought me an antique spinning wheel as a New Year present. Being well over two hundred years old and having stood as part of a collection for a considerable time, it needed renovation at first. A leather strap for the treadle and the "footman" (the bar which joins the foot treadle to the main wheel) were missing, and the bent nails which held the thread as it passed along the bobbin were rusty. My husband made the missing parts, replaced the nails and generally oiled and overhauled the wheel. Unable at the time to find pure linen thread easily, we used fishing line for the drive band, which worked very well and it was ready to spin even if I had still to learn. The design of the wheel itself appeared to be a hybrid of Scottish and Irish wheels of the period, but there was no doubt from the hole left for the bowl of water on the swinging arm of the wheel and another for the pole distaff on the lower platform, that this had originally been designed for spinning flax rather than wool.

Courses on spinning flax were not, however, available and so first I learnt to spin wool on a day course in Weardale, where I saw my first Great wheel, otherwise known as the Walking wheel. The sight of this huge wheel, mounted on its stand with the long spike of a needle sticking straight out to take the thread was impressive. The spinner walks first one way to draw out the fibres, turning the wheel with their other hand as they go and then back again to wind the spun thread onto the needle. Not unnaturally, it brought us to discuss the connection between this predecessor of the modern spinning wheel and the fairy tale of Sleeping Beauty, for the Princess could only have pricked herself on a Walking wheel. Predictably, another fairy tale came to mind and we recalled the tale of the Princess and the Eleven Swans in which the Princess must spin nettles and weave the fibre into coats in order to change the swans back into human form.

The class began, and as I struggled with my first lumpy yarn and each one of that busy group of would-be spinners seemed to move forward across the stone floor until our wheels clashed in the centre and we all had to move apologetically backwards, I mused on the first use of my wheel for flax and the challenge of flax and of nettles to come.

Nettles

Spinning wool soon proved an enjoyable and relaxing pastime and for several years the flax and nettle spinning remained a dream. Then, ten years ago, I decided to research nettle spinning and began writing away for advice. First I tried the Royal Botanic Gardens at Kew and received a reply detailing five methods of preparing the fibres. I read that in Russia early in this century, the nettles were cut and dried and then passed through a machine with fluted and smooth rollers to separate the fibres from the useless parts of the stalks. The greenish fibre could then be stripped, combed, spun and bleached. It sounded simple, but I had no machine with rollers. I read on - in India the nettles were cut, left out in the air and then boiled with ashes - this, I decided was equally unsuitable for home repetition.

A further recipe from F. Oakley's book, **Long Vegetable Fibres**, included partly drying the stems and then boiling them in a soda lye. This recipe became more and more impractical for me as chloride of lime and weak sulphuric acid solutions followed on in drawn-out processes, before the final assurance that the fibre might come away freely.

The letter went on, detailing a Viennese method involving three machines and quoted those in use in hemp factories as suitable. Finally, from a Kew source, a further record of nettle fibres being prepared for spinning as for hemp or flax, by retting and then separating the fibres was given.

The last note was to the effect that there seemed to be considerable diversity of opinion as to whether the nettle should be dried, retted, boiled or treated with chemicals. Not surprising when we consider that almost 50 different methods of preparing nettle fibres were patented between the beginning of the First World War and the end of the Second World War. In this century at least, that time of hardship seems to have seen the hey-day of the nettle. In Germany, for example, some garments in army uniforms were made of 85% nettle fibres, with the other 15% of ramie which also belongs to the nettle family and thousands of tons were harvested for spinning.

Looking back in history, the stinging nettle had been stripped of its fibres for spinning as early as the Bronze Age, for nettle cloth was found wrapped around the bones of a Danish burial from that period. There were no machines or vats of sulphuric acid then, although of course the stems might easily have been retted in ponds and then beaten with stones or other implements. I found references, too, to the use of nettle cloth, homespun and woven in Scotland in the 17th and 18th centuries. This was made into tablecloths and sheets. A letter to the Victoria and Albert Museum brought the disappointment that they had no samples of nettle cloth, but a quote of "Nettell clothe" at one shilling a yard in an inventory of 1572, from **The Draper's Dictionary** in 1884. Little else was forthcoming and letters to textile museums in England and Scotland brought no joy.

Just as my enthusiasm was dying for lack of fuel I made a breakthrough. At about this time I had also sent out queries to Spinning and Weaving Guilds, to find whether anyone else might be searching for ways to spin with nettle fibres and been more successful. This brought a reply from a spinner in Essex who, to my great delight, wrote back to me with her methods of preparing nettles and a slide of cloth woven with a blend of nettle fibres, flax and hemp.

Unable to find a detailed method, her first experiment had been to dry the nettles for some three weeks and then peel the thread down from the stem. Numerous experiments later she was still recommending this way, although admitting it was tedious, but could produce 6.5 metres (7 yards) of thread from a single nettle cut either in late June or on through July into August. It was several years later before I found, in **The Weavers Garden** by Rita Buchanan, the American Indian method of preparing wood nettles and stingless nettles for making fishing nets - leaving the dead stalks laid in the weather to rot through the autumn and then peeling the fibres from the dried stems. By then I had already discovered that nettles cut and left out through a wet autumn and early winter could produce, by January, or a little later, perfectly prepared fibres with all the useless vegetable matter rotted away.

As long as an untidy corner of the garden is not a problem, this is much the easiest way, but the stems can come to grief if your dog or other animals decide to curl up in the middle of it at some stage, damaging the fibres. If you simply can't wait for spring, Rita Buchanan recommends cutting the nettles while green and peeling away the outer fibres and skin to ret down. In this case, I prefer to dry them first to remove the sting. However they are prepared, nettles have given fibres for fishing nets and cordage, a substitute for linen in sails for boats, clothing, tablecloths and sheets, a fine mesh for sifting and filtering and even been woven into a velvet fabric. The best nettles for fibres will be those growing to 1.85-2m (6 or 7ft) in the bottom of ditches or really well-fed, moist ground. If harvesting, gather those with few side branches which are mature and well coated in a fine lint, but not aged to the extent that the stems have become woody. Unless you have a pond or large tub you can use in the garden, or a mown area you can give up for a few days for dew retting, I would try drying the stems first and then peeling. Or perhaps you may come up with a better way . . .

Spin as for flax with a wetted thread, as the nettle fibres are set end to end with a length of some 2-6cm (¾ to 2½in), and do not have the microscopic hooks which wool fibres have to cling to each other as you spin.

Ramie

Ramie, which is a member of the nettle family, less hardy than the common nettle, looks very like it, but is stingless and grows in China and Southeast Asia. It has been spun there since prehistoric times and has fibres some 15cm (6in) long. It can be bought ready-prepared from suppliers. When I first saw the pure white silkiness of ramie I delighted in it. This was my first experience of spinning with a fibre other than wool and running the long sausage-like rolag of prepared fibres through my fingers, I couldn't wait to try. Try was the operative word at first, for I had become accustomed to spinning wool with my attention on the conversation rather than what my fingers told me of my progress.

This, I soon found with ramie, results in all the fibres in your hand coming to a sudden and disastrous end at the same time, with the thread flying ahead of you back towards the wheel and a good deal of wetting of both thread and fibres needed to rejoin.

I have learnt to spin ramie with the length of fibres over my shoulder and down ⌐ the basket, or keeping it on a table alongside, and no longer use water. In fact the ⸝est way to begin spinning ramie is to card it with wool, taking advantage of the natural microscopic hooks on the wool to give extra clinging quality. You can safely use about one-third of wool to two-thirds of ramie. Taking the continuous length of ramie fibres, pull away short lengths which will just fit across the depth of your carder. Lay these across the spikes until it is almost covered, then take some unwashed wool and spread this thinly over the top with the fibres running in the same direction. Card once only. Do not transfer the wool and ramie mix to the other carder as you would with wool on its own.

You will now have all of the fibres running in the same direction. Taking a little wool alone at first to join into the thread on the wheel, continue feeding in from the blended wool and ramie. This will give slight colour changes from pure white to cream as one or the other is dominant. By the time you have filled a bobbin you will have developed a feel for the qualities of ramie and lost some of your apprehension about its slippery nature. You may like the blend so much that you decide to continue spinning the two together. This is a good method of blending the fibres and gives a most acceptable result which can be both warm when woven or knitted into garments and offer comfortable summer clothing at the same time.

When beginning to spin pure ramie on its own, keep a little unwashed wool handy and use tiny amounts of this held with the ramie thread wherever you need extra grip. The trick is to keep lightly pinching the fibres between the fingers of your right hand to be sure you keep a steady thin line of thread running between the fingers of your left hand and up to the wheel. If the twist runs down past your left hand into a thicker wad of ramie you may have to cut this away and start again with a little wool mixed in. Ramie fibres are, in fact, stronger than flax and too strong to pull apart once partly spun. The slight shuffling action is soon part of your technique and produces a fine, white thread which can be knitted, woven or used as crochet thread. As with nettle, ramie has also been used for nets and cording. The fibres dye well.

Flax

Spinning flax came next and proved even more difficult at the beginning. It may be easier to learn to spin flax first, as I am sure spinning wool spoils you for the extra effort needed in dressing a distaff. The distaff supports the prepared flax in position for the spinner to draw fibres steadily from the mass without tangling them as the thread is spun. Spreading the bundle or strick of flax around what is usually a conical shape and attaching it with ribbon is called dressing the distaff. Once you gain enthusiasm for spinning flax you may even wish to grow your own plants if you have a spare plot of land, so let us begin at the beginning.

The Swiss Lake dwellers spun flax for clothing 10,000 years ago and the ancient Egyptians made linen clothing their ideal. The Romans imported much of their linen, and after the fall of the Roman Empire flax cultivation dropped until the eighth century when the Emperor Charlemagne, champion of so many useful herbs, revived it. The linen industry later thrived in northern Europe with flax spun in many ordinary households and when settlers went to America they took flax and their skill in spinning, weaving and dyeing with them.

At a household level flax was, and still is, grown by enthusiasts in America. A minimum area of 4.5 x 3m (15 x 10ft) is needed for fibres to prepare, spin and weave into a linen shirt. Rich, slightly acid soil in open sun is best for the necessary growth. When sowing for line flax, which is flax of the best quality for spinning, seed to give 200-250 plant stems per square foot is recommended in an excellent publication, **Flax Culture from flower to fibre** by Mavis Atton. The flax is ready for harvest when two-thirds of the stem has turned yellow and the seeds have begun to ripen. Several plants are then pulled from the ground in handfuls of similar length stems, tied together into bundles and dried hanging upside down. The seeds may be combed away from the stems straight away, or after drying, this process being known as rippling. The flax is then retted either by standing the bundles in a crate and lowering them into a pond or river, or otherwise weighting them down, or by laying them on mown grass for the action of the dew to break down the stems. The temperature of the water is critical in the first method which rules out shallow water because this is subject to sudden changes of temperature. Left on grass, the process takes from 3 to 5 weeks, while in perfect conditions in a tub, running water or a still pond, it may be finished in 4 days. In either case you are seeking to encourage a natural fermentation which removes the adhesive from the stems. During this process, the stems will change colour to reach the required grey appearance. The fibres must separate easily from the stems when tested before the next stage.

After retting, the fibres are rinsed and dried very thoroughly so that they become quite brittle. This is to enable a special wooden tool called a break to be used. Breaking the flax in this case involves bringing down the upper frame of the break over the flax stems so that the bars which form the jaws on the upper and lower frames chop along the length of the stems to remove the pith and cuticle from the fibres that remain. Using a fluted mallet will have the same effect but is, of course, harder work as it involves repeated hammering. The final preparation is scutching which involves scraping the bundles of fibres with a smooth, wooden knife as they are held against a wooden board. This removes any remaining unwanted material.

Combing is then required to untangle any matted fibres and is done with a hackle which is rather like a heavy-duty wool carder. There are several grades of hackle, according to how far apart the spikes are set into the board. The widest grade is used first and the flax progresses to being combed in the fine hackle which has spikes set very close together. Just as when combing hair or wool, a residue of shorter fibres is combed out. This coarser material is called tow and can be bought for spinning at a cheaper price than a strick of line flax.

Having combed out the tow you are left with a strick of flax which, thankfully for most spinners who have less time and space nowadays, can be bought ready to spin. I have known people leap away from a strick as I take it from my basket, since it does look very like a thick ponytail of human hair and it is easy to appreciate where the description "flaxen hair" came from when flax was commonplace. I think it is rather beautiful laying neatly with all the fibres side by side.

Having said your flax is ready to spin, there is still dressing the distaff to master, although spinning from flax wrapped loosely in a towel is an alternative. Dressing a distaff requires a section to itself and I am not sufficiently experienced to deal with it here. A much simpler distaff to dress and use is the comb distaff as seen in the diagram on page 162. Take a little less than half of the flax in one strick and gently ease the fibres apart at each end of their length. First lay the root end of the flax over the teeth at the top of the comb. As the strick is used up the flax can be moved down across the lower teeth. Tie loosely with a ribbon wound around the body of the comb so that the flax hangs down from the distaff ready for spinning. Small comb distaffs have been used tucked into the spinner's belt or waistband so that he or she can walk freely carrying a drop spindle, moistening the thread with saliva and spinning along the way. This is by far the simplest method; however, passing flax thread between your lips is not to be recommended. The fairy tale which portrays the three spinning ladies, one with a big foot from treadling the wheel and one with a big thumb from holding it against the thread, fails to tell us that the third lady with the big lip from moistening the thread was saying yukh as she did so.

For spinning with a wheel, either a lantern distaff or a pole distaff will be needed and, in my opinion, the best publication for detailing these and the methods of dressing them is **Handspinning Flax** by Olive and Harry Linder. Full particulars are given in the bibliography.

A simple method to try spinning flax and to find out whether you wish to go to the expense of buying a distaff - or the trouble of making one - is the towel method, also described in **Handspinning Flax.** Simply take the strick and lay it on a large towel, fold in the towel over the root end of the strick to hold it in place and then bring the material across the length of the strick so that the longest fibres are left sticking out at the open end. Lay the bundle next to you on a table which is slightly higher than your elbow and draw the fibres a few at a time from the towel opening, moistening with water and spinning.

Once you have conquered spinning ramie and flax and feel in need of a new challenge, you may like to look to the garden for other fibres. Nettle, of course, is the obvious alternative, but there are more.

Mallow
Few works on vegetable fibres seem to mention it, but the mallow family has also supplied thread. The common mallow was used by the Romans, who were also fond of eating mallows and later, in 600 A.D. we find a cloth called "melocinea" made of mallow thread. This cloth was still made into the last century in Spain and was sufficiently soft for shawls. My father found mention of 40 acres of another member of the mallow family, the hollyhock, being grown in North Wales for fibre production in the last century. This experiment appears to have soon been abandoned, but offers us a clue to a herb which may give sufficiently good results for home-produced, if not commercially viable cloth. Having left hollyhock stems to weather outside, I find the fibres peel away relatively easily and give the advantage of being very long. At worst, they can be left for papermaking should they prove too much for the would-be spinner.

Lupin
Again, a herb to be found in the herbaceous border of many gardens - the lupin - has provided stem fibres to be made into paper and spun into thread sufficiently durable for weaving tablecloths. As has already been mentioned in the cultivation details for the lupin, wartime saw the investigation of this as a possible source of cloth also. I have as yet to try lupins, but imagine the preparations already discussed will prove suitable.

Sunflower
Our last herb is even taller and may seem, at first glance, to be just as unlikely - the sunflower. The potential this herb offers for spinning fibres both from the leaves and the tall stems appears to have been explored to the greatest extent in China. Both coarse fibres and those soft enough to be combined with silk are recorded. Again the

American Indians discovered and used the textile properties of the sunflower, just as they had also harvested and spun flax before settlers brought new crops of the plant. Interestingly, burning sunflower stalks produces quantities of potash to be spread on the soil, a mineral important for flax growth. The stems of sunflowers, if the herb has been left to flower at the end of the season, are harder to break down than either hollyhocks or nettles. I have tried retting them beneath the hedge for weeks on end and, when paper-making, usually have to resort to boiling the chopped stem with caustic soda to obtain the fibres. However, given the bonus of a very wet winter with sharp, frosty spells, the weather can triumph in at least preparing the whole stem to be broken down more easily. Here, as with the nettle, peeling comes into its own.

This section has not explored every possible vegetable fibre, hemp has been left aside and other little known fibre sources may be worth further investigation. I hope, however, that I have provided sufficient ideas and information to motivate more spinners to enjoy experimenting.

Comb distaff

Herbal Paper-making

WHILE paper-making is not as ancient a craft as basketry, it was certainly known by the Chinese about 105 A.D. Then it was made by steeping bark fibres and flax in water to soften them in preparation for beating to pulp. This soggy mass was levelled and dried in the sun as sheets of paper. Several centuries passed before the art reached Europe. Indeed, paper mills were not in operation here until the 14th century.

As the craft slowly spread from one country to another, different fibres were explored. By the 18th century over 80 possible raw materials had been identified. Since many of these are garden herbs, anyone with an interest in textures, colour and original design in paper-making can explore this cornucopia of opportunities at their leisure.

The mallow family, which includes wild and cultivated mallows and hollyhocks, is particularly rich in useful fibres in both the leaves and stems. Sunflowers also provide liberally for the paper-maker, along with fennel, nettles, mullein, golden rod, grasses, St. John's wort and many more. Towards autumn, when the best of each crop has already been harvested for other uses, you will find the mature herb garden still has much rampant growth remaining. This will soon inspire you to find more sources of materials as each herb conveys something of its own individual nature into the finished paper.

By experiment, a selection of decorative papers can be built up to use in greeting cards, to act as a background to display pressed flowers or other art work, to line gift boxes and so on. Both fragrance and colours can be incorporated into the finished product. The equipment needed is very simple and paper-making kits are readily available from charity catalogues and craft shops etc. The kit will provide a minimum of a wooden frame and matching deckle through which the paper is strained, 2 smooth boards to enclose the pile of wet paper sheets and absorbent cloths to separate the layers. Should you wish to improvise, use an old wooden picture frame for the mould (at least 2cm (¾in) deep) and a second picture frame of the same size which is made into a deckle by attaching a fine mesh stretched tightly across it. These and the boards should be approx. 21 x 25cm (8 x 10in) to supply sheets of paper of a useful size.

To make paper of herb fibres

Harvest the stems and leaves in late summer or early autumn, when the herb has already given its choice leaves, flowers or seeds. Cut down to a few inches above the ground, as you would in preparation for winter, and store the cut material in plastic bags beneath a hedge or at the back of the border where they will remain damp and out of view. Long stems such as hollyhock and sunflower can be chopped into several lengths in order to fit them into the bag which should also contain a little rainwater before it is loosely sealed.

A few weeks later the soft tissue around the fibres will have begun to rot away and the fibres are easily removed and chopped into short lengths for boiling with caustic soda. First, however, set them in a bucket of water and leave again for a couple of days.

Before following the next stage it should be remembered that using caustic soda needs special precautions. Thick rubber gloves should be worn and even sunglasses will give the eyes protection from splashes if goggles are not available. The fumes should not be inhaled and so good ventilation is necessary, preferably with an extractor hood, or by boiling the mixture out of doors. The pan used must be of stainless steel or pyrex. Other materials will react chemically with the soda. **Caustic soda must be kept out of reach of children and pets.**

You will need:

a pyrex or stainless steel pan which takes 2½ litres (4½ pints) or more
a large wooden spoon
a blender (saved for this purpose only)
an old oblong or square washing up bowl
a sieve
caustic soda
thick rubber gloves
protective glasses
a papermaking kit
newspapers
a rolling pin

When preparing to make the paper remember that time must be allowed for the paper-making process to be finished before preparing or setting out food in the same room. Wearing gloves and goggles, pour 1.2 litres (2 pints) of cold water into the pan and add 3 tablespoons of caustic soda. Always add the caustic to the liquid in order that only diluted caustic soda comes into contact with the pan. Next, add the chopped stems and fibres until it is half full. Cover and heat slowly to bring to the boil, remaining in the room until the liquid is boiling gently and steadily. At this point the need for ventilation will be appreciated. Boil the stems for at least 2 hours, checking the water level frequently and topping it up as necessary.

Remove the pan from the heat and allow the mixture to cool. The excess water should then be poured away down an outside drain, using the lid as a strainer. A pyrex container is safer as you can see how much water is left and will be warned of the bulk of the stems falling forwards. Refill with fresh water sufficient to cover the stems and rinse again, straining the liquid using the lid. Do this three times to wash away most of the remaining caustic soda. Put the stems, a few at a time, into an old sieve and wash thoroughly again under a running tap. When cleansed, tip them in small quantities into a blender goblet which should already hold 500ml (18fl. oz) of cold water, or slightly less if this quantity may overfill your blender. Blend each for 45 seconds and pour the pulped fibres and liquid into the washing-up bowl.

If you wish, colourings may also be added to the blender in the form of elderberry juice or dye solutions. These are obtained as for wool dyes - by simmering suitable flower heads such as dahlia, *Coreopsis* or *Tagetes* for 20 minutes in 850ml (1½ pints) of water and straining the liquid. One teaspoon of alum should be mixed in a little hot water and added to the dye to increase fastness. Further use of the blender should be remembered however, and you may prefer to add dye to the pulp at the next stage, when all the goblets of blended pulp have been poured into the washing-up bowl. Include this quantity in your liquid calculation in either case. Alternatively, the dye liquor may be spooned over the wet paper as it drains on the deckle and some dye petals sprinkled over the pulp. Or the finished paper can be dyed after drying.

With the pulp mixture in the washing-up bowl, bring up the level by adding a further 3.5 litres (6 pints) of warm water. Stir well. Set one smooth wooden board on the drainer covered by a damp, absorbent cloth. Holding the deckle mesh side upwards, place the frame squarely on the top and dip both down to the bottom of the bowl, holding them firmly together and allowing the pulpy mixture to flow over the deckle. Rock them back and forth to raise any herb fibres which have settled to the bottom. Bring both frames upwards together, keeping them level so that on surfacing an even layer of pulp is left on the deckle, enclosed by the frame.

Place this on the drainer for a minute or two to allow the excess water to run away. If the pulp is unevenly distributed, simply tip the frame back into the bowl and begin again. Once you are satisfied, remove the frame and line up the top and bottom edges of the deckle with those of the board and cloth, which should be laid next to it. Flip the deckle neatly over to place the paper sheet squarely onto the absorbent cloth. Press down firmly across the full width and length of the mesh to release excess water, before rocking the deckle back and forth and lifting it away to leave the paper on the cloth.

If any large bubbles have formed, or the surface is torn, scrape the pulp back into the bowl and repeat the process. Smaller creases can be removed by gently pulling at the edge of the cloth nearby. Lay another absorbent cloth over the paper sheet and return both frame and deckle to the bowl to repeat. Continue in this way, covering each sheet with an absorbent cloth until the pulp will no longer cover the deckle completely. Place the second smooth board on top of the last cloth and press down heavily to squeeze out water held in the paper.

Open out several layers of newspaper onto an adjacent worktop. Remove the top board from the pile of papers, and then the top cloth. Take each sheet of paper still laid on its supporting cloth and set these on the newspaper to dry. Leave for an hour or so and then turn the sheets face down onto fresh newspaper. Roll with a rolling pin before carefully easing the cloth away from the damp paper, using a cocktail stick or tweezers at the edges and corners if necessary. The damp paper is left to finish drying and then pressed flat in a flower press, or between the pages of a large, heavy book.

Dried paper can be further fragranced by storing it in a sealed box with strongly scented herbs and a little orris root, or with a cotton wool pad which has had 1 or 2 drops of essential oil added.

To dye finished paper with elderberry juice

Heat together 75ml (2½fl. oz) malt vinegar, 150ml (5fl. oz) cold water and 1 teaspoon of alum until the alum is dissolved. Cool. Pour this liquor into one shallow tray and the strained elderberry juice into a second. Take each sheet of paper in turn, immersing it, with one side upwards and then the other, in first the vinegar and alum mordant followed by the juice. Allow to drip and then rinse in cold water before setting to dry pegged to a line out of doors or laid on a smooth surface which can be stained without nuisance.

Recycled paper-making

A simpler method of paper-making is to recycle used paper. This can be enlivened by adding herb leaves or flower petals to the paper pulp to give the appearance of a "designer" paper. Embossed papers are easily made by pressing distinctive stems, flowers and leaves (not necessarily all from the same plant) between two sheets of drying paper. The edges can be bonded together giving an exceptionally attractive natural design. To give a personal touch, tiny pressed flowers can also be rolled into sheets of home-made notepaper in the top corners or centre top of each sheet as it dries. The sources of paper for recycling in the home are: used computer paper, unused wallpaper, newspaper with black and white print only, and sheets of used typing or copy paper. Of these, the computer and typing papers will give a smoother end result than wallpaper or newspaper.

You will need:

a paper-making kit as described on page 163
a plastic bucket
a blender (one saved for this purpose alone)
a measuring jug
a large washing-up bowl
a thick newspaper
some 85g (3oz) of unwanted paper for your first experiment

First, the paper needs to be completely saturated in water. This is achieved by tearing it into pieces and placing in the bucket, which is then filled with water and left to stand for several hours. The soggy paper will now come together into individual balls with the pressure from your closed fist. Make the balls with the capacity of your blender in mind. Drop them into it one at a time, adding a measured quantity of water. Generally some 500ml (18fl. oz) will enable the blender to turn the paper into a thick, soupy consistency. Take care not to overfill the blender. Repeat with each crushed ball of paper and tip all of the resulting pulp into the washing-up bowl. If you wish, colourings may again be added to the blender in the form of elderberry juice, or dye solutions. See instructions on page 164. If dye is added, again make sure the quantity is measured and included in calculating the filled bowl which should be brought up to 5 litres (8½ pints) with warm water.

With dyed or plain paper, you may now wish to add two or three handfuls of flower petals or small herb leaves for decorative effect. In the case of rose, safflower, *Tagetes* or pot marigold petals, some colouring will also appear around them in the finished sheets of paper. Stir well.

Set a smooth board on the sink drainer and cover this with a damp, absorbent cloth. Any fineweave absorbent cloth can be substituted for cloths supplied in kits. Set the wooden frame on top of the deckle, mesh upwards, and plunge them both straight down to the bottom of the bowl, holding them together while allowing the pulp solution to flow over them. Rock them back and forth beneath the surface to catch the fibres from the paper pulp. As you bring them back up to the surface it is important to hold them completely level. This ensures an even thickness of the finished sheet of paper.

Do not worry if the first try emerges with a thicker layer at one end of the deckle. Simply dip the frame and deckle again, tipping away the pulp and repeat until you are satisfied with the result. Once you have an even layer of pulp on the deckle, stand it briefly on the drainer to allow the excess water to run away. Lift off the top frame and flip the deckle face down to land the wet paper sheet squarely onto the cloth and board beneath. Run your fingers across and down the square of mesh to release trapped water before carefully removing the deckle with a steady, rolling movement. If there are any small creases in the sheet, these can be carefully removed with a gentle tug at the nearest edge of the cloth. Large air bubbles or tears are more difficult to remedy. If these appear, it is best to scrape the pulp back into the bowl and begin again. The knack of producing even sheets comes readily with practice.

Before dipping the frame and deckle for the next sheet, lay a second absorbent cloth, dry this time, over the sheet of paper you have now produced. Your second sheet will be laid over this, again lining it up with the board, and therefore, the sheet below as closely as possible. Continue until there is not sufficient pulp left in the bowl to give a full sheet. Lay an absorbent cloth over your last sheet of paper and place the second smooth board on top of this. Press down hard on the pile of paper and cloths to release the water.

Open out several layers of newspaper on a smooth worktop nearby. Remove the top board and first absorbent cloth from the pile of wet sheets of paper. Take the top sheet supported by the absorbent cloth beneath and lay this with the cloth still in position on the newspaper. Repeat with each cloth and sheet and leave to dry - unless you wish to add more decoration.

For decorative papers, lay pressed flowers and leaves in position after the paper has been drying for half an hour, and press them carefully into the paper fibres. Small arrangements are the most effective, with delicate mint flowers, forget-me-nots, hyssop, yarrow, the smaller clary sage bracts and flowers, oregano or thymes. Violets, pot marigold petals, *Tagetes* and other dye petals can add areas of colour around their edges.

When positioning the herbs, remember the edge will need to be trimmed away for notepaper. As each sheet dries, turn them over face down onto the newspaper and roll the back of the cloth with a rolling pin before cautiously peeling it away. A cocktail stick can be useful to ease the corners and edges of the sheets if necessary.

Embossed papers are also made while the paper is still wet. The whole of a pressed herb stem with leaves and flower can be laid onto the first wet sheet. Another sheet with its cloth backing laid on top then encloses the natural material. Alternatively, flowers, leaves and stem from different herbs can be laid next to each other to form an imaginary plant design or an abstract shape. As before, the enclosed plant material between the two sheets is rolled before the backing cloth is removed from the top sheet. Roll the embossed paper at each edge to seal.

Dried lavender or other scented herbs could also be sprinkled between sheets of paper, giving both pattern and a subtle fragrance. Lavender and seeds can add a

167

further design dimension to the surface of drying papers, creating various textures with their indented forms before being scraped away when the paper has dried. Further fragrance can be sprayed onto the drying sheets using diluted essential oils.

Dry sheets of paper need only to be flattened for use. This can be achieved either by placing them in a large flower press or book press, or setting them between the pages of a large book and piling more heavy volumes on the top. In either case leave them for one or two days before removing. The finished recycled paper will take ballpoint pens but not the ink from fountain pens, unless it is further sized with gelatine.

You may like to try the challenge of making your own ink, the recipe below gives a really lovely purple ink which will keep for several years if you do not rush to use it all at the beginning.

Elderberry ink
300ml (10fl oz) elderberry juice
2 teaspoons alum
1 dessertspoon of salt

The method is very simple. Pick 1.4kg (3lb) of elderberries when they are sufficiently ripe to hang down in clusters. Remove all thick stalks and place the berries in an enamel pan. Heat them very slowly without added water, so that the juice flows readily. This can also be done in the oven with the temperature no higher than 100°C. Cool. Strain through a fine nylon sieve. This will give about 300ml (10fl. oz) of juice. Return the juice to an enamel pan and sprinkle on the alum, stirring. Bring to the boil, still stirring the liquid. Set to cool. Dissolve the salt in 2 tablespoons of hot water. Stir into the cooled mixture. When cold pour into small screwtop jars. Store in a dark cupboard. Suitable for most fountain pens.

Herbal trees in Woodcrafts

THE appreciation of herbal trees, and correspondingly of herbal woods, is a relatively new area of interest, both for me and for the modern works on herbs which leave it mostly unexplored. The exception is Mrs. Grieve's A **Modern Herbal,** which is truly encyclopaedic. If we look back to the 17th century we find Culpeper including holly, yew, hazel, ivy, oak, hawthorn, walnut, mulberry and blackthorn in his herbal, not to mention chestnut and ash. Trees also appear in the herbal works of preceding centuries. Most certainly, trees were included in the range of natural medicines and in a rural economy they would, until relatively recent times, have formed part of the everyday country life and herbal lore.

Now that town living has erased the immediate knowledge of their properties and household uses – and a reminder of the dangers of yew and laburnum in particular, seems timely – I feel it doubly important to pass on an appreciation of the nature of herbal trees, together with information on their qualities and woodworking potential. This, I hope will arouse the interest of those who enjoy either woodcarving or woodturning as a hobby.

Since field enclosures began, country hedges have abounded with hawthorn, alder and blackthorn - the latter pre-dates the last ice age in Britain and perhaps previous ice ages. Early hedges were strong with an interwoven mix which might also include elder and hazel amongst others. Even in towns, hawthorn remains a contender for boundary hedges despite, or perhaps because of, its intimidating thorns.

Hawthorn - Crataegus monogyma

To most people hawthorn is simply - a hedge. I have already given some details of its further possibilities in the herb cultivation section. It has been best known as a cardiac medicine, especially successful in treating hypertension. On the other hand, its vicious nature will be familiar to anyone with hawthorn to clip. This ferocity is balanced by the old use of the distilled water of hawthorn to draw out thorns and splinters. Both the flowers and berries have found a place amongst country liqueurs and wines, but the Latin name *Crataegus* relates to none of these uses or properties – it means strength and refers to the wood of this long-lived tree.

When hawthorn was felled in the past, the most obvious use must have been firewood, since it gives an exceedingly hot fire when burnt. Thankfully some hawthorn, root and wood included, also caught the eye of woodcarvers and turners who succeeded in producing beautiful boxes, combs and decorative, delicate bowls such as the one illustrated on page xxiv, which I was delighted to find for sale in the north of England. Although the timber reaches no great size, and is therefore a source of small items only, the wood takes on an exceptionally fine polish which shows the grain to perfection.

Holly - Ilex aquifolium

Another tree which is still in flower when the hawthorn blossom whitens the hedgerows is holly. This is one of my favourite trees, both as an undercanopy in deciduous forests, where I associate it with parts of the New Forest and deer sightings, and as an ornamental feature in the hedges of my own garden. It took a magical May morning some years ago to broaden my conception of the holly beyond the familiar image of dark green leaves and bright red berries and to see it as a wonderfully fragrant, flowering herb. Walking through the New Forest I found myself in a sunny glade filled with the most delicious perfume. Even though it wasn't quite the scent of honeysuckle, I still searched for some, because I was unable to see anything else which might account for such a lingering sweetness. Only oak rose high above a magnificent thicket of holly and, giving up on the early honeysuckle fantasy, I moved closer to the dark spiny leaves. There, at the leaf axils, were the tiny white flowers I had so often missed noticing – the source of this delightful perfume.

It also took me time to discover the role of holly in furniture-making and, to my surprise, also in such objects as the black handles of metal teapots - before these were succeeded by plastic imitations. Holly is not only the whitest known timber, it takes staining well and has an almost featureless grain. For these reasons it has formed an important inlay wood, being used in Tunbridge Ware amongst other decorative patterns. The hardness of holly was an advantage for producing blocks for printing, for "true" mathematical instruments and for walking sticks.

Anyone who has burnt holly on the fire will know that it retains its sap over a long period and will need to be carefully dried and seasoned before it is suitable for the woodworker. In the garden it is not only a source of branches for Christmas decorations but also attracts small pretty holly blue butterflies and, if Pliny is to be believed, the branches may protect both us from witchcraft and our house from being struck by lightning. Medicinally, the berries were once used as a purge, a practice discontinued since their effects may be dramatic and toxic. The leaves were formerly administered for rheumatism and fevers.

Elder - Sambucus nigra

Elder is as familiar in the hedgerow as hawthorn or holly, and carries with it the ever present "darker" side of its nature still kept alive in superstitions. Until very recent times it was believed unlucky to chop down an elder tree, and certainly the use of its wood in household furniture was restricted. To make a cradle with elder was definitely forbidden as it begged for misfortune. The superstitions linking elder with witches and evil - even with the crucifixion of Christ as the tree on which Judas reputedly hung himself - take us back in time to the pre-Christian era. Then the elder was a sacred tree dedicated to Hulde-Moer a Scandinavian goddess who was believed to have taught women to spin. Permission was still asked of her spirit to fell each elder, centuries after her identity had been forgotten. Fortunately, and rather cunningly, her assent was shown by a lack of any appreciable response.

Taking branches of the close-grained white wood for whittling skewers, needles with which to weave nets, combs, shoemakers pegs and the ever-popular pipes which might produce simple music or be used to blow darts, seems to have been an entirely different matter. Nowadays, when almost anything we touch appears to bear a warning label regarding its toxic nature, making blowpipes of elder is frowned upon for the very good reason that elder contains anthocyanins. Just as eating raw elderberries is not a healthy thing to do, sucking on the hollowed-out branches is no longer considered safe, although generations of children have done both with little ill effect. My own collection of elderwood includes the bowl illustrated on page xxiv and a wool bobbin, both of which confirm the tendency of the wood to split if not extremely carefully chosen and seasoned. The white wood is attractive, if not as hard and durable as holly.

The soft pith removed from young branches when making pipes and popguns has had its own uses. Made into small balls it has provided toys, while specimens for analysis have been secured between layers of elder pith in laboratories. The elder tree has been close to the heart of herbal lore and famed across Europe. Firstly, it has been known as the "medicine chest of the country" for the many uses of its flowers and berries in cold cures and ointments. Secondly, as the "cosmetic tree" from the properties of elderflower water and the application of the flowers in various other skin preparations. Thirdly, as the source of elderflower champagne and wine and elderberry port, and lastly as a source for dye, ink, basketry material and a gentle pest control for the gardener. In addition, it is also a herbal tree for the woodworker who enjoys experimenting.

Ivy - Hedera helix

Ivy is mainly seen as a parasite or, at best, a decorative climber. It hardly ranks as a herbal tree in most people's appreciation of the scheme of things. As mentioned in the cultivation section, however, the herb is extremely long-lived. At an age of several hundred years we may expect the trunk or main stem to have achieved considerably more girth than the slender exploratory tendrils which are so useful as basketry weavers. This trunk can be as large as 30cm (1ft) across, although one this size would be a rarity.

In previous centuries, ivy was certainly used to fashion cups which were serviceable drinking vessels and it was considered an aid to good health to use them frequently. For troubles connected with the spleen, Culpeper recommends leaving your drink to stand in an ivy cup for a time before drinking. (The spleen seems to have received rather more attention in those days than now - in the eyes of the patient at any rate.) Ivy was strongly linked with easing drunkenness and the after effects of a surfeit of alcohol. Dedicated to Bacchus, a Greek/Roman god of wine on one hand, the ivy bush was much used as a sign outside alehouses while elsewhere cups of ivy wood were popular to filter out the strength of the wine. The porous wood tended to absorb colour from wine left standing in it and this seems to have encouraged the belief that alcohol was also being extracted.

Ivy cups were not only thought to make drinking less of an abuse to the system: one hangover cure required more of the same wine taken the night before to be stood in an ivy cup and then drunk to counteract the effects. Other extremely dubious and, possibly, dangerous remedies which involved eating the berries were also indulged in and are definitely not recommended.

Sadly, wooden items of ivy are not easy to come by; the softness of the wood and rarity of really sizeable pieces have left woodturners more likely to choose from the many woods which are more readily available and appealing. My search for a cup turned from ivy continues . . .

171

Yew - Taxus baccata

When thinking of long-lived trees, the yew naturally comes to mind. These ancient trees fascinate me, particularly in winter when the dark green needles of the leaves are edged with frost, and the just as poisonous berries show bright against them. Passing a large yew tree almost every day, seeing another magnificent specimen from my kitchen window and having, as a consequence, a number of "bird delivered" seedlings in my garden has removed some of the "dark dread" of the yew suffered by many. This probably began with the spooky nature of old yews in churchyards - which often form a child's first impression of the tree, along with stern warnings from anxious mothers not to touch.

The warnings are perfectly right of course, yew can kill swiftly and has taken the lives of many children and animals who have eaten leaves or berries. It acts quickly to depress the action of the central nervous system, the dangerous part of the berries being the seed rather than the pulp. There is no apparent support for the old belief that falling asleep underneath a yew leads to death, since no toxic gas has been discovered leaking from the leaves.

In the past few years, severe gales have brought down a number of old yew trees, providing a source of wood for eager woodturners who have increased their sales with numerous valued souvenirs. The mushroom shape of yew illustrated is one of these, turned from a tree which had stood on the nearby Butser Hill for centuries.

Yew is exceptionally attractive since it is extremely hard and, where there is a straight grain, relatively easy to work. The contrast of the white sapwood (which holds the food for wood-boring insects) with the red heartwood makes it a wonderfully dramatic timber for decorative pieces. For items which need durability, however, the heartwood only may be chosen.

Mulberry - Morus nigra

The mulberry is thought to have originated in Persia and, true to its warm preference, is known as the wisest of trees from the habit of being one of the last to open its leafbuds in spring - which by then is almost summer. My own young mulberry opened its leafbuds in the second week of May this year.

The earliest suggested date for the introduction of the mulberry from Southern Europe is the Roman period, for the Romans were fond of eating mulberry fruits at their feasts. They dedicated the tree to Minerva, goddess of wisdom and the arts. Our next definite record of mulberry appreciation was in the ninth century when Charlemagne, Emperor of the Roman Empire, ordered mulberry trees to be cultivated along with myriad other useful herbs on the Imperial farm.

When we see giant old mulberry trees alongside beautiful 17th century houses, their great crown of leaves sometimes spreading to 7m (20ft) across, we may appreciate their romantic charm. The enthusiasm of James I for supporting home-produced silk by having thousands of mulberries planted in his grounds, and encouraging his subjects by various means to plant the trees as food for silkworms, is largely responsible for many of the oldest and largest trees. Sadly for this project, the black mulberry was imported rather than the white and in this climate the silkworms, with less than an ideal host, did not thrive. The black mulberry proved a better choice from other aspects, however, for once they have reached some 15 years old, the trees give a delicious harvest of fruits to eat, preserve, make into wine or use as a dye. Both unripe and ripe berries have been given medicinally in the past - the ripe to "open the body" and unripe to "bind it". Syrup from the berries also relieved sore throats and the juice of the leaves in vinegar soothed burns.

Appreciation of the wood for turning is well documented by an interesting incident recorded by Mrs. Grieve. She writes that Shakespeare had planted a mulberry from the garden of James I in his own garden at Stratford-on-Avon and that when Shakespeare's home was demolished in 1752, the Rev. Gartrell, who owned the property, also had the mulberry chopped down to keep sightseers away. This famous mulberry then supplied wood for many souvenirs of snuff boxes, cups etc. which must now be even more valuable as collector's items.

The mulberry cup illustrated on page xxiv is my own and has a rather less celebrated history. The wood is hard and durable and takes on an excellent polish. A relative of the black mulberry is the paper mulberry: it also provides fibres from its bark for paper-making.

Lime - Tilia cordata

The lime is unfortunately mostly noticed for the drips of sticky resin which fall from its canopy onto cars that have foolishly been parked beneath. The honeyed sweetness of flowers from the *Tilia cordata* and other limes - also known as linden blossom - makes a soothing tea, and the name limeflower is more commonly connected with wholefood and healthfood shops than the garden in Britain. The wonderfully scented blossoms, which might be harvested here as readily as on the Continent, have tonic, nervine and hypotensive effects. For this reason they are included in herbal medicines to lower blood pressure and are also administered for catarrh, headaches (including migraine) and as a soothing night-time drink to give relaxation in preparation for sleep.

The wood from this lovely tree, which can reach some 40m (130ft), is easy to work and smooth with a pale, creamy veneer. More readily available to the amateur craftsman than many herbal woods, it is included in marquetry and inlay decoration. Lacking the strength for everyday objects that must be durable, lime is blessed with more precious properties which enable woodcarvers to give their work the finest detail. Carvings of figures and flowers alike have a rare beauty in this wood and have been included in the decorations of both St. Paul's Cathedral and Windsor Castle.

Other craftsmen have found lime suitable to meet the varied demands of piano and organ manufacture and making charcoal for artists. The inner bark has a further offering of fibres for coarse matting and baskets, while in Sweden it has been macerated to provide fibres for fishing nets.

Oak - Quercus robur

As a child I loved both the old, spreading oak trees in the countryside and the solid oak antique chest in which my father kept some of his many documents. With the passing of time I also watched for the best oak leaves as the one midsummer week approached when it is traditionally the right time to make oak leaf wine - a rare treat if left to mature for a year or two. Nowadays I search also for oak galls with which to make ink and use oak apples in dyeing wool.

As a timber, the oak was felled in winter for best results and was of prime importance in earlier centuries for shipbuilding. In turn, this high demand reduced the oak forests dramatically and, since oak was also popular for constructing timber-framed houses, occasionally old ship's timbers were re-used in house building. The bark from the felled trees has always been a popular tanning agent for the leathermakers. Medicinally, it was administered to patients suffering from malaria as a substitute for quinine. In addition, distilled water was prepared from the buds to treat fevers and influenza. The oak platter illustrated was made from one of the floorboards in the manor house where I once lived.

Walnut - Juglans regia

If there is a herbal wood better for furniture than oak, it must surely be walnut, which also supplies wood for small turned objects. The walnut tree grows slowly to some 20m (60ft) tall with a spread of foliage almost as great as the mulberry and a harvest of nuts to rival that of the mulberry fruits. In the herbalist's eyes, the walnut has been a source of medicinal fruit, leaves and bark. The green fruits which later ripen into the familiar walnuts so popular in the Christmas nut bowl since they are the easiest to crack, were gathered unripe as they were considered to have more virtues. The likeness of the shape to that of the human brain led to them being given for epilepsy in earlier times. In more recent medicine, the leaves and bark have produced remedies for a variety of skin problems including herpes and eczema.

The green fruits are still the preference of those seeking dyes, although the leaves can also be simmered to give a brown dye. The still-soft outer shell has been steeped in urine to dye chair frames with a typical walnut stain. Walnut oil has been used by painters to thin varnish and, today, is seen on the grocery shelves as a cooking oil.

A walnut tree is almost as long term an investment as a mulberry, since it too may live to be several hundred years old. The wool bobbin in the illustration shows the unpolished wood.

Box - Buxus sempervirens

One wood which my collection still lacks is box. In England, we are mostly familiar with very low box hedges, although occasionally a tall hedge tightly encloses a kitchen garden, or even an outer boundary. On the Continent, box trees are more common and it is from these that the typical smell we find complained of in old herbals is noticeable. Boxwood is pale and yellow and, not surprisingly, the sawdust was once used to dye hair. The wood itself is exceptionally hard and heavy. Being so dense it was found the best timber for the wood-engraver to work with and both printing blocks and engraving plates were made of it. Musical and mathematical instruments were of box, for the same qualities were of great importance to their exacting requirements. Chess pieces and, of course, boxes are also made from box and it may be thinly applied in inlay work. In modern medicine, box has been more used in homoeopathy than herbal remedies; once seen as a medicinal agent to purify the blood, the herb is recognised as being far too toxic to administer in its natural form.

Rosemary - Rosmarinus officinalis

A herb which is also powerful, though only toxic in overdose, is rosemary, and perhaps this holds the most romantic dream of all the herb woods. Although classified as a perennial shrub rather than a tree, a very large, old rosemary can supply wood for small, thin objects. A delicate box might be made from rosemary and the tradition that making a box of rosemary and opening it each day to smell the perfume would preserve your youth must have set many searching for this treasure.

Lilac - Syringa vulgaris

A likely herbal wood in the garden setting is lilac. The wood is not commercially available as far as I know, but has been well recommended by woodturners who have found themselves with access to a felled tree. With care in seasoning it is described as being hard and beautiful. The lilac flowers have been sprinkled on salads and added to dishes as a garnish as well as providing the lovely perfume.

Laburnum - Cytisus alpinus

In the case of laburnum, the branches may be cross-cut for veneering and, as can be seen from the illustration on page xxiv, beautifully patterned turned articles are also possible. Yew and laburnum share both a common use of their wood in oyster veneer on tables and drawer fronts and the worst reputation as garden poisons, being especially dangerous to young children. Although the leaves have been administered medicinally, the cytisine in laburnum gives it an action similar to that of strychnine.

Other woods could have been added to this list, for I have said nothing of hazel, blackthorn, ash, cherry or field maple. The last is seen as a wool bobbin in the illustration. The bark has yielded a lotion for sore eyes, meriting the field maple's inclusion in lists of medicinal plants. Here, with the herbal woods, is the beginning of an enjoyable search for more knowledge and experiment in the future.

Twenty herbal gifts

There is a great satisfaction in giving and receiving home-made presents, especially when they show real thought and creativity. This selection contains both the quick and easy, and more elaborate projects which leave room for your imagination and ingenuity to blossom. There are natural ties between this section and others in the book, with opportunities to use skills in basketry, dyeing wool, flowercrafts, papermaking, stem baskets and needlework design. The Christmas hamper could equally well be filled with your choice of recipes from the cookery and wine and liqueur sections in the form of home made-sweets and candied roots, a bottle of herb syrup, liqueur or wine; bags or jars of herb peppers or other seasonings, herb jellies, rosemary shortbread or savoury biscuits.

Flower basket

Fragrant and attractive, this gift will be particularly welcomed by anyone who spends the coldest months indoors.

You will need:

a basket - preferably one with a tall handle to frame the taller herbs. This can be bought at small cost, made of bunches of herb stems on a frame (see page 109) or, if you are a basketry enthusiast, from materials detailed in the basketry section a block of oasis which can be cut to fill the basket to within 5cm (2in) of the top herb flowers and foliage

You may like to assemble a colourful display of herb flowers with a seedhead here and there for effect. The basket in the illustration on page xxv was made by setting the tall lady's mantle and sea holly to make a curve which follows the line of the handle. Next, the helichrysum, Jerusalem sage flowers and seedheads, and teazle seedheads were set to form eye-catching points of interest. Lastly, in the front of the basket, the mass of yellow yarrow, tansy and curry plant added bright colour, with a centre of pink Tudor immortelles and mints and occasional stems of lavender. Behind the lady's mantle, seedheads of St. John's wort provide a rich, tan background.

In the stem basket illustrated on page xvi I have selected herbs to enhance the silver effect of the cotton lavender in the basket sides. Again, I began with the taller lady's mantle, peppermint and mint close to the handle and then grouped chives, helichrysum, bergamot, thrift and Tudor immortelles, with their shades of pink to purple, to display soft colour. The spaces between and at the ends of the basket were filled by the white of sneezewort and yarrow. This keeps the whole display light and delicate in appearance.

To give a Christmas effect which need not look out of place when the decorations have come down, use a good proportion of silver foliage and one or two seedheads sprayed with silver paint, amongst the more colourful herbs. Seedheads to spray silver are: poppy (carefully emptied of their seeds first), sorrel, golden rod, fennel and dill. Where there are seeds that are likely to fall later, the paint will help to hold them together. See the Christmas table decoration illustrated on page xxxii.

Snowman

A soft, cuddly toy with a Christmas message and soothing fragrance, the snowman is perfect for over-excited children at bedtime. It can be made in two sizes.

You will need:

¼m (¼yd) white fur fabric
crochet or strong thread in white
¼m (¼yd) butter muslin
scraps of red and black felt
a few lengths of wool to plait for a scarf
card to make patterns for a 19cm (7½in) or 38cm (15in) circle
and a 13cm (5in) or 26cm (10in) circle
fragrant dried herb filling - very fragrant rose petals,
lavender, or a blend of two-thirds lavender and one-third chamomile flowers, with ½-1 dessertspoon of pounded dill seeds and ½-1 dessertspoon orris root (depending on the size chosen)

For each snowman cut 1 large and 1 small circle of white fur fabric and butter muslin for the body and the head. Edge each circle by machine oversewing. With a knot on the end of the thread (to remain on the outside of the material), gather each circle 1½cm (½in) in from the outer edge. On the body, leave one long end of crochet cotton to attach the head later.

Fill the muslin circles with fragrant herbs and pull the gathering tight, tying and then stitching to secure the ends. Place the fragrant bags of filling inside the fur fabric circles and repeat, tying and stitching these ends in the same way. Cut circles of black felt for the eyes and nose and a shape from the red felt for the mouth, glueing these in place on the head. For a small child these are safer stitched in place or embroidered on. Stitch the head to the body very securely with back-stitch (see diagram on page 140) using the crochet cotton from gathering and a further length if necessary.

Plait six strands of brightly coloured wool, each 1m (1yd) long to make a scarf which will go around the neck at least once with long ends to hang down. Wind the scarf around the neck to cover your earlier stitching. **Please note:** Not to be made for children suffering from asthma.

Kitchen plait

This bright decoration is welcome in any kitchen, with the bonus of herb blends to be enJoyed by the enthusiastic cook in the New Year.

You will need:

6 lengths of coloured raffia and 12 lengths of plain raffia each approx. 1.25m (48in).
18cm (7in) diameter circles of Christmas material and butter muslin for bags
1 garlic head with length of stem
1m (1yd) of narrow red or green ribbon
fine, strong, gold thread and a strong, small-eyed needle
gold balls,
helichrysum flowers and florist's wire (optional),
cinnamon sticks, nutmegs, narrow gold braid and star anise.

Fold all of the lengths of raffia in half and lay them side by side in a group of 6 plain, 6 coloured and 6 plain. Tie them together about 2½cm (1in) below the folds, with a short length of raffia. With the raffia on a flat surface, holding the folded end down, work a tight plait bringing the lengths to the right over the centre group and then from the left over the group now in the centre, until the ends start to become thin, at about 36cm (14in). Tie again with a short length of raffia just above the end of the plait. Trim.

Make the Christmas bags by taking each circle and turning under a small hem. Stitch this neatly in a contrasting thread. Next, work a row of gathering stitches 1½cm (½in) in from this edge using crochet cotton or strong thread. Draw up to form the circle into a round bag.

These can be filled with fragrant or mixed culinary herbs, such as the herb pepper, (on page 216). Fill and tie closed. Stitch the bags to the raffia plait with strong thread at intervals, taking the stitches through to the back of the plait. Sew the garlic head in the same way, taking the stitches through the stem of the garlic and the plait. Add decorations of ribbon bows over the raffia ties.

Between the bags add interest with pieces of cinnamon stick decorated with several gold balls threaded onto the gold lurex used to stitch them to the plait, star anise decorated with a gold ball at the centre in the same way, helichrysum flowers attached to the plait with florist's wire (be sure to bend the ends over and push well in), or more elaborate combinations. Two pieces of cinnamon stick with star anise laid over them can be most effective, or a nutmeg in gold braid (see diagram 2 on page 183). Additionally, before attaching the decorations you may like to spray a plait of plain raffia, gold; or wind narrow gold braid around it in a long spiral which binds cinnamon sticks on the way.

Mulled wine basket

A versatile present, this is suitable for almost any age and either sex. The recipe with the ingredients can be for an alcoholic or non-alcoholic wine.

You will need:
red tissue or crepe paper
small or large gold doílies to cut to size
a small oblong basket, approx. 15-20cm (6 x 8in), or a round one with an 18cm (7in) diameter
a helichrysum or dried rosebud
small self-sealing polythene bags (optional)
clingfilm
card to make a 13cm (5in) diameter circular pattern
paper glue
a large label (wine labels are suitable)
small amounts of nutmegs, cloves, coriander seeds, root ginger and cinnamon sticks
scissors and a stapler (optional)

Using your card pattern, cut 5 circles through 5 thicknesses of red paper. Note that for varying sizes of basket the diameter of the circles will need altering. With tiny dabs of glue, secure one small gold doily at the centre of each of the top circles. Alternatively cut the edging of a large doily to fit the circles as a decorative fan. Pinch the circle at one side to fold in half with all 5 thicknesses of tissue held together. Fold lower flap against the open shell shape and Glue or staple as shown in diagram 1. Repeat with all 5 circles.

Place them together side by side with the points towards the centre. You now have a flower shape with each red "petal" lined with gold doily. Glue each one to the next, one-third of the distance from the centre to the outer edge and about half way up. The placing of this glue is crucial to the success of the finished shape.

Set this paper lining inside the basket. Make up the fillings for each petal: 3-6 nutmegs, cinnamon sticks broken into several lengths, 3-6 pieces of root ginger and as many cloves and coriander seeds as will neatly fill the open petals. To keep the herbs and spices in place you may wish to put them into small self-sealing, labelled bags, setting each in the basket. Add the dried flower in the centre of the paper flower shape and write out a recipe for mulled wine on the wine label. This can be alcoholic or non-alcoholic (see Christmas cookery page 214). Lastly, slip the recipe between the flower shape and the side of the basket at one end, turning in the edges. Cover the whole with clingfilm.

Christmas pot-pourri
With their symbolic meanings, the herbs below bring together all the ingredients of a good Christmas in a rich, spicy, fragrance.

You will need:
a glass jar with a thick cork, or covered glass or china bowl
red or green ribbon or lace to trim
a large gift tag
dried herbs - 1½ tablespoons marjoram, 2 tablespoons lemon balm, 1 tablespoon thyme (dried flowering if possible), 2 tablespoons rosehips, 2 tablespoons dried fragrant rosebuds, 1 dessertspoon sprigs of rosemary, ½ tablespoon sage, 1 teaspoon aniseed, ½ tablespoon orris root, 2 drops essential oil of cinnamon, 2 drops essential oil of orange or mandarin.
Blend the herbs, flowers and rosehips. Pound the aniseed before stirring in. Next add the powdered orris root and stir again. Lastly, drip in the essential oils, one drop at a time, as too much can spoil the pot-pourri. Keep sealed in a dark glass container in a warm, dark cupboard for 6 weeks before the gift will be opened. Swirl the jar a little at intervals during this time.

Before giving the present add the ribbon and write the following on the gift label:

Christmas pot-pourri bringing marjoram to wish you joy, lemon balm for peace, a good thyme, roses and rosehips as the flowers and seeds of love, rosemary for happy memories, sage to wish you a long life, aniseed to give sweetness, orris root to preserve all you value, and oils for fruity richness and the spice of life!

Flower coasters or paper weights

A pretty gift which offers a glimpse of your summer garden, these coasters or paperweights may hold special memories for the person receiving them.

You will need:

clear coasters or paperweights from a craft shop
adhesive felt for the backing
thin, stiff card, in white or a pastel shade
paper glue, tweezers, scissors and cocktail sticks
a selection of pressed herb flowers which might include forget-me-nots, golden rod, oregano, woad, clary sage bracts, violets, cowslips, gold lace polyanthus, chive petals, basil thyme, St. John's wort, hyssop, avens and carnation or pink petals
pressed herb leaves which might include - sweet cicely, white jasmine, small golden hop, sweet woodruff, fennel and silver *Artemisias*.

Cut the thin card to fit the indented circle in the coaster or paperweight exactly. Select flowers and foliage and, using the tweezers if liked, experiment with arrangements until you are satisfied. If you are trying to achieve a complex effect and have sufficient materials, it is best to repeat this on a second circle of card, using the first for reference.

Squeeze a little glue onto a scrap piece of card. Take tiny dabs from this onto the end of a cocktail stick and carefully apply to the back of the flowers with this. Particular care needs to be taken with violets, pinks or members of the heartsease family as the petals easily curl up when the glue is applied. With the flowers and leaves fixed to the card, wipe away any excess glue with a tissue. Cut the adhesive felt to fit behind the card, slightly overlapping the edges. Peel away the backing paper and press the felt firmly into place, trimming if necessary. Finally polish the coaster or paperweight with a clean duster.

Fragrant Jewellery

A unique present to give lasting pleasure, for those who have everything. This gift combines frankincense, sandalwood, spices, seeds and roots with other ingredients for a real winner. As the skin temperature of the wearer heats the beads, so they give out more perfume.

You will need:

a heavy duty grinder, or pestle and mortar
a tablespoon, dessertspoon and teaspoon for measuring
a bowl
a small screwtop glass jar
a darning needle and thread
small boxes
cotton wool
greaseproof paper

herb ingredients - 2 tablespoons of ground dried lavender, 1 dessertspoon cinnamon flakes, 1 dessertspoon sandalwood chips, 1 dessertspoon safflower or pot marigold petals, or a few strands of saffron, 1 tablespoon of gum benzoin, powdered, 1 teaspoon coriander seeds, 1 teaspoon lovage seeds, 1 teaspoon star anise seeds, 1 teaspoon ground rosemary, small piece of dried angelica root to give 3 teaspoons of ground powder, gum tragacanth (available from cake decorating shops),1 tablespoon of gum benzoin (available from a good herbalists)
2fl. oz water or rosewater
olive oil
essential oils - basil, sandalwood and frankincense
First make the mucilage of tragacanth which is used to bind the other ingredients together. Add the gum tragacanth powder and a pinch of gum benzoin, to one of the waters in a screwtop jar. Shake the ingredients well and set aside for one or two days, shaking the mucilage again at least twice a day. Grind the spices, roots, remaining gum benzoin, sandalwood and seeds together using a powerful electric grinder or pestle and mortar, and add them to the already ground lavender and rosemary in a bowl. Stir in the mucilage of tragacanth which should bring the dry ingredients to a workable paste. Finish the mixing with your fingers. Drip the oils in one by one, with particular care, mixing between each oil. Add 3 drops of essential oil of basil, 5 drops of essential oil of frankincense and 7 drops of essential oil of sandalwood.

Note. Care should be taken to wear rubber gloves if you have sensitive skin, as some people may experience an allergic reaction, especially when adding the drops of essential oil to the paste and working these in.

Divide the paste into portions. A mustard spoon gives the correct amount of paste for a small bead about 1.25cm (½in) in diameter. The beads can be made in several sizes and different shapes - perhaps cubes, diamonds or oblong blocks. While the paste is still drying, thread the needle with crochet cotton or linen thread and moisten this with a little olive oil before tying a knot in the end and threading the beads onto it, leaving good spaces between them while they finish drying.

Lay the strings of beads on greaseproof paper on a tray and store away from direct light and heat where there is a good airflow, for 1-2 weeks. Check and turn the beads every day or so, wiping away any mould which may appear in damp conditions, using a drop of essential oil on a tissue. Pack the beads in cotton wool in small boxes for a further 2-3 weeks to mature and fix the fragrances. They are then ready to fit into jewellery settings or thread for a completed necklace, bracelet or belt. This amount will make about 30 assorted beads.

Herb design pincushion on wristband

The perfect present for a friend or relative who is a keen needlewoman. Quick to make, the pincushion also shows thought.

You will need:
a small square of tapestry canvas, approx 13 x 13cm (5 x 5in)
a square of felt or velvet of the same size
30cm (12in) length of velvet ribbon, 2cm (¾in) wide
1 hank each of crewel wools:

colour	D.M.C.	Appletons crewel wools
orange	7919	624
lemon yellow	7726	552
lilac	7262	451
purple	7247	105
sage green	7404	641
leaf green	7361	543
darker green	7427	355

scissors, and tapestry needle
a small frame to keep the canvas taut as it is being worked
bran and lavender to fill
First mark the centre lines of your canvas, both horizontally and vertically, with tacking stitches in cotton that are later removed. Diagonal lines worked in the same way will guide you to the corners of the design. Following the graph on page 183 work the heartsease flowers and background in tent stitch (see diagram 1a on page 140).

Place the completed needlepoint face down on the right side of the velvet or felt and trim to the same size. Taking two 15cm (6in) lengths of ribbon, lay these between the right sides of the materials to stitch firmly into opposite seams. Take care to fold the remainder of each length away from your stitching. Tack and machine along the exact edge of your needlepoint stitches on three sides. Turn right side out. Stuff the pincushion with bran and lavender mixed together until it is hard. Neatly handstitch the fourth side closed. Work an additional row of blanket stitch in sage green crewel wool over all four edge seams.

Sew two press studs or attach a short strip of velcro to the ribbon band to fasten, oversewing the ribbon ends to prevent fraying.

Miniature herb garden

Delicate and fragrant, this is a present which can really show your artistic flair. The beauty of these tiny gardens is that, covered for most of the time, they will last and last.

You will need:

a decorative oval box, at least 10cm (4in) across
a block of dry oasis
a few dried herb flowers chosen from: oregano, cotton lavender, curry plant, lavender, tansy, statice and wild yarrow and seedheads of horehound or thrift
dill weed
scissors, glue, tweezers (optional), sharp knife
Use the box to impress its own shape into the block of oasis. Cutting to these lines with a sharp knife, cut the oasis to fill the depth of about two-thirds of the container. Push the oasis down into the box and, following the diagram, mark out the area of grass onto the oasis with a cocktail stick or sharp pencil. A patchwork template could also be used to make the impression, or a biscuit cutter if you have one to size.

Mulled wine basket

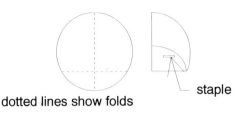

dotted lines show folds staple

gold braid on nutmeg

Pattern for Pincushion

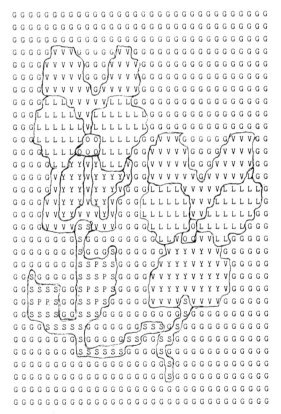

G – Green (sage)   V – Violet   Y – Yellow   L – Lilac
O – Orange   S – Stem green   P – Pale leaf green

Prepare the herb flowers by cutting the stems to a length of about 1½cm (½in) and placing each separate herb on small saucers or tin lids. Apply glue to the grass area and pour dill weed over to cover quite thickly. Press down gently before turning the box upside down over a sheet of paper to remove any excess. Add a little extra glue and more dill to cover any bare patches and repeat.

Next push the central flowers into the oasis, always working out towards the sides. With these firmly set, begin the outer border for the oval garden by setting the thrift or horehound heads and yellow curry plant flowers in place at intervals. Fill the spaces between them with oregano and statice. The clumps of tansy add the finishing touches, as in the illustration on page xxvi.

Selection box

A scrumptious gift that could be for a whole family, or anyone with a sweet tooth

You will need:

a Christmas gift box, clear plastic container or used chocolate box which is clean and can be covered as necessary with Christmas paper
small paper cases for chocolates
ribbon
card or a large label for details
A selection of home-made sweets chosen from the recipes in the Christmas cookery on pages 218-220. Chocolates should be consumed within a few days as it is difficult to bring the chocolate to the exact temperature needed for a lasting, perfect, glaze. Candies and fudge will keep and travel better if the present is to be posted. They are all at their best eaten within 10-14 days, but this should not be a problem for anyone receiving the gift! With the box filled, make a guide on a large label, outlining each candy and giving them mouthwatering names such as sweet cicely delight, tipsy apricot surprise and melting marigold soothers. A ribbon bow on the outside of the box adds a touch of luxury.

Cosmetic basket

Fun to make, the natural ingredients ensure this will be a popular gift.

You will need:

a round basket approx. 23cm (9in) in diameter
either, a small decorative jar, a round earthenware or china dish approx. 8cm (3in) in diameter for the soap, and another dish of similar size or larger for the handcream
or, a set of three matching containers
a small pan and heatproof dish
a square of butter muslin 18 x 18cm (7 x 7in)
a grinder or pestle and mortar
herb ingredients - for the talcum: 4 tablespoons of powdered orris root, 2 tablespoons of fragrant rose petals and 1 level teaspoon of ground cloves. For the soap: a 100g (4oz) bar of plain unscented soap, 9 fresh pot marigold flowers, 25g (1oz) each of fresh applemint and lemon balm leaves, 10fl. oz boiling water, 5 drops essential oil of

melissa or geranium. For the handcream: 15g (½oz) of anhydrous lanolin, 2fl. oz peach kernel oil, 1 tablespoon of strong pot marigold infusion, 6 drops essential oil of frankincense.

To make the talcum, mix together the powdered orris root, finely ground rose petals and freshly ground cloves. Pour into a glass jar or box. Old, kitchen spice jars which have been sterilized can be re-used and will have an inner top which allows only a little powder out at a time. A larger box or open-necked jar could be provided with a powder puff, set in the top.

To make marigold, mint and balm soap, pour the boiling water over the petals from 9 fresh pot marigolds and torn applemint and lemon balm leaves, already set in an enamel pan. Simmer gently, covered, for 15 minutes. Leave to stand for 2-3 hours. Grate the bar of unscented plain white soap, or use the same quantity of pure soapflakes. Strain the herb decoction over the soap into a heatproof bowl set over a pan of hot water, simmering gently on a low heat. Melt the two together, stirring frequently. Remove from the heat. Cool slightly. Add the essential oil of melissa or geranium. Stir well in and pour into greased moulds to set. The moulds can be old buntins, shells or dishes. Leave the soap for 3-5 days before unmoulding it and wrapping in greaseproof paper. Keep in a warm, dry place for 2 weeks before wrapping in clear film and placing in a dish or container in the completed basket.

To make the marigold handcream, melt the lanolin in a heatproof bowl over a pan of gently boiling water. Add the peach kernel oil slowly, trickling it down the side of the bowl and stirring briskly. Remove the bowl from the heat and add the herb infusion just as cautiously. Stir gently as the cream cools until you can comfortably touch it. Drip in the essential oil, one drop at a time and pour into containers, covering immediately.

Seed selection

When friends or relatives have enjoyed visiting your garden in summer, it will be a special pleasure to receive seeds of the plants they have admired...

You will need:

a packet of plain brown wages envelopes
seeds gathered from your garden
pressed flowers or foliage from the same herbs
paper glue

Smaller envelopes can be bought for those herbs that are familiar to your friends and need little in the way of instructions. A wages envelope will give you the space for a pressed flower decoration and written instructions for cultivation. You may even wish to write a favourite short recipe with some herbs.

Seeds must be gathered on a dry day, preferably when the weather has been consistently fine. Empty the seeds out of the seedpods onto labelled saucers or trays set in the sunshine and leave open for several further days to be sure they are absolutely dry. They can then either be sealed in aluminium foil first, or poured straight into the wages envelopes, sealed and labelled.

Beneath the name of the herb (you may like to add its Latin name) write Annual,

Perennial or Biennial, Height, When to sow - indoors or outdoors - whether it likes sun or shade, and any good companions or special attention it needs. Below this you might write uses in cookery, fragrances etc - whatever information you think makes it of particular interest to the recipient. For example:

Hyssop - Hyssopus officinalis. Perennial. 60-90cm (2 to 3ft) tall. Sow indoors Feb-Mar, outdoors from April. Plant 15cm (6in) apart for low hedging or at 45cm (18in). Good protection for beans against blackfly and brassicas against cabbage white butterflies. Likes sun and poorish soil. Bee herb. Flowers June-August. Cut back late summer. Tangy bean seasoning.

Herbs that will give you plentiful seeds and press well are biennial clary sage, oregano, salad burnet (leaves), meadowsweet (leaves), marshmallow, chamomile, hyssop, water avens, red or yellow cowslips, elecampane (flower petals can be pressed as a small spray, the whole flower is more difficult), dyer's chamomile, motherwort (the lovely pink flowers at either side of the stem are especially effective when pressed with a leaf or two) and lady's mantle.

Aromatic teacosy

A welcome present for anyone who enjoys a good cup of tea and sits chatting next to the pot.

You will need:

¼m (¼yd) of cotton fabric, lining, butter muslin and wadding
thread and scissors
shaped paper pattern 25cm (10in) top to bottom, and 35cm (14in) at the widest point, see diagram on page 188
herb filling of rose petals with 1 tablespoon of orris root and 2 drops essential oil of rose (optional),
lavender
or a blend of two-thirds lavender to one-third lemon verbena with 1 tablespoon of orris root and 1 drop of essential oil of lavender and 2 drops of essential oil of lemon

Using the paper pattern, cut 2 shapes from the cotton fabric and lining. Cut 2 pieces of butter muslin to fit the top part of the teacosy marked (a) on the diagram on page 188. Next, cut 1 full shape from the wadding and a second piece to fit the bottom part of the teacosy marked (b) on the diagram page 188. Cut a single strip of cotton fabric 7.5cm (3in) wide and 112cm (44in) long. Neaten each end with a small, machine stitched hem. Fold the strip in half with the wrong sides together and gather a little less than 1.25cm (½in) in from the long edge. Lay one piece of cotton fabric right side up. Pin and tack the gathered frill along the centre of the curve following the seamline 2cm (¾in) in, with the frill fold away from the seam. Lay the second cotton fabric piece right side down against the first. Next, lay the two lining pieces, right sides together, on top. Pin and tack through all five layers. Machine the complete curve. Machine the butter muslin all around the edges, leaving a gap only 5cm (2in) wide for filling. Turn right side out.

Blend the lavender and lemon verbena, or other herbs of your choice with orris root and add the essential oil with care. Fill the muslin sachet with the material laid flat on a tray to a depth of approximately 1.5-2cm (½ to ¾in) and sew the opening closed. Do not crowd the herb against the curved edge of the sachet as you will need to stitch along this later. With the sachet still laid flat make large back-stitches diagonally across the sachet in one direction and then stitch again in lines at right angles, to give diamond sections. Adjust the depth of herb as you work to keep the distribution even. This will stop the herbs falling to the base of the sachet when the teacosy is in use.

Take the larger piece of wadding and trim away 1.25cm (½in) all the way round the edge. Place it between the lining and the outer material. Lay the herb sachet and the smaller piece of wadding on top of the lining material. Handstitch these in place into the seams and overstitch the edges of the muslin and wadding where they meet, to leave a smooth join. With your thumbs between the right sides of the outer material, turn the teacosy right side out. Turn up the bottom hem with the right sides of cotton material and lining together. Tack and machine. Seal the teacosy in a polythene bag for 2-3 weeks before Christmas to fix the perfume.

A wallet of colours

So often we search for just the right shade to work a flower or leaf. Give your friend or relative a treat with natural colours in wools to weave a small picture, or work into a needlepoint canvas. The wallet to keep them tidy during use has a scented lining, takes 8-10 hanks of wools and is made to hang from a tapestry frame.

You will need:

¼m (¼yd) cotton fabric
2m (2yd) contrasting or matching ribbon 2cm (¾in) wide
¼ m (¼yd) wadding, and a scrap of butter muslin
lavender
selection of dyed wools
Cut a piece of cotton fabric 34 x 53cm (13½ x 21in), and a smaller piece 14 x 12.5cm (5½ x 5in) for the pocket. Cut 2 lengths of wadding, each 15 x 19cm (6 x7½in), and a piece of butter muslin 14 x 16.5cm (5½ x 6½in). Turn hems at the edges of the pocket of cotton fabric to neaten, with a double hem at the top edge. Machine. Fold the large piece of cotton fabric in half lengthways and mark the fold with pins at the centre. Open out. Fold again horizontally to find the centre and mark again with pins. Place the pocket as shown in the diagram on page 188, to lay at the centre of the completed wallet. Machine, leaving the top of the pocket open and ensuring the pocket is attached only to one thickness of material.

Fold the cotton fabric of the wallet in half, with right sides together, and machine the ends closed, leaving a 2cm (¾in) seam allowance. Turn the right way out. Machine three sides of the muslin and turn right side out. Fill with lavender, or another chosen herb, until full but not bulky. Handstitch the fourth side closed. Set between the pieces of wadding to lie behind the pocket. Having turned in a small hem along the long, open side, machine closed. If the herb is to be replaced at a later date, leave a 4cm (1½in) gap close to the pocket, which can be handstitched or closed with fasteners.

Cut 2 lengths of matching or contrasting ribbon, each 27cm (10½in) long. Turn the end of the first under and place it along the centre line of the wallet as shown in diagram on page 188, starting 1.25cm (½in) in from the edge. Backstitch in place.

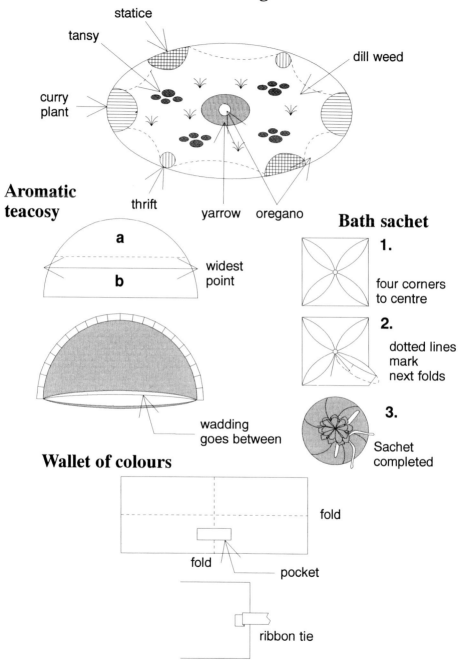

Miniature herb garden

statice

tansy

dill weed

curry plant

thrift   yarrow   oregano

Aromatic teacosy

a

b

widest point

wadding goes between

Bath sachet

1.

four corners to centre

2.

dotted lines mark next folds

3.

Sachet completed

Wallet of colours

fold

fold

pocket

ribbon tie

Lay a hank of wool next to the ribbon and pass the ribbon over the top, pinning it to hold the hank in place. Backstitch. Repeat 4 times, working towards the pocket. Place the second length of ribbon and stitch in the same way at the other side of the pocket. Cut a third length of ribbon, 34cm (13½in), backstitch this in place on a centre line 2.5cm (1in) in from the edge of the wallet. Cut a fourth length of ribbon 53cm (21in) long and backstitch this in place 24cm (9½in) from the other end so that you now have a "tie" at either end of the wallet. See diagram on page 188. To close the wallet it is rolled and the ribbons tied in a double bow which can then be used to hang it from a frame.

Christmas herb candles

Christmas is never quite complete without candles and what better way to make this gift memorable than by decorating candles with herbs.

You will need:

green, red or white candles
a selection of pressed herb flowers and foliage
tweezers and a dessertspoon
a small quantity of paraffin wax (sold by the kilo in craft shops)
an old pan or heatproof bowl and a larger pan
a thermometer
a small watercolour paintbrush

Before heating the wax, choose which herb flowers and leaves you wish to use and plan exactly where they are to be placed on the candle. Have a kettle of hot, but not boiling, water to hand. Warm the spoon in the water for a few seconds and then dry it quickly. While it holds the heat, gently press the herb flowers and leaves into place on the candle with the back of the spoon. As the spoon cools, warm it again and continue. Silver leaves such as the delicate *Artemisias,* silverweed and cotton lavender are most effective on green candles. White candles are needed for really colourful, pretty sprays of herb. Simple variegated leaves or a single flower will stand out best against the red.

When the decorations are complete, pour the wax flakes into the heatproof bowl or smaller pan and heat this over the larger pan of boiling water. The water should not come further than half way up the sides of the smaller pan. Stand the thermometer in the melting wax. Never leave a pan of wax on the stove unattended. It is very unlikely to catch fire, but if it does, then cover the flames to smother the fire and turn off the heat. Do not move the pan immediately or pour water on the flames.

When the wax has reached a temperature of 95-97°C it is ready to be painted over the flowers and leaves, using the small paintbrush. With coloured candles it will appear as a white film and can be effective as a mock frosting painted heavily over silver leaves on green candles. Fragrance can be added at this stage with a few drops of candlemaker's oil, such as rose, lavender, jasmine, sandalwood or violet. Stir well in with the thermometer and carefully paint a thin layer of wax over the herbs. Hold the candles by their wicks when moving them to avoid damaging your work. A large amount of herb can act as a wick itself as the flame reaches it and so always add a little note to the label to burn safely in a suitable container. Herb flower arrangements can also be kept low down on the candle for better safety, although if you think your friend or relative unlikely to burn it, the herbs could be placed up to the top with the precaution of a warning label. The finished candles should be packed in boxes, surrounded by soft packing or rolled in clear film.

Spicy lavender sacks

A gift for the man who has everything. The exotic, slightly heady fragrance of these simple sacks makes them perfect to hang in a man's car, sit amongst his books in a study or lay with socks and woollens in a drawer.

You will need:
¼m (¼yd) of hessian or fine canvas
58cm (23in) length of green Seasons Greetings ribbon 2cm (¾in) wide
6 tablespoons lavender
1 teaspoon cloves
2 cinnamon sticks
a star anise
essential oil of cinnamon, frankincense or sandalwood
glue
Cut a piece of hessian 24 x 22cm (9½ x 8½in). Turn down a double hem of 1.25cm (½in) along one short side which will form the top of the sack, and machine. Oversew the other raw edges. Fold the material with right sides together, machining again to form a sack. Turn right side out and fill with lavender. Add a teaspoon of pounded cloves, a few star anise and 2 drops each of essential oil of cinnamon and either the essential oil of sandalwood or frankincense. Stir these into the lavender with one of the cinnamon sticks and then place both sticks pointing diagonally into the sack into the bottom corners. These hold the sack in the correct shape. Pack the herbs well down and tie the neck with the Seasons Greetings ribbon in a double bow. Decorate the front of the sack by fixing a star anise, perhaps with a gold ball at the centre, with a dab of glue. Keep sealed in a polythene bag for a few days before wrapping, or give double wrapped in polythene and Christmas paper to fix the fragrances.

Decorated Box

This is an exceptionally attractive present which might be used to store writing paper, special letters from friends, bottles of essential oils etc.

You will need:
a plain wooden box (obtainable from craft shops)
clear varnish (preferably a spray)
clear glue
pressed flowers (those that press really flat will give the best results)
Choose your herbs from amongst biennial clary sage, forget-me-nots, wild strawberry flowers, cowslips, sweet cicely leaves, golden hop and white jasmine leaves and the petals of pinks. Golden rod, water avens and hyssop are all lovely but should be included only if the box will not be in regular use.

Decide on your design using the herbs available and glue these firmly in place. Set the box outside on a still, warm day if possible, or indoors on sheets of newspaper, well away from furniture. Spray or paint with clear varnish. Give another coat when the first has dried, and a third if necessary.

Notepaper and elder ink
To someone who enjoys writing elegant letters, this will be a real treat.

You will need:
Either a carved or plain wooden box
lengths of narrow ribbon to tone with the colours of your paper
24 or 36 sheets of elderberry dyed paper
a small bottle of elder ink
For the recipes for dyeing paper and making the ink, see the craft section pages 163-168. It is more effective if several shades of blue through pink to purple can be achieved. The paper might be home-made or bought. Ensure the ink is in a very well-sealed bottle and the paper protected adequately from any spillage. Roll wads of the finished paper and tie with the ribbons for a perfect presentation.

Bath sachets
A small and pretty present which could be hung on the tree. Although designed for use in a scented bath, the sachets can be enjoyed in a bedroom on the dressing table or set amongst clothes in drawers.

You will need:
One fine handkerchief for each sachet
1m (1yd) of matching ribbon 1.25cm (½in) wide
a large label
a polythene bag
5-7 tablespoons herb filling, depending on the size of the handkerchief
For a very personal present, buy plain, lace edged handkerchiefs and embroider your choice of herb in one corner, see the craft section, pages 134-136 for ideas.

Spoon the mixed herbs, which may have a base of rose petals, lavender or lemon verbena, with a half quantity of one of the following herbs - marjoram, lemon balm, eau-de-cologne mint, limeflowers, lemon mint or pot marigold petals - into the centre of the handkerchief and bring the four corners together at the centre. Take the four corners now left and bring those also to the centre (see diagram 1a on page 188). Tie the ribbon firmly round to hold these in place, leaving one very long end. Tie in a double bow and pull any remaining stray edges of handkerchief well through. At the other end of the ribbon make a small loop with a slipknot which will hang the bag from the bathtap.

Write a label giving these instructions: "Hang from the hot tap so that the water runs through the sachet. Dip in the fully run bath and squeeze dry. Leave on an open dish to re-use within 48 hours."

You might also like to add the names of the herbs in the sachet. Seal in a polythene bag before wrapping.

N.B. Do not give a herbal bath sachet to anyone who suffers from asthma, eczema or has skin problems as they may have a reaction to one of the herbs included.

Christmas hamper

A delight for anyone who appreciates good cooking, the contents can be a source of new and useful ingredients, or ready made delicacies.

You will need:

A basket or hamper at least 24 x 19cm (9½ x 7½in)
oddments of raffia or snippets of coloured crepe paper for packing and lining
scraps of Christmas fabric
lengths of red and green ribbon or ric-rac braid
labels
decorative small jars and bottles
a small box covered in Christmas paper
herb fillings
Part of the joy of this present is that it will always be personal, both to you and the recipient. For it will contain your choice from your own store-cupboard of good things made during the year. You might include, as I have in the basket illustrated on page xxviii, small jars of pot marigold and rose sugar, herb pepper and other seasonings, small bags (made as for Christmas bags in the kitchen plait on page177) filled with bouquet garni, soup seasoning or ground rosemary, a large jar of herb jelly, a small bottle of liqueur, and candied roots and flowers.

Other ideas could be a pot of herb mustard, a bottle of herb vinegar or oil, a small china jar filled with your own blended herb tea, mincemeat fragranced with essential oil of rose geranium, rosemary shortbread - the list could go on and on. The gift may even encourage your friend or relative to begin their own exploration of the world of herbs and their many uses.

Flower basket.

Gifts

Hexagonal and oval boxed miniature gardens.

(Left) *Herb design – pin cushion.*

Pressed flower coaster.

Gifts

Basket of talcum, hand cream and soap.

(Right) *Fragrant jewellery.*

(Below) *Aromatic tea cosy.*

Gifts

Hamper of sugars, jelly, seasoning, etc.

(Below left) *Wallet of natural colours.*

Mulled wine basket of seeds and spices.

Pressed flower decorated box.

Elderberry notepaper and ink.

Gifts/decorations

(Left) *Spicy lavender sack, and curtain tie.*

(Centre) *Pot pourri and decorations.*

(Bottom left) *Kitchen plait.*

(Bottom right) *Herb candle.*

Decorations for hanging.

(Top right) The tree.

(Right) Spicy sacks on a string.

Rosemary bower.

Cookery

(Top) *Herbal sweets to celebrate.*

(Below) *Decorated table.*

(Centre) *'Pears in velvet' candies and syrup.*

(Below) *Christmas buffet.*

Herbs at Christmas

CHESTNUTS roast in the embers. while holly and ivy arch over the fireplace enriched by adding boughs of gilded rosemary tied with red ribbons. Herb-scented candles fragrance the air with spices and frankincense; bay and mistletoe hang above doorways to admit all in a spirit of friendship and goodwill and surely here we have the essential elements to revive the traditional spirit of Christmas.

Preparations that restore the past - when herbs and spices flavoured mulled ales and wine, festive cakes were baked with rosemary, coriander and caraway, and herbal jellies, sweetmeats, preserves and decorations graced laden tables - are perhaps the ideal so many of us reach for. Clove-studded pomanders, home-made Christmas crackers and a tree hung with bright, fragrant decorations can provide a perfect backcloth for the celebrations.

What of this past we look upon with such nostalgia? How far back does it reach? Evergreens were cut and taken indoors at mid-winter long before the date of Christmas was set in the fourth century by Pope Julius 1. Evergreens with berries were sacred as fertility symbols, carrying life when the sun's light was dying. They were taken in as refuges for the wood spirits.

Holly, ivy and especially mistletoe were all originally pagan boughs. Holly was adopted first by the church, then ivy, but mistletoe - the golden bough which opened the door to the underworld - remained pagan. Christians said that Christ's cross had been made of mistletoe and after His death it had shrunk to its present size in shame.

In the good old days when the plant was plentiful rather than plastic, men picked a berry from the bough each time they kissed the girl beneath it. When all the berries were gone the girl was released and a new bough brought in for the next couple. It was very unlucky to refuse a kiss under the mistletoe. After twelfth night, one sprig was always left hanging up until the following year for luck. The custom of kissing under the mistletoe may simply come from its association with fertility, but there is another possible origin. In Norse legend, evil Loki tricked Hödr, the blind god, into killing Balder, the son of Odin and god of peace, with a shaft of mistletoe. Although Balder was brought back to life, mistletoe was shamed, as in the Christian story, and made to promise never to harm anyone again. The reputation of mistletoe tells us that it not only receives in friendship, but keeps away evil spirits, thunder and lightning.

Mistletoe was, and still is, a medicinal herb, once honoured by the Druids. It was used by the physicians of Myddfai in South Wales in the Middle Ages to treat nervous diseases, epilepsy, paralysis and dropsy, and generally to restore strength and all the senses. In modern herbal medicine it is still recognised as effective for epilepsy, hypertension and water retention.

Holly has many superstitions and rituals woven around it. While Christians likened it to Christ's crown of thorns and even the burning bush, it also had connections with the supernatural. It was believed it could reveal to young girls who they would marry: sprigs of holly were tied to each upright of four poster beds and the daughter or daughters of the house solemnly ate their roasted apples before laying down to dream of their future husband.

They could also try pricking the initials of three favourite boys into three holly leaves and setting these under their pillow - again to induce a prophetic dream. A really desperate girl could finally turn to the most uncomfortable method, which must surely have taken some courage. This was to sew nine holly leaves onto their nightgown and retire to bed wearing it. We can imagine the inevitable results and perhaps it is not surprising that on this occasion the future husband appeared in a vision rather than a dream!

Purely as a Christmas decoration, holly was brought in along with the yule log, mistletoe and ivy on "Adam and Eve's Day" - that is, Christmas Eve. The name Adam and Eve's Day was said to come from the birth of Christ taking away the sin of Adam and Eve. Evergreens, including holly, had previously been brought in for the Roman festival of Saturnalia. This honoured sowing seeds, and began on 17th December, lasting for seven days. In early times, bringing the greenery in before Christmas Eve would suggest the household was celebrating this festival, rather than the Christian Christmas.

You may have noticed that some holly leaves are comparatively smooth and these were known as "she" holly, while the very spiky leaves were "he" holly. Care should be taken to bring in he or she holly according to who you wish to rule the house for the following 12 months. To come across a broken branch of holly while gathering it could mean a happy surprise. To drop a sprig of holly as you were bringing it in was considered unlucky, possibly because you were likely to tread on it shortly afterwards. Taking holly down after Christmas also required a cautious approach. Then the herb must be burned, buried or, strangely - given to cows. The first two seem sensible precautions, the third mysterious, unless it relates to the idea that throwing holly after an animal would make it lie down quietly. All decorations must of course be down by Plough Monday (the first Monday after Twelfth Day).

Holly also is a medicinal herb. It was used in early times against smallpox and fevers, and the berries administered as a rather dangerous purge. (Care should be taken not to allow children to eat berries from holly decorations). Modern research confirms the herb's application in reducing fevers and, administered cautiously, to treat diarrhoea. It is not a herb for home treatment.

According to tradition, ivy has an entirely different nature to holly. In some symbolism the herb is seen as having a feminine, clinging role, while holly is masculine. Dedicated to Bacchus, Roman god of wine, ivy was hung as wreaths around his statue and worshippers at his festival. The connection with Bacchus reminds us of the biblical story of Moses, since Bacchus was also abandoned by his mother - this time being hidden in ivy rather than bulrushes. Ivy remained a herb associated with wine, although none could be made from it and ivy bushes were hung outside early taverns as signs. We still have numerous public houses called "The Ivy House" from this custom.

Medicinally, ivy was used for dysentery and modern research recommends ivy tincture to treat whooping cough and other preparations for neuralgia, rheumatism and so on. In large doses the berries are poisonous.

Another ancient herb decoration, associated first with the Roman Kalends which later became our New Year, is bay. This was nailed over the doorways as a peaceful greeting in a similar manner to mistletoe. Bay still makes a lovely door decoration in the form of a wreath, together with other herbs, spices and ribbons.

Bay can also be a most attractive table decoration. Using a small tree brought in for the winter for protection against frost, tinsel and light ornaments can be hung from the twigs without harming the tree. Keep well watered and, if possible, in plenty of light during this time. Do not site your decoration in a dark corner.

Rosemary is the one herb used for Christmas decorations that is specifically Christian and has no pagan history. It seems sad that this is also the herb which was almost lost from the celebrations in the last century. With herb gardens once more becoming a frequent sight and large rosemary bushes no longer a rarity, we can return to the delight of using rosemary boughs, whether left to dry naturally as they hang or gilded.

There is a tradition, which may well be Spanish, about the origin of the name. This tells anew the story of the flight into Egypt from Herod's soldiers. The Virgin Mary and Jesus were almost caught but a rosemary bush folded its boughs around Mary and the babe, and hid them. It is said the blue colour of rosemary flowers comes from the colour of Mary's robe and its scent from the contact with the baby Jesus.

Rosemary, then, has a very special connection with Christmas and the Christ child. To emphasise this, I always use sprigs of the herb to form a green and fragrant "bower" for our crib figures. Rosemary was also a herb that was carried and used in quantity at all large gatherings. Its antiseptic properties could then be used for protection against the spread of disease. Favoured also as a herb of remembrance and friendship, it can join bay and mistletoe with welcoming thoughts at doorways.

Decorations to make
A door wreath

You will need:
for the base - a metal coathanger and lengths of ivy, as long as you can find or a bought base of raffia or vines
sprays of bay leaves, juniper or holly
15cm (6in) sprigs of rosemary
cinnamon sticks, whole star anise, pine cones
small gold balls
2m (2yd) red ribbon 2.5cm (1in) wide
florist's wire and wire cutters
If you are making your own base, form the coathanger into a circle, removing the hook unless you are planning to make a very wide wreath which will cover it. Twine the freshly gathered ivy stems around the wire and after the first couple of times around the whole circle - in and out of each other, to build up a firm circular shape, at least 7.5cm (3in) across.

Remove any ivy leaves which seem to crowd the circle, leaving some for effect. Begin adding sprigs of greenery at intervals around the wreath, using as much bay or holly as possible. Place the sprays of rosemary and juniper to show against the plain leaves and carry across into the centre and then out to the edge.

Add sprays of spices. Make these as follows. Take 2 cinnamon sticks, a whole star anise, a gold ball and a length of florist's wire. Thread the wire through the gold of the star and twist it once below the star seedpod, leaving the two ends pointing in opposite directions. Lay the star anise across the cinnamon sticks, placed side by side and wrap the florist's wire around them and again twist it once or twice below the sticks, leaving the two ends still just over 2.5cm (1in) long. Push these into the wreath base, twisting each around ivy or vine and hiding the sharp end safely.

Beech mast, pine cones and nuts can also be wired and added with or without cinnamon sticks, or the cinnamon sticks can simply be wired to the wreath and the wire covered with narrow red or gold ribbons. With pine cones, take a wire loop around the cone, just above the base and between the scales, twist and attach as before. For beech mast, the florist's wire is taken down, between the open "petals" and round the stem. To attach nuts, drill a hole through one end of the nut to insert either wire or a cocktail stick which can be pushed into the wreath. Nutmegs can also be drilled to take a cocktail stick which is glued in place.

A large bow of red ribbon is added to hang below the wreath on the door.

Christmas swag

Swags of herbs look wonderfully effective in old houses, where they can be hung along beams, but they are also attractive hung vertically against a velvet background on a modern wall. If you have a wide pelmet to your curtains, one can be looped above it; or, for a very grand Christmas buffet, swags may be attached to a heavy table drape.

Ready made swag plaits can be bought from florists in varying lengths. The swag in the illustration is 1m (40in) long. First gather your materials together:

You will need
One or more swag plaits
dried herbs selected from - oregano, tansy, curry plant, double feverfew, hyssop, winter savory, mints, thymes, cotton lavender (foliage and flowers), sneezewort, yarrows, germander (flowering with foliage), purple and tricolor sage, juniper, rosemary (sprayed with gold paint), lavenders, bay, helichrysum, small bags of Christmas material to fill with lavender, spices or a rose blend
narrow ribbons cinnamon sticks
Each swag should be unique. From the herbs above it is possible to produce one with the accent on red helichrysum, green juniper, bay and silvery leaved cotton lavender with tiny bags of Christmas spices between and ribbon bows scented with essential oils as a final touch.

Equally effective would be a combination of the purple tones of oregano, thymes, yarrow and bergamot with silver-grey leaves - perhaps sages and cotton lavender. A swag bright with yellow curry plant amongst helichrysum can be left hanging through the dark January days if the tinsel or ribbons added for festive effect are later removed and replaced with extra herbs as in the illustration on page xiii.

Small bunches of herbs should be prepared first, ranging from just wide enough to give the swag covering, to double the width. Make at least six, together with any small bags of Christmas material and spices, and try the effect of laying these together on the plait.

It is best to lay the bunches facing in the same direction until you have some practice, as it is easy to create an untidy appearance where stems are left uncovered if you try to be too creative. Tie each bunch with crochet cotton leaving an end which can be stitched into the plait, or use florist's wire to bind the bunches on. Think about any spaces to be left for ribbon bows, tinsel, Christmas bags or cinnamon sticks, and set these in place as you work.

A horizontally hung swag will require a different appearance to one hung vertically. With a horizontal swag, it is most effective to mark the centre and perhaps sew in a large ribbon bow or a collection of small bags with a spray of greenery behind, leaving one bag at each side or a length of ribbon unattached to cover the stems of the nearest herbs. The bunches of herbs can then be repeated at either side of this marker, working in towards the centre. For a vertical swag there is no need to be as symmetrical in your design.

Pomanders
You will need:
an orange, or large lemon
approx. 25g (1oz) cloves
1m (1yd) of 1.25cm (½in) red, green or gold ribbon
2 tablespoons orris root
1 dessertspoon cinnamon
2 teaspoons ground nutmeg
essential oil of mandarin or lemon
essential oil of cinnamon or clove
essential oil of frankincense (optional)
a large darning needle, or bodkin
1m (1yd) of bias binding or plain tape
a brown paper bag

Mix the powders of orris root, cinnamon and nutmeg together in a dish. Add 2 drops of cinnamon or clove and the matching essential oil for the fruit used. Add 2 drops of essential oil of frankincense if liked.

Roll the orange or lemon in this powder, rubbing it well into the surface. Wrap the plain tape once around the fruit, twist the two ends round each other, and then wrap them around the fruit at right angles to the first circle. Either stitch the ends at this point, or make a hole through the tapes and into the orange, pushing in a clove to hold the tape in place.

You can now begin adding the cloves in vertical lines to fill each of the four sections. To look effective this must be done by beginning at the centre of each section and working outwards to meet the tape at either side, keeping the lines as straight as possible. The cloves should be almost touching. Make a hole for each clove first if necessary with the bodkin or needle. A traditional pomander is covered only in cloves, however the changes can be rung a little by making some rows of holes at regular intervals which are left open and adding heads of lavender or other herbs into these when the pomander is cured and ready to hang.

When the pomander is completely stuck with cloves, hold it just inside the brown paper bag and spoon over the spiced powders once again, turning it as you do

197

so. Gather the open edge of the bag around the tape and pin, having left all the spiced powder inside the bag. Hang from a rack in the airing cupboard to cure for at least 3 weeks. Open the bag and check on the condition of the orange at intervals. It should dry slowly and steadily, shrinking the cloves closer together. Check beneath the tape for any sign of mould and if there is a problem remove the tape, rub again with spices and retie with fresh tape before rehanging in the cupboard. A warm, dry atmosphere should, however, be sufficient to check decay.

When the pomander is fully dry, remove the tape and replace with ribbon or ribbon and lace. The pomanders can be hanging decorations, or set in a bowl for guests to take home.

Christmas tree mats

These are just as pleasing and decorative hung on the wall with the mat attached or, with a card backing inserted into the tree, stood on a shelf amongst Christmas cards.

You will need:

1 raffia place mat, 30.5 x 23cm (12 x 9in)
or stiff card to approx. the size of tree chosen
¼m (¼yd) or two 30cm (12in) squares of green felt
½-1m (½-1yd) Christmas trim braid, approx. ½cm (¼in) wide
2 cinnamon sticks
wadding or herb filling of lavender, ¼-½ teaspoon of ground clove
1 drop per tree of essential oil of mandarin
circles of Christmas material, 5 or 2.5cm (2 or 1in) in diameter
threads and needle
glue
short lengths of florist's wire
gold thread and tinsel
a few star anise seedpods
liquorice stick (optional)
tiny gold balls and stars

The trees can be made in three sizes. The largest is designed to be backed by the mat, and the two smaller ones with a card backing. Cut 2 Christmas tree shapes from the green felt 24cm, 21cm or 18cm (9½in, 8in or 7¼in) tall. Stitch the side edges together, sewing in the end of the braid trim if you wish to zig-zag it back and forth across the tree.

When using card and wadding for the smaller trees, or wadding for any size, cut this to the tree shape, trim away just over ½cm (¼in) and perfume it with a drop of essential oil before laying it between the felts and stitching. Cut a channel in the wadding for the tree trunk of cinnamon and glue in place. For the lavender filling, mix the ground clove with the lavender in a bowl, adding the drop or drops of essential oil, and stir before filling the tree or trees. Set the tree trunk between the felts amongst the herb just before stitching the base closed.

Small bags of Christmas material can now be made by trimming the raw edges with pinking shears or a tiny hem, and then working a circle of gathering stitches close to the edge in strong cotton. Pull the gathering slightly to form the circle into a bag. Fill with coriander seeds or cloves and tie off the ends to enclose the filling. Sew 1-3 of these tiny bags onto each felt tree as a decoration. Glue or stitch a gold star at the top of the tree and add other lengths of tinsel, braid and beads as desired. Tiny bows and twists of coloured braid or ribbon can be stitched onto the zig-zags of tinsel or braid see – the illustration on page xxxi.

Final decorations are used to attach the largest tree to the mat. Cut 2.5cm (1in) lengths of cinnamon or liquorice stick. Take a length of florist's wire twice around the stick, leaving equal lengths of wire hanging beneath. Twist the two ends together just below the stick to secure. Twist another length of wire around each star anise seedpod, taking the centre of the wire across the front of the pod and down between the star arms on either side. Twist below the seedpod as before. For extra effect a gold ball can be threaded onto the wire to sit at the centre of the stick or star.

With the tree against the mat, push the wires of stars and sticks between the coiled raffia on alternate sides of the tree where the felt shape is indented. Open these wires out at the back of the mat, tucking them back into the raffia so that no sharp ends protrude. The mat can be hung from one of the gaps between the raffia coils. To decorate the smaller trees, spices can be attached by stitching them in place with strong gold thread.

Table decorations

It is always a delight to be able to make a table decoration which is original. One that will take friends and neighbours by surprise and really hold their attention. If it is made up of seedheads and dried flowers from your garden, and perhaps a few nut husks and seeds from the hedgerow, it will be even more appreciated.

You will need:

a block of dry oasis approx. 23 x 10cm (9 x 4in)
green felt or Christmas material to cover the sides of the block and extend away from it
a raffia place mat, 30.5 x 23cm (12 x 9in)
a Christmas cracker (for a home-made, fragrant cracker see below)
glue
scraps of tinsel and Christmas material
cinnamon sticks, beechmast, star anise and pine cones
seedheads chosen from dill or fennel, poppies, golden rod, sorrel, cardoon and elecampane
dried flowers chosen from helichrysum, Tudor immortelles, *Eryngium,* bergamot, double feverfew, yarrow and sneezewort
optional foliage could be juniper, rosemary, holly or bay with silvery-leaved lavenders, or cotton lavender for a lighter touch
Begin by shaping the ends of the oasis block if liked. Cut the felt or fabric to cover the sides of the block. One piece of material can be cut in the shape of a Christmas tree and used at the front of the oasis so that it extends over the mat. With fabrics which could fray, stitch or glue turnings as you work.

One or two impressive seedheads are needed as a central focal point. In the decoration illustrated on page xxxii I have used a cardoon sprayed gold to emphasise its armour-like quality. Another, totally different seedhead, slender and quietly elegant, is a sorrel top with most of the seeds already gone, gathered from the edge of a field and sprayed silver. To counteract what might seem a stark effect, several tiny bags of Christmas material can be made and filled with coriander and dill seeds, to hang from the delicate stems, together with fragments of tinsel. If you don't have a suitable seedhead available, you might use an ornamental gourd, a large pine cone cut in half or a dried globe artichoke. Alternatively, many florists stock large seedpods for arrangements.

With the centrepiece in place, set a number of poppy heads, sprayed silver or gold into the block of oasis, to mark out the shape of the arrangement. Around the base of the cardoon, I chose to add a splash of colour with helichrysum, placing softer yarrows and white feverfew further onto the block.

If your arrangement is to stand in the centre of a table you will need to keep turning it as you work, giving thought to its appearance from all sides. You may wish to create entirely contrasting effects as it is turned, or to mirror them with two cardoons and a central sorrel. Place the dill or fennel and golden rod seedheads last as these are easily damaged. An edging of cinnamon, beechmast and spices, wired as for the Christmas tree on the mat, is especially effective with small silver or gold poppy heads or helichrysum buds set amongst them.

With the arrangement finished, add the cracker, or two crackers one at either side, and pine cones and spices as decorations. To keep the block steady on the mat, use wired spices as before to secure the felt or material and add one or two pushed into the edge of the block and down through the mat.

Fragrant Christmas cracker

Simple to make, these can be set on a table, around the base of the tree or amongst other decorations. After Christmas they are perfect to add fragrance to clothes in drawers or a wardrobe, or to add a feminine touch to writing paper.

You will need:

a cardboard roll which can be the inner of a kitchen paper towel roll, or made to size
Christmas fabric, or plain red fabric and red net, cut with pinking shears, to approx. 7.5cm (3in) longer than the roll and wide enough to pass one and a half times around it
2 lengths of gold braid, narrow red ribbon or Christmas trim
a piece of butter muslin the same size as the Christmas fabric
glue
a gold Christmas-cake paper trim (optional)
fragrant filling, essential oil star anise (optional)
Fold the butter muslin in half lengthwise and sew across one short end and up the long, open side to form a tube. Turn right side out and fill this loosely with fragrant rose petals, lavender or a blend of herbs - to which you have added a teaspoon of orris root (lavender will not need this) and 2 drops of essential oil of orange, cinnamon or

the dominant herb in the filling. (Only 1 drop is necessary if this is rose.) Oversew the tube closed.

Pierce holes in the cardboard roll at intervals all around and along its length. Push the muslin tube filled with herbs inside the roll so that it fills it and slightly overhangs at either end. Centre the roll close to the long edge of the Christmas or plain red fabric, and dab glue in a line along the cardboard. Roll the cardboard in the fabric smoothing the glued area as you do so. Glue again at the long raw edge, being careful not to use too much which might stain the fabric. If covering again with red net, repeat this last step. Tie at either end, just beyond the roll, with the ribbon or trim. For further decoration, a star anise or gold shapes cut from the Christmas-cake trim can be glued on or around the centre of the roll.

The crackers will hold their fragrance best if they are made one or two weeks early and kept sealed in a polythene bag for that time. They will then give lasting pleasure.

Rosemary bower
This is most effective for giving crib figures a definite background. Over the years I have made numerous "stables" with a variety of materials for my children to set the figures against. Recalling the legend of rosemary protecting the Virgin Mary and Jesus, one year, I decided to make a green and fragrant setting for them instead. The result was so lovely I have repeated it each year since.

You will need:
a horseshoe-shaped or round flower arrangers bowl
water-absorbent oasis or sphagnum moss
sprigs of rosemary of varying lengths
one or two lengths of ivy
more moss, plain raffia cuttings or pieces of straw to lay as a base
a gold star
a set of crib figures
Cut the oasis to fit the container and soak in water. Set a series of the ivy stems to arch from one side of the semi-circle to the other, making a "roof". Take 2 long, narrow ivy stems, stripped of their leaves and weave these around the back of the semi-circle in and out of the other stems, making sure either end is slotted in away from the front edge. Add the sprigs of rosemary, weaving these gently in and out of the ivy supports as you work.

Cover the base with snippets of straw coloured raffia, straw or moss and set the figures on this. Make sure the front of the container, if it is a round one, is completely covered in moss, or set short sprigs of rosemary into the oasis. Hang the gold star from the topmost point of the arching ivy above the figures.

Herb trees
Two herbs - rosemary and bay - are perfectly suited as small table decorations. A well-shaped rosemary bush can be potted up a month or so in advance and kept in a

greenhouse or conservatory until it is wanted indoors. Do not give the plant the double shock of digging it out of the garden to be potted and immediately bringing it into an entirely different temperature. A 30-45cm (12 to 18in) bush can appear very similar to a miniature pine Christmas tree and will not drop needles everywhere. Many very light tree ornaments are available or you can make your own, see below. A few of these together with some light tinsel and a decorative pot will surely make your tree a talking point.

Just as attractive in a different way, is to decorate a small bay which may have been brought in out of danger of frost. With both herbs it is important to give them a little water and ensure they have plenty of light.

Handled carefully, the plants will benefit from the time inside when the garden can be frosty. Return them to the outside gradually, or keep in a greenhouse until spring. If the change of temperature is very great, water with one or two drops of Bachs Rescue Remedy (available in healthfood and wholefood shops generally) to a jug of water.

Tree decorations

There are a wealth of tree decorations for sale in the shops each year which are bright and eye catching. Yet it remains a treat to make your own, original items. The following are sufficiently simple to be made while watching television, or chatting over a cup of tea with friends.

Fragrant cubes

Made in minutes, these have proved the most popular decorations, since my daughter devised them.

You will need:

¼m (¼yd) of Christmas fabric which has a squared pattern
1m (1yd) of thick gold thread or narrow Christmas trim
herb filling - lavender with a ¼ teaspoon of ground clove and 1 drop of essential oil of mandarin
needle and thread
pinking shears

For each cube, you will need to cut out an elongated cross shape which is 4 squares long and 3 squares across on your patterned material (see diagram 1 on opposite page Before you cut, however, add on a seam allowance of ½-1.25cm (¼ to ½in) to the outside edges of the cross shape. To make up, bring the side arms of the cross to meet the top square, right sides together as in diagram on opposite page. Stitch, following the straight line of the outside of the square on the pattern. This will give you an open box. Turn this right side out and fill with the lavender mixture, packing it down tightly to maintain the shape.

With the cube almost filled, sew the two ends of a 7.5cm (3in) length of trim or strong gold thread into one corner of the cube. Turn the seam allowance inside as you work and stitch the cube closed, adding a little lavender when you reach the last open side to make the shape symmetrical. When finished, the cubes can be hung from the branches of a Christmas tree, inside wreaths, from swags or amongst other decorations.

Spicy sacks on a string

These can be made as tiny or as large as your tree requires, in colourful Christmas fabrics or plain canvas, and trimmed with brilliant gold and silver thread or braid or tied with softly coloured green ribbons. When finished, the smaller sacks are most effective when attached to a gold or brightly coloured braid. The braid can be kept simple with bags of herbs alternated with nutmegs held in loops of fine gold trim along its length; or made more decorative by adding ribbon bows, cinnamon sticks with star anise and the fragrant cubes hanging from heavy loops of tinsel.

You will need:
¼-½m (¼-½yd) fabric
at least 1m (1yd) tinsel or braid
ribbons
thread and needle
glue and trim (optional)
a choice of cloves, cinnamon sticks, coriander and caraway seeds, dried rosemary and bay leaves, star anise, nutmegs, root ginger, orris root, essential oils for fillings
Cut pieces of fabric roughly twice as long as they are wide: for example, 10 x 6.5cm (4 x 2½in), 15 x 9cm (6 x 3½in). Fold in half lengthwise and stitch the side seams firmly. Turn down a hem at the open end and stitch, or leave cut across with pinking shears if the material will not fray. Turn right side out.

Half fill smaller sacks with a mixture of pounded cloves, coriander and caraway seeds and a sprinkling of orris root. Add 1 drop of essential oil of cloves or cinnamon to each before tying closed with strong thread. Alternatively, the larger sacks can be filled with pounded dried rosemary and fragments of bay leaves or root ginger, pounded cloves and cinnamon.

Glue a star anise on the front of larger sacks, or use fragments of tinsel, gold or silver stars on smaller sacks. With the sacks made, sew them to a length of thick braid or tinsel, leaving space to attach wired star anise (see page 198), pieces of cinnamon stick, ribbon bows fragranced with essential oils, fragrant beads (see page 180) or nutmegs between them. To attach the nutmegs to the braid, take a 30cm (12in) length of gold trim and, starting 5cm (2in) from the end, wrap it round the nutmeg once, glueing it to the nut as you go. Bring the braid back down for a quarter of a turn, over the braid already glued down and then wrap it around the nutmeg to make a full circle at right angles to the first circle, again glueing as you go. With the nutmeg now encircled by trim, both horizontally and vertically, take the free end of trim and thread this through a loop in the braid or over the tinsel. Make a loop, glueing the free end to the trim at the back of the nutmeg.

Hang the string of decorations around the tree or over the fireplace where the rising warm air will bring out the full fragrance.

Fragrant cubes

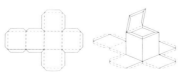

1. cross of squares with seam allowances

2. side arms of the cross meeting top and bottom squares, to form cube

Hanging sachets

A simple touch of colour for the tree, these can also be hung from wreaths and, after Christmas, can be hung in the wardrobe for fragrance, or used as a pincushion.

You will need:

scraps of Christmas fabric with a small pattern such as holly leaves or tiny toys
28cm (11in) of red or green ribbon for each either, approx. 30cm (12in) gold braid or approx. 60cm (24in) narrow lace and 30cm (12in) each of broderie anglaise and 1.25cm (½in) red or green ribbon to thread through it
lavender herb filling

For each hanging sachet, cut 2 circles of Christmas fabric 9cm (3½in) in diameter. For a sachet trimmed with gold braid, place the two circles right sides together and machine, leaving an opening of 2.5cm (1in). Turn right side out and fill with lavender, using a pointed spoon. Insert both ends of the ribbon into the opening and pin, before stitching it closed to hold the hanging ribbon securely. Handstitch the gold braid around the edge of the sachet to give it a firm, round shape.

To make the lace-edged sachets, tack the narrow lace to the right side of one of the Christmas fabric circles, with the outer edge of the lace facing into the centre of the circle. (Lace which is gathered and has a solid edge gives the best effect.) Next, thread the narrow ribbon through the broderie anglaise and lay this over the narrow ribbon. Tack. These are then enclosed with a second layer of narrow lace and the second Christmas fabric circle - which is laid, face down on the top. Tack again, before machining. As before, leave an opening of 2.5cm (1in) for the filling. Machine. Unpick the tackings and turn right side out. Fill the sachet, remembering to insert the hanging ribbon before handstitching the opening to close.

Seed star

An unusual star for the top of the Christmas tree, or to set amongst tinsel further down in the branches, this is quick and easy to make.

You will need:

thick card
loose star anise seeds
whole star anise seedpods
silver or gold trim to edge the star
glue

Cut a 5-pointed star-shape from the card. A star is 18cm is right for a medium-size tree, (7in) at the widest point, but both larger and smaller stars can be made in this way.

Begin by placing a whole star anise at the centre of the shape and glueing this to the card. Add others around it until they fill the central area, leaving the arms of the star still as plain card. Next, glue the loose seeds in place, beginning at the very tip of each point and covering the remaining area. The seeds have a shiny lustre which makes them very attractive. When all the seeds and seedpods are secure, glue the trim to the edge of the star. One which has loops to one side is particularly suitable as these stand up, hiding the edges of the card completely and protecting the seeds when picked up.

Perfumes and flavours

ESSENTIAL oils can transform the atmosphere of a room as dramatically as a whole host of streamers, balloons and boughs of greenery. The oils most closely identified with Christmas are mandarin, orange, cinnamon and clove (the last two are almost identical) and pine. To these we could add rosemary, myrrh and frankincense. Myrrh is not a particularly pleasant perfume alone and should be added with caution to blends. Frankincense is heady and strong, but in an entirely different way. Care should be taken not to give children a bottle of essential oil to hold. The oils are very concentrated and particularly dangerous if they come into contact with eyes.

However, diluted in a room spray or humidifier they can give a delightful perfume to a home before the party begins. They may be added to decorations as in the fragrant cubes and sacks; or to other tree decorations. To scent pine cones, seal them in a polythene bag for 2 days with a ball of cotton wool perfumed with 1 or 2 drops of essential oil of pine before attaching them to the branches. Ribbons can also be scented with a drop or two of essential oil and kept enclosed in a bag in the same way, before tying them to the tree.

Even before candles represented the yule log, they were given as presents by the Romans at Saturnalia. Later, they became an essential part of Christmas, reminding us of the power of light over darkness, good over evil. Drops of essential oil can be added to the wax. Care must be taken, however, never to drip the oil onto the flame or the wick as essential oil is highly inflammable. Wait until the candle has melted a pool of wax around the wick and then snuff out the candle before adding 1 or 2 drops of oil to this pool. The candle can then be relit.

The rich, spicy flavours - Christmas puddings, gingerbread, sauces and stuffings - always invoke memories of past years. There are elements of comfort, excitement and joy which we can all appreciate in making and eating them. Just as the taste of a home-made mince pie or mulled wine brings our senses to life, putting us in the mood for a celebration, so scents from the past affect us. Who can smell essential oil of mandarin or orange, oil of cinnamon or clove and not think of Christmas? For the very young perhaps, these associations are not as strong, but they can soon become so.

If we follow history further back than our own lifetimes, we soon reach a time when caraway sauce over roasted apples would be as evocative of a firelit scene and holly decorations. Then gingerbread was spiced, not only with ginger, but with caraway and coriander. Rosemary-flavoured Christmas cakes, brought out the full richness of the fruit and stuffings were heavy with sage, thyme and other antiseptic herbs to counteract the possibility that the meat might be over-ripe. Comfits of sugar-coated caraway seeds were eaten after the huge meals to relieve indigestion, and fruit, such as oranges, which were then a treat for Christmas only, were enjoyed with a sense of excitement we can only imagine.

Imagine the pleasure of opening your store cupboard in early December to find it ready-stocked with jars of candied flowers and leaves, crystallised angelica and lovage stems, or candied sweet cicely root, with its rich liquorice flavour - all ready for making special Christmas treats. Coloured and fragrant herb sugars of pot marigold, rose and lavender for decorating trifles and cakes or to include in home-made chocolates and candies. Ranged on the shelves might be jars of sweet herb jellies, from lemon-scented geranium to spicy elderberry and rose-hip for cake fillings. Luscious syrups of aniseed-flavoured sweet cicely, wine-rich angelica, clove pink and rose and dark elderberry.

Beneath the shelves, on the cool floor, stand bottles of wine to accompany or flavour the meal. Lemon balm and lemon thyme, a favourite with fish, sweet dessert wines, such as blackcurrant and curled mint or marigold and peach, may double as flavourings in winter fruit cocktails and, for a very special occasion, rosemary spring liqueur with melon as a starter, or peppermint liqueur with ice cream after a heavy meal.

By Christmas there will be a host of opportunities for small gifts to be taken from these shelves to show appreciation of dinner invitations or to contribute to parties. Most home-made chocolates and sweets are best eaten within two weeks of being made, but your essential ingredients will all be to hand in that last rush of preparations. The Christmas pudding, given extra flavour by ground rosemary and coriander, chopped, candied sweet cicely root and angelica and, perhaps, home-made apricot brandy, will stand wrapped on the shelves for weeks before the holiday.

Some essential oils of herbs can be used as flavourings, powerful as they are. Peppermint, and ginger will come as no surprise to most cooks. However, rose geranium for cakes, ice cream, rice pudding and even to lend a touch of magic to mincemeat for mince pies at Christmas is a new experience for many. Lavender is even stronger in flavour but is also suitable for home-made sweets, fruit desserts, white meat, fish and vegetable dishes. Fennel, dill, basil, marjoram, spicy coriander, anise, extravagant rose and jasmine - all have their own individual qualities to offer. With these additional flavourings and a little imagination in the use of dried herb blends, herb syrups and honeys as healthy winter tonics, you cannot fail to create original recipes.

Essential oils in cookery

This is a new area for most cooks and one which is satisfying and exciting to explore. Essential oils are exceedingly powerful flavourings having been distilled from huge quantities of herbs. One or two drops, therefore is usually sufficient. Care should be taken to store bottles containing essential oils away from the reach of children, and preferably in a cool, dark cupboard, rather than on a shelf in the hot, steamy atmosphere of the kitchen. Care should also be taken not to allow drips to run back down the side of the bottle since, of those essential oils suitable as food flavourings, only lavender can be dabbed directly onto the skin. If the bottle does not have a dropper set into the top, use a straw as a pipette to draw the oil up and then release it. However, do take the precaution of dripping it onto a spoon, as the pipette method makes measurement very difficult. One drop too many can spoil a recipe.

With these cautions noted, a tiny quantity of essential oil can transform a simple recipe into a treat. Once you are accustomed to using them, you will wonder why they have not been used in the home before. Simple recipes such as custards, plain sauces, rice pudding, jams and jellies, butter icing, and vegetable or meat stocks provide suitable mediums for experiment. Cooking oil, vinegar, mayonnaise, butter and cream cheese or puréed fruit can also be flavoured and enhanced with oils.

206

Oils to use

For sweet dishes
coriander
jasmine
lavender
melissa
peppermint
rose
rose geranium

For savoury dishes
basil
dill
fennel
marjoram
melissa

The essential oils of parsley, rosemary, sage and thyme can all be used in cookery, but are so powerful that I prefer to use the herb. Essential oils from spices such as nutmeg, clove, cinnamon and ginger are also very strong, together with that of black pepper.

Christmas recipes

Main dishes for the buffet
Savoury Plait

1 tin 439g (15.5oz) chestnut purée
50g (2oz) wholemeal breadcrumbs
3 sticks celery, chopped finely
1 medium carrot, grated approx 75g (3oz)
1 beaten egg
50g (2oz) spinach or nettle cooked lightly in a little water for 3-4 minutes and chopped
1 heaped tablespoon chopped fresh parsley
1 sage top of young leaves chopped (heaped teaspoon)
1 heaped teaspoon chopped coriander
1 teaspoon thyme
1 teaspoon herb pepper for meat
½ teaspoon celery salt or salt to taste
½ teaspoon ground rosemary
450g (1lb) puff pastry

Mix all the filling ingredients together in a large bowl. Roll out the puff pastry into an oblong, laying the filling down the centre, starting 5cm (2in) from the top and with an equal strip of pastry uncovered at each side. With a sharp knife cut in diagonally from each of the top corners towards the filling, stopping some 1.25cm (½in) away from it. Make more cuts moving down the roll at about 2.5cm (1in) intervals until the other end is reached. Bring each strip of pastry over the centre, crossing them to give a plait effect. Bake for 10 minutes uncovered at 220°C, until the pastry is golden brown, then cover with foil and bake for a further 20 minutes. Serves 6.

Rice and herb loaf

1 cup Basmati rice
1 small onion
1 tablespoon olive oil
2 cloves of garlic
1 large carrot, diced
1 large mushroom
1 small courgette
1 cup sweetcorn
1 beaten egg
1 large bay leaf
85g (3oz) Cheddar cheese
½ teaspoon herb pepper for vegetables
1 drop essential oil of marjoram
2 teaspoons chopped fresh parsley

Place the rice in boiling water with a large bay leaf torn in half. Cook according to the instructions on the packet, or until tender. Drain. Fry the onion lightly in the olive oil with the chopped cloves of garlic, add the diced carrot and courgette. Sprinkle with the herb pepper as they are frying and, when softened, add the chopped mushroom for the last few minutes.

Mix the fried vegetables, cooked rice and sweetcorn together with the grated cheese and chopped parsley. Stir the drop of essential oil of marjoram well in. Add sufficient beaten egg (you may need 2) to bring to a soft mix. Bake in a moderate oven, 180°C for about 40 minutes.

Pasta with wine sauce

225g (8oz) pasta shapes
olive oil
25g (1oz) margarine
1½ dessertspoons cornflour
6 dessertspoons chopped tomatoes with their juice
6-8 dessertspoons white wine
3 teaspoons chopped fresh basil
a bunch of watercress

Pour a few drops of olive oil into the pan to grease it before adding boiling water and the pasta. Set the pan on the heat and bring to the boil. Turn down the heat and simmer until cooked. Meanwhile melt the margarine in another, smaller pan and stir in the cornflour. Add the chopped plum or fresh tomatoes with their juice and stir until the sauce thickens. Steadily stir in the wine just before the pasta is ready. Add the freshly chopped basil and pour over the strained pasta. Serve with a side-salad of watercress.

Side dishes

Sage bread
275g (10oz) wholemeal flour
25g (1oz) margarine
½ teaspoon celery salt
2 teaspoons thyme
¼ teaspoons chopped sage
¼ teaspoon herb pepper
½ small onion
25g (1oz) Cheddar cheese
½ teaspoon sugar
¼ pint of milk and water, mixed
1 dessertspoon dried yeast
Add the sugar and dried yeast to the warmed, diluted milk and stand to rise until it is frothing well up the sides of the jug. Rub the margarine into the flour and stir in the chopped herbs, grated cheese, finely chopped onion and seasonings. Add the frothing yeast and mix well. Knead the dough for 10 minutes and set in a covered bowl in a warm place to rise until it has doubled in volume. Knead again for 5 minutes and this time place the dough in a greased and floured loaf tin. Cover and leave it in the warm for a further half an hour. Sprinkle with sesame or lovage seeds if liked and bake at 200°C for 20 - 25 minutes, or until the loaf leaves the tin easily and sounds hollow when you tap the underside. Serve warm if possible.

Tipsy Dip
100g (4oz) mature Cheddar cheese
40ml (1½fl.oz) elderberry port
2 dessertspoons of chopped walnuts
Grate the cheese finely. Add the elderberry port, mixing well. Stir in the chopped walnuts. Chill and serve.

Tomato and basil dip
2 beef tomatoes
225g (8oz) tub cottage cheese
3 button mushrooms
1 tablespoon chopped chives
scant ¼ teaspoon herb pepper for vegetables
1 drop essential oil of basil
Cut the tops off the tomatoes and set these aside as lids. Scoop out the centres, reserving 1 tablespoon of the fruit to add to the mixture. Stir the chives, seasonings and finely chopped mushrooms into the cottage cheese. Set the lids on the tomatoes and chill before serving with a tray of freshly sliced carrot, cucumber, celery and cauliflower florets.

Savoury biscuits

The following recipe makes tangy, flavoursome small biscuits. I have given them the merry name as saffron has long been thought of as a herb of mirth. Cutting them out in strange, silly shapes can add to the fun.

Saffron chuckles

100g (4oz) plain white flour
1½ teaspoons ground coriander
2 good pinches of saffron
50g (2oz) butter
2 tablespoons pure orange juice
1 drop of essential oil of mandarin
a little beaten egg

Mix together the sieved plain flour, ground coriander and saffron. Add softened butter and blend. Stir in 2 tablespoons of orange juice with the single, carefully measured drop of essential oil of mandarin, and lastly the beaten egg to mix to an elastic dough. Roll out on a floured board and cut into shapes. Bake on a greased baking tray at 170°C for 5 -10 minutes, until golden.

Somehow, cheese straws of one kind or another seem to be expected at parties and they are quick and easy to make at the last minute. These are at their best when served straight from the oven, but they can be reheated.

Thyme twists

170g (6oz) plain flour
85g (3oz) Davidstow cheddar cheese grated finely
100g (4oz) butter, warmed
2 heaped teaspoons of fresh lemon thyme leaves (stripped from the stems and chopped)
½ beaten egg

Mix the warmed butter, sieved flour and grated cheese together. Stir in the 2 teaspoons of chopped thyme, with all the stems removed. Add the beaten egg to mix. Set in the fridge to rest for ten minutes. Then, taking small quantities of the mixture form into rolls, cut in half lengthways and roll again with spread fingers to give a twist effect. Bake at 170°C for about 10 minutes until golden. Serve warm.

The biscuits in the recipe below look as if they should be sweet biscuits. However you will find them a good companion together with the saffron chuckles and thyme twists for a real contrast of textures and flavours.

Rosemary and walnut biscuits

25g (1oz) finely chopped walnuts
100g (4oz) unsieved wholemeal self raising flour
50g (2oz) oats
1 level teaspoon ground rosemary
50g (2oz) soft butter
1 tablespoon honey

a little egg to mix

Stir the flour, oats and the ground rosemary together. Add the softened butter and blend. Stir in the chopped walnuts, honey and egg and finish mixing. Form small balls of mixture into flattened cakes about 4cm (1½in) across and bake on a greased baking tray at 170°C for about 10 minutes.

Sweet biscuits

The flavouring in the next biscuits comes from essential oils and makes a good introduction to their use for the cautious cook.

Carob surprise biscuits

100g (4oz) margarine
85g (3oz) raw cane sugar
1 egg
200g (7oz) fine wholemeal flour
25g (1oz) carob flour
essential oil of peppermint
essential oil of lemon

Cream the margarine and sugar until light and fluffy. Add the egg with a little of the sieved flour and carob. Stir in the remainder of the flour and carob until the mixture is stiff. Divide the biscuit dough in half, making a well in the centre of each shape. Add 2 drops of essential oil of peppermint to one ball, kneading it well into the mix. Roll out the soft dough and cut into biscuit shapes, baking on a greased tray for just 5 minutes at 180°C.

Take the second half of the mixture and in the same way add 2 drops of essential oil of lemon; mixing well before rolling out and cutting as before. Bake. The biscuits can, if liked, be sandwiched together in pairs with a layer of icing flavoured with 1 drop of the appropriate esssential oil.

No Christmas would be complete without gingerbread, whether this is used to make a gingerbread house, or cut out as people, robins, Christmas trees, or the figures of the three Wise Men and shepherds.

Coriander gingerbread

170g (6oz) margarine
170g (6oz) soft brown sugar
2 level tablespoons black treacle
1 level tablespoon honey
¾ level teaspoon ground coriander
1½ teaspoons ground ginger
½ teaspoon ground caraway
325g (12oz) self raising, fine wholemeal flour

Cream the margarine and sugar, beat in the treacle and honey. Sieve the flour and spices and fold into the mixture, adding a little milk if necessary to mix to a firm paste. Turn onto a floured board and knead well. Roll out to ½cm (¼in) thick and cut into gingerbread men and ladies, robin shapes, Christmas trees etc.

The next recipe is another Christmas favourite - often a useful alternative or accompaniment to mince pies.

Rosemary shortbread

170g (6oz) butter
85g (3oz) caster or ground raw cane sugar
¾ -1 teaspoon ground rosemary
275g (10oz) plain flour
1 beaten egg yolk

Cream the butter with the sugar, adding the egg yolk together with a little of the flour. Continue adding the flour gradually until a firm dough is reached. Press into a greased and lined square tin. The top may be brushed with a little of the remaining egg and pricked with a fork. Bake at 170°C for about 40 minutes, until firm and very lightly browned. Sprinkle with sugar and cut into squares. Leave in the tin to cool. You may find the spicy rosemary flavour becomes more pronounced with keeping the shortbread sealed in a cake tin for a day or two.

Cinnamon oatcake

100g (4oz) margarine
2 dessertspoons honey
2 dessertspoons golden syrup
1 tablespoon wholemeal flour
170g (6oz) oats
2 dessertspoons sunflower seeds
1 dessertspoon sesame seeds
1 drop essential oil of cinnamon
1 drop essential oil of ginger

Melt the margarine, honey and syrup together in a thick-bottomed pan, over a low heat. Stir in the wholemeal flour and then most of the oats. Add the seeds and sufficient oats for the mixture to cling together and leave the sides of the pan clean. Stir in the drops of essential oil with the pan removed from the heat. Bake at 170°C in a shallow tin for about 20-30 minutes, until golden brown. Cut when slightly cooled.

Desserts

Rosemary apple cream

4 large cooking apples
125ml (5fl. oz) whipping cream
1 level teaspoon ground rosemary
sugar to taste
flaked almonds
candied angelica
herb sugar or crystallised flowers to decorate

If using fresh rosemary, dry a little in the microwave between two pieces of paper kitchen towel until crisp. Check after 1 minute, removing the wet under-tissue and replacing with dry. A second minute should be sufficient. See your microwave booklet for instructions. The dried rosemary can then be ground along with the sugar and the two added together to the peeled and sliced apples in a pan with a little water. Alternatively, ground rosemary can be bought as a powder. Cook the apples until soft, strain and cool. Either blend with the whipping cream in a liquidizer, or mash the apple to a purée and swirl in the cream. Spoon into individual dishes, decorating with candied angelica and herb sugar or nuts and crystallised edible flowers. Serves 3-4.

Pears in velvet
The elderberry coating can be made simply by thickening 125ml (5fl.oz) of ready-made elderberry syrup, or with the following ingredients.
325g (12oz) stalked and washed elderberries
5 cloves
¼ teaspoon ground nutmeg
¼ teaspoon ground ginger
1 rounded tablespoon brown sugar
½ level tablespoon of powdered arrowroot
1 tin 410g pear halves in fruit juice
flaked almonds
a little coconut if desired
Bring the elderberries to the boil in 2 dessertspoons of water, with 5 cloves added. Simmer for about 3-5 minutes, to encourage the juice to flow. Leave to infuse for 10 minutes, stirring occasionally. Strain to remove the berries and cloves, being sure to press out all of the juice. Return the strained juice to the pan. Mix the arrowroot, ground nutmeg, ground ginger and 1 tablespoon of cold water. Bring the juice to the boil, pour over the arrowroot mixture and return to the pan. Sweeten to taste and bring back to the boil. Set the pear halves in individual dishes and pour the thickened elderberry syrup over to cover. Decorated with flaked almonds set with their pointed ends into the pears, these can be made to look like hedgehogs with dried elderberries for eyes, or only three flaked almonds for ears and tails on each pear can be seen as a mouse or rabbit. Sprinkle a little coconut around the pear halves if liked.

Angelic temptation
Marzipan base
100g (4oz) ground almonds
50g (2oz) caster sugar
1 egg yolk
a pinch of saffron
2 dessertspoons of rosewater
Filling
mincemeat with 1 drop of essential oil of rose geranium added and stirred in
1 large cooking apple

a little sugar
½ teaspoon ground coriander
1 tablespoon of lemon juice
125ml (5 fl.oz) angelica syrup (see preserves)
a little herb sugar (see preserves)
Mix the ground almonds, caster sugar and saffron together. Add the whisked egg yolk and rose water to form a marzipan paste. Roll this out on a board sprinkled with a little icing sugar and line a small round casserole dish or pie plate. Bake at 130°C for 10-15 minutes. Cool slightly. Peel and slice the apple, cooking it gently in the lemon juice and a little water if necessary, with the ground coriander and only a little sugar. Fill the base with a layer of mincemeat topped with cooked apple slices laid neatly in an overlapping ring. To thicken the angelica syrup, mix a little with 2 teaspoons of cornflour or arrowroot in a dish and heat the remainder in a small pan. Pour the heated syrup over the blended cornflour and return to the pan for a moment or two, stirring all the time. Pour the thickened syrup over the apples and cool slightly. Return to the oven briefly. Sprinkle with pot marigold sugar or decorate with crystallised flowers and candied angelica before serving hot or cold. Serves 4-5.

Mulled wines
1 bottle blackcurrant and curled mint wine, (or other red wine)
rind of 1 lemon
1 teaspoon ground nutmeg
1 teaspoon cloves
1 drop essential oil of cinnamon
1 drop essential oil of coriander
150ml (¼ pint) water
1-2 tablespoons sugar
Wash the lemon well and peel it finely with a potato peeler. Pour the wine into a large pan, adding the spices, essential oils and lemon peel. Heat to boiling, then simmer gently for a few minutes. Strain and serve.

Non-alcoholic punch
600ml (1 pint) red grape juice
600ml (1 pint) ginger ale
1 bottle rose non-alcoholic wine
1 drop essential oil of cinnamon
1 nutmeg
half an orange
a few cloves
a few coriander seeds
Pour the grape juice into an enamel pan with the spices, essential oil and fruit. Stick the coriander and cloves into the orange to make them easier to remove later. Bring to the boil. Turn down the heat and simmer slowly for 15 minutes. Add wine and ginger ale and serve hot or cold with a small sprig of rosemary in the bowl.

Preserves

Herb syrups are a most useful preserve in that they may be diluted as drinks in winter or summer, added as a flavouring to ice cream, sorbets, stewed fruit, home-made sweets and cakes; or taken by the teaspoonful to soothe sore throats.

Sweet cicely syrup

100g (4oz) sweet cicely leaves
325g (12oz) sugar to each pint of liquid
1.2 litres (2 pints) cold water
Pour the water into a pan. Wash the herb leaves and tear these into the water. Simmer gently for 1 hour. Measure the remaining liquid as you strain it and leave to cool. Add 325g (12oz) sugar to each pint of liquid and dissolve over a low heat. Bring the syrup briefly to the boil and pour into sterilized bottles.

Angelica syrup

325g (12oz) angelica stems and leaves (about equal parts of each)
1.2 litres (2 pints) water
550g (1lb 4oz) sugar
Pour the water into a large pan. Wash and chop the leaves and stems and add to the water. Simmer gently for 1 hour. Strain and measure. Make up the liquid as necessary with cold water to make 1.2 litres (2 pints). Pour into the cleaned pan and slowly dissolve the sugar into the liquid. Bring briefly to the boil and remove from the heat immediately. Pour into sterilized bottles.

Elderberry syrup

1.8kg (4lb) elderberries
approx. 450g (1lb) sugar
a piece of root ginger the size of a walnut
9 cloves
Place the stalked elderberries in an enamel pan or casserole dish. Add 2 tablespoons of water and bruise well with a wooden spoon. Heat on a low setting, stirring all the time and mashing the fruit at intervals. Bring slowly to the boil. Boil for 5 minutes. Set aside to cool. Squeeze the pulp through a fine mesh bag. Add the root ginger and cloves. Return to the cleaned pan. Simmer for 10 minutes. Strain. Measure and return to the pan.

To each pint of juice add 325g (12oz) sugar. Stir over a low heat until the sugar is completely dissolved. Pour into rigid containers to freeze or into sterilized bottles with screw tops.
N.B. Syrups are best kept in the fridge after opening.

Elderberry jelly

1.8kg (4lb) elderberries
450g (1lb) brambles
juice of 1 lemon
½ stick of cinnamon
9 cloves

Stalk the elderberries and brambles and put into a pan with 1 pint of water, the juice of the lemon and spices. Simmer for 45 minutes. Pour into a straining bag and leave to drip overnight over a large bowl. Next day measure the juice, adding 1 cup of sugar to each cup of liquid. Heat gently to dissolve the sugar and boil until it reaches setting point. Pour into prepared jars.

Rose or lemon geranium jellies can be made simply by pouring a plain apple jelly over a large, torn leaf of either herb in the bottom of each prepared jar.

Mincemeat

85g (3oz) sultanas
85g (3oz) raisins
50g (2oz) chopped dates
25g (1oz) candied sweet cicely root
2 tablespoons puréed apple cooked in lemon juice
25g (1oz) ground almonds
50ml (2fl.oz) rum
1 drop essential oil of rose geranium

Chop the candied sweet cicely root finely and mix with the dried fruits. Pour over the rum and leave covered for 3-4 hours. Stir in the puréed apple, ground almonds and essential oil. Spoon into small, sterilized jars.

Herb peppers

Make up the herb peppers with 4 teaspoons each of black and white peppercorns ground together. Grind the pepper again with one of the following blends of dried herbs.

for fish	for meat	for vegetables
1 tablespoon lemon balm	1 tbsp basil	1 tbsp savory
1 tablespoon marjoram	1 tbsp parsley	1 tbsp parsley
½ tablespoon dill weed	½ tbsp tarragon	½ tbsp thyme

Store the peppers in labelled jars to use at table or in cooking. Remember they have a large proportion of pepper when adding to dishes, and add cautiously until you can judge their strength. The added seasoning powers of the herbs make these invaluable in the kitchen.

Home-made confections

HOME-made candies are always special, whether intended as a thoughtful gift, or simply to enjoy in solitary luxury on dark winter evenings. A selection can be created to tempt every taste, sweet or spicy, rich or subtle, vibrant with colour or wrapped in smooth chocolate.

Candied sweet cicely roots are spicy with aniseed sweetness. Elecampane root prepared in the same way, is powerfully fragrant with only a few drops added to flavour cough sweets. Marshmallow root is milder altogether and offers the joy of making real marshmallows by blending the boiled root with icing sugar and gum arabic.

Herb syrups can be added to flavour candy, toffee, or fudge and herb sugars are also a source of colouring. Rose petals offer sugar shades of pink to purple, often turning a mixture a soft green with pink flecks. The soft yellow of primroses may accompany subtle flavours, while a brighter orange from pot marigold petals is well partnered with rose geranium. A lilac shade can be obtained with violet petals, either from *Viola odorata,* or the strongly flavoured Parma violets which are so pretty with their mass of petals puffing out the flowerhead. Lavender flowers give a soft grey if crushed with sugar when dried; or green, pounded when fresh.

What tastier luxury than a soft centre flavoured with flower sugar and wrapped in chocolate or marzipan and topped with a crystallised violet or rose petal?

Roots, syrups and seeds can all be included in toffee or fudge recipes. Coriander should be ground before adding and many people prefer to grind caraway seeds. The nutty flavour of sunflower seeds may be brought out by toasting them for a few minutes under the grill before sprinkling them onto hot toffee as it sets. Such a toffee, spiced with ground coriander and caraway, or even a little ground rosemary makes a perfect sweet for Halloween or Christmas.

For those seeking powerful flavours, a drop or two of essential oil of peppermint, lavender or rose geranium may be added to an icing base. Citrus oils are also useful although care should be taken with these very strong flavourings, adding drops one at a time and taking frequent tastings.

Each recipe may be varied by substituting flavourings similarly prepared from other herbs. The table below shows the possibilities . . .

seeds	roots	syrups	sugars	oils
aniseed	elecampane	angelica	clove pink	citrus
caraway	marshmallow	clove pink	cowslip	coriander
coriander	sweet cicely	elderflower	lavender	lavender
dill		elderberry	pot marigold	melissa
lovage		peppermint	primrose	peppermint
sunflower		rose	rose	rose
		rose geranium	violet	rose geranium
		sweet cicely		

Candied sweet cicely root

l00g (4oz) cleaned and chopped sweet cicely root
170g (6oz) sugar
300ml (½ pint) water
When the root is dug, small shoots are discarded, along with any discoloured parts. The healthy main root is peeled and chopped into small cubes. Add the root to the water with 50g (2oz) of sugar over a low heat until the sugar dissolves. Then bring to the boil and continue boiling gently for about 20-25 minutes until soft enough to allow a fork through the cubes. Set aside to cool. Strain the root and layer with an equal quantity of sugar in a covered dish. Leave for 2 days as when candying angelica. Pour the syrup and root back into a pan and bring to the boil briefly. Strain out the root and sprinkle with sugar before setting on a rack to dry in a just warm oven. Store in layers between greaseproof paper in screwtop jars.

Candied elecampane root

l00g (40z) cleaned and chopped elecampane root
170g (6oz) sugar
450ml (¾ pint) water
Dissolve all the sugar in the water over a low heat. Add the cleaned, peeled and chopped root and simmer until tender. Remove from the heat. When cool, liquidize and add ½ tablespoon of brandy. Store in a sterilized jar in a cool place and refrigerate once opened. A few drops may be added to candy to make cough sweets.

Herb sugars

Add an equal quantity of fresh, washed and dried edible herb petals, to the caster or granulated sugar. Make sure all green parts are removed from the flowers first. Lavender has the strongest flavour and is best added dried and in half quantity. Fresh lavender gives a green colour, whereas the dried produces grey. Pound the herb flowers with the sugar until they are quite absorbed and the sugar is coloured. Spread the herb sugar on foil on a large plate or baking tray and set this in the oven with the door ajar and the setting no higher than 50°C. Once dried through, pound briefly again and store in screwtop containers until needed. Grind if using for icings, or leave in granules for decorating sweets and cakes.

Pot marigold soothers

1½-2 cups icing sugar
1 egg white
50g (2oz) pot marigold sugar
1 drop essential oil of rose geranium
Break up the egg white with a fork and then add half the sieved icing sugar using a mixer. Stir in the pot marigold sugar and essential oil before adding the remainder of the icing sugar. This should be sufficient to make a firm paste which can be rolled out on a clean surface sprinkled with icing sugar, to about 1.25cm (½in) thickness. Cut shapes out of the paste and lay these on greaseproof paper to dry out for about 1 hour. Turn and dry again before storing in a chocolate box or decorating with chocolate and candied root or crystallised flowers.

Sunflower and rosemary fudge

100g (4oz) white chocolate
approx. 550g (20oz) icing sugar
100g (4oz) sunflower margarine
4 tablespoons evaporated milk
½-1 level teaspoon ground rosemary
2 tablespoons sunflower seeds

Melt the broken chocolate and margarine over a low heat. Stir in the evaporated milk and ground rosemary thoroughly. Add the sieved icing sugar gradually, stirring all the time and when the mixture starts to thicken add the sunflower seeds. The remainder of the icing sugar will now bring the mixture to a stiff paste which can be pressed into a lined, shallow tin to set. Place in the fridge for about 20 minutes before cutting into squares, Store in an airtight tin or sealed box in a cool place.

Lavender coconut roll

100g (4oz) unsweetened coconut
25g (1oz) lavender sugar
100ml (4fl.oz) condensed milk
1 drop essential oil of lavender
50g (2oz) pot marigold sugar
50g (2oz) icing sugar
100g (4oz) ground almonds
1 egg
dark chocolate

Sieve the icing sugar and ground pot marigold sugar and add to the ground almonds. Make a well in the centre to take the beaten egg and mix thoroughly. If using plain sugar the marzipan can be coloured by adding a pinch of saffron instead. Mix to a smooth paste and roll out on a clean surface that has been sprinkled with icing sugar. Form into an oblong approx. 2cm (¾in) thick. Stir the milk, lavender sugar and coconut together over a low heat. Set to one side before adding the essential oil and stirring well in. Spread half of the coconut blend in a line down the centre of the marzipan and lay candied root or angelica on top, again following a central line. Mould the coconut mixture around the root or candied stem, adding more as necessary to make a central core. Wrap the marzipan around this to cover, and trim. Leave the roll on greaseproof paper for a few hours to dry out before covering in dark chocolate. To make the chocolate base, simply spread a thick layer of chocolate on the greaseproof paper beside the roll, shaping it to approximately the same size. When the chocolate is almost set pick up the roll on a palette knife and lay it on the chocolate, adding a little extra melted chocolate to seal the joins. Mark lines for rounds or cut into smaller bars while the chocolate is still slightly soft.

All kinds of combinations are possible with these ingredients, chocolate boxes can be made by spreading chocolate on greaseproof paper to make squares to form the four sides and the flavoured icings providing a solid base. Fillings from variously flavoured coconut and fudge can make these "chocolate surprises". Crystallised flowers are decorations for the chocolates and candies. These are made by washing and drying edible herb flowers, removing their green parts and dipping them into gum arabic and rosewater before sprinkling with sugar and drying. The gum arabic powder can be bought in cake decorating shops and is always added in the proportion of 1 teaspoon to 1 tablespoon of rosewater from a dispensary. This is shaken in a wide necked bottle to dissolve the gum arabic before each flower is immersed to coat it completely. Liqueur chocolates can be made by steeping apricots or other fruits in home made liqueurs, or simply with sugar in brandy and then adding a tiny piece of the drained fruit to a marzipan centre. The possibilities and discoveries go on.

Bibliography

Herb Cultivation
The Encyclopedia of Herbs and Herbalism, Edited by Malcolm Stuart, pub.
Macdonald & Co., 1967.
A Modern Herbal, Mrs. M. Grieve, Edited and introduced by Mrs. C. F. Leyel, pub.
Savvas Publishing, 1984 in association with Jonathan Cape.
Gerard's Herbal, Edited by Marcus Woodward from the 1636 Edition, pub. 1973.
The Illustrated Flora of Britain and Northern Europe, Marjorie Blamey, Christopher
Grey-Wilson, pub. Hodder & Stoughton, 1989.
Plants From The Past, David Stuart and James Sutherland, pub. Viking, 1987.
Culpeper's Complete Herbal, 1815 Edition, London.
Five Hundred Points of Good Husbandry, Thomas Tusser, Text from 1580 edition.
Oxford University Press, 1984.
Garden Shrubs and Their Histories, Alice M. Coats, pub. Vista Books, 1963.
Plants in Garden History, Penelope Hobhouse, pub. Pavilion Books Ltd. 1992.

Herbs in Wines and Liqueurs
Home-Made Wines, Cordials and Syrups, Dr. F. W. Beech, W.I. Books 1979.
Updated 1988.
Home Winemaking from A - Z, Les Zanelli, and Ward, London, 1971.
Making Your Own Liqueurs, Joyce van Doom, Prism Press 1980.
Spirits, Apertifs and Liqueurs, Their Production, S. M. Tritton, Faber and Faber, 1975.
Liqueurs, Peter Hallgarten, Wine and Spirit Publications, 1973.

Flowercrafts
The Complete Book of Pressed Flowers, Penny Black, pub. Dorling Kindersley,
1988.
The Complete Book of Dried Flowers, Malcolm Hillier & Colin Hilton, pub. Dorling
Kindersley in association with The National Trust, 1986.
Flowercraft, Violet Stevenson, pub. Hamlyn Publishing Group, 1977.

Basketry
Baskets From Nature's Bounty, Elizabeth Jensen, pub. Interweave Press, 1991.
The Complete Book of Rush and Basketry Techniques, Margery Brown, pub.
Batsford, 1983.

Herbs in Needlework Design

The Royal School of Needlework and Embroidery, General Editor, Lanto Synge, 1st pub. Collins, 1986.
Erica Wilson's Embroidery Book, Erica Wilson, pub. Faber and Faber, 1973.
The Embroiderer's Garden, Thomasina Beck, pub. David and Charles, 1988.
Stumpwork, Muriel Best, pub. Batsford, 1987.
The Craftsman's Plant Book, Richard Hatton, pub. Chapman and Hall Ltd., 1909.
The Canterbury Tales, Geoffrey Chaucer.

Dyes for Wools

Dyes From Plants, Seonaid Robertson, pub. Van Nostrand Reinhold Co. N.Y., 1973.
The Woad Plant and Its Dye, J. B. Hurry, pub. Oxford University Press, 1930.
Traditional Scottish Dyes, Jean Fraser, pub. Cannongate, 1983.
Vegetable Dyes, Ethel M. Mairet, pub. Faber and Faber, 1952.
The Colour Cauldron, Su Grierson, pub. by Mrs. S. Grierson, 1986. Reprinted 1989.
A Dyer's Manual, Jill Goodwin, pub. Pelham Books, 1982. Reprinted 1990.
A Weaver's Garden, Rita Buchanan, pub. Interweave Press Inc., 1987.
Medieval English Gardens, Teresa McLean, pub. Barrie & Jenkins, 1989.

Spinning Herb Fibres

The Craft of Hand Spinning, Eileen Chadwick, pub. Batsford Ltd., 1980.
Flax Culture from flower to fabric, Mavis Atton, pub. The Ginger Press, 1988.
Handspinning Flax, Olive and Harry Linder, pub. Bizarre Butterfly Publishing, Arizona, 1986.
The Spinner's Workshop, John Mercer, pub. Prism Press, 1978.

Woodcrafts

The International Book of Wood, Hugo Johnson, pub. Mitchell Beazley Publishers Ltd., 1976.
The Craftsman Woodturner, Peter Child, pub. Unwin Hyman, 1987.
Agar to Zenry, Ron Freethy, pub. The Crowood Press, 1985.

Spinning and Dye Suppliers:

Fibrecrafts	*Fibrecrafts*
Style Cottage	Elterwater
Lower Eashing	Ambleside
Godalming	Cumbria
Surrey GU7 2QD	LA22 9HW

Index

G

226

228

T

231

_N O T E S_